THE POLITICS OF THE PAST IN AN ARGENTINE
WORKING-CLASS NEIGHBOURHOOD

ANTHROPOLOGICAL HORIZONS
Editor: Michael Lambek, University of Toronto

This series, begun in 1991, focuses on theoretically informed ethnographic works addressing issues of mind and body, knowledge and power, equality and inequality, the individual and the collective. Interdisciplinary in its perspective, the series makes a unique contribution in several other academic disciplines: women's studies, history, philosophy, psychology, political science, and sociology.

For a list of the books published in this series see page 285.

The Politics of the Past in an Argentine Working-Class Neighbourhood

Lindsay DuBois

UNIVERSITY OF TORONTO PRESS
Toronto Buffalo London

© University of Toronto Press Incorporated 2005
Toronto Buffalo London
Printed in Canada

ISBN 0-8020-8844-9

Printed on acid-free paper

Library and Archives Canada Cataloguing in Publication

DuBois, Lindsay
The politics of the past in an Argentine working-class
neighbourhood / Lindsay DuBois.

(Anthropological horizons)
Includes bibliographical references and index.
ISBN 0-8020-8844-9

1. Authoritarianism – Argentina – Buenos Aires – History – 20th
century.   2. Labor movement – Argentina – Buenos Aires – History –
20th century.   3. Civil-military relations – Argentina – Buenos Aires –
History – 20th century.   4. José Ingenieros (Buenos Aires, Argentina) –
History.   5. Argentina – Politics and government – 1955–1983.   I. Title.
II. Series.

HN270.J68D82 2005   306'.0982'11   C2004-904537-7

This book has been published with the help of a grant from the Canadian
Federation for the Humanities and Social Sciences, through the Aid to
Scholarly Publications Programme, using funds provided by the Social
Sciences and Humanities Research Council of Canada.

University of Toronto Press acknowledges the financial assistance to its
publishing program of the Canada Council for the Arts and the Ontario
Arts Council.

University of Toronto Press acknowledges the financial support for its
publishing activities of the Government of Canada through the Book
Publishing Industry Development Program (BPIDP).

To my parents, Sarah Buchanan and Macy DuBois

Contents

List of Illustrations   ix

Acknowledgments   xi

1 Introduction   3
2 'This Is Not a Shanty Town'   20

Histories
3 The Toma, Its Origins, and the Early Years, 1968–1976   47
4 Repression and Reorganization, 1976–1982   85
5 After Reorganization, 1982–1992   113

Memories
6 The History Workshop: An Exercise in Popular Memory   133
7 Narrative Truths   158
8 Of Memory, Trash, and Politics   178
9 Conclusion: The Weight of History   205
Epilogue   214

Appendix A: Peronist Identities   221

Appendix B: Chronology   230

Glossary   233

Notes   237

Bibliography   263

Index   279

Illustrations

Maps
2.1 Location of José Ingenieros 21
2.2 Plan of José Ingenieros, NHD 4-5-6, 17, and 18 32
2.3 Plan of José Ingenieros, NHD 19 33

Figures
6.1 *Taller de Memoria* Time Line, Yellow Group 142
6.2 *Taller de Memoria* Time Line, Orange Group 145
6.3 Painting the *Taller de Memoria* Mural 153

Plates (*colour plates follow page 146*)
1 *Taller de Memoria* Mural
2 Restored *Taller de Memoria* Mural

Acknowledgments

In writing this book I have incurred innumerable debts. First and foremost, to my friends and acquaintances in José Ingenieros. It is amazing that they should have put up with me with such generosity and good humour. The people I call Anahí and Marisa, in particular, took me under their wings, looking out for and guiding me, but also trusting me to come to my own understandings and make my own judgments. I cannot imagine having produced this book without their support, their friendship, and their insight. The commitment and compassion of those I call Juan, Malena, Magdalena, Roberto, Miguel, Gloria, and María, among many others, give me reason for optimism despite Argentina's rather bleak prospects. Although she did not live in José Ingenieros, Alejandra's contribution to the community was evident, and her help, experience, conversation, and friendship enriched my understanding.

Many other friends received me warmly and helped me understand Argentina while I was there. As a fellow graduate student who shared my interest in popular memory, Rosana Guber befriended me when I knew almost no one in Argentina. Gloria Vitale and Analía Gutierrez taught me Spanish but also *porteño* culture and politics. Likewise, many in Buenos Aires suffered through my early days of halting Spanish and then my halting understanding of Argentine society and politics. Among them were Hermana Laura Amate, Marilú Bou, María Cecilia Cangiano, Nora de Cortiñas, El Grupo de Teatro Catalinas Sur, Laura Gingold, Ana González, Clelia Guiñazú, Ester Kaufman, Cecilia Luvecce, Alicia Martín, Norberto Méndez, Sofía Tiscornia, and Liliana Zuloaga. I received more formal, but no less important, support and assistance from the people at CODESEDH, CELS, El Equipo de

Antropología Forense, EURAL (Centro de Investigaciones Europea Latinoamericanos), and Madres de Plaza de Mayo, Linea Fundadora. I owe a special debt to Norberto Liwski, whose history in José Ingenieros and personal insight pointed me in the right direction on several occasions. The interview with Dr Liwski from which I quote extensively in chapter four was recorded, transcribed, and edited as part of a much larger project on human rights and the transition to and consolidation of democracy in Argentina. The interdisciplinary project was undertaken by a team of researchers at CEDES (Centro de Estudios de Estado y Sociedad) in Buenos Aires and funded by the Ford and the John and Catherine T. MacArthur Foundations. Some of the findings were published in *Juicio, castigo y memoria* (Acuña et al. 1995). Many thanks to all those involved in the CEDES project, especially Elizabeth Jelín, who allowed me to sit in on this interview and to work with a copy of the transcript. Thanks especially to Norberto Liwski himself, who gave me permission to attend the interview and to make use of his words here.

Nancy Powers and Judy Lawton were fellow-travellers in all the best senses, especially in our early months in Buenos Aires. I am especially grateful for Nancy's continuing companionship across the disciplinary divide. Julie Taylor was particularly generous with her assistance and advice stemming from long experience and deep knowledge of Argentina.

I acquired a bundle of debts in North America, both before and after fieldwork. My long graduate studenthood was informed and enlivened by the personal and intellectual comradeship of Elena Arengo, Jennifer Burrell, Kim Clark, Mimí Doretti, Bruce Grant, Garth Green, Julie Hunter, Nikolai Houston, Robin LeBaron, Chandana Mathur, Anne Meneley, Jane Miller, Abby Scher, Gregory Tewksbury, the late Hernán Vidal, and Donna Young.

The influence of my professors at the New School for Social Research is so pervasive that I did not know how to cite them in the following pages. I know, though, that I understand the world differently because of Rayna Rapp, Deborah Poole, Talal Asad, and the late William Roseberry. In his quiet and incisive way, Bill not only taught me much of what I know about anthropology, but also imparted a vision of anthropology and a commitment to the people with whom we work which I struggle to emulate. As external examiner, Donald Scott raised important and provocative questions helping me think all this material through. Thanks to the New School, which nurtured me, and Dalhousie University, where I finished my dissertation and turned it into a book. The support of colleagues and friends there has made all the difference.

This book has benefited tremendously from the attentions of friends and colleagues who took time away from their own work to think about mine. In particular Anne Meneley and Bruce Grant, with characteristic generosity, gave me detailed comments on the entire manuscript. I want also to thank the anonymous reviewer for University of Toronto Press, and two other anonymous reviewers who helped me think about its overall shape. I have received constructive comments on portions of my work from Elena Arengo, Pauline Gardiner Barber, Jennifer Burrell, Teresa Caldeira, María Lagos, Tania Li, David Nugent, Antonius Robben, Karen Robert, Gavin Smith, Joel Stillerman, Steve Striffler, and Donna Young. Portions of some chapters have been published previously as journal articles. An earlier version of chapter 6 appeared in *Anthropologica* (1997) as 'Past, Place and Paint: A Neighbourhood Mural Project in Suburban Buenos Aires.' A portion of chapter 7 appeared previously in *Oral History* (2000) as 'Memories Out of Place: Dissonance and Silence in Historical Accounts of Working Class Argentines.' The argument developed in 'Valiant Ladies: Gendered Dispositions in Argentine Working Class Memories' runs throughout the book and was originally published in *Social Analysis* (1999). I am especially grateful to editors and reviewers for their constructive comments and their support. In addition, many conference papers related to this work have received helpful comments from discussants and audience members. On many occasions the able assistance, kindly offered, of Donna Edwards, Mary Morash-Watts, and Lori Vaughn saved me from myself. My research assistants Suzanne Hindmarch, Mary Gaudet, and Meaghan MacIntyre not only picked up many pieces, but also made many helpful comments on the manuscript.

Financial support has come from many places over the years. I received dissertation fellowships from the New School for Social Research, the Wenner Gren Foundation for Anthropological Research, the Social Sciences and Humanities Research Council of Canada, the Harry Frank Guggenheim Foundation, and a Grant-in-Aid of Research from Sigma-Xi, the Scientific Research Foundation.

I have to thank my many families, especially my parents, Sarah Buchanan and Macy DuBois, and also Helga Plumb. It remains a mystery how my brother, Mark DuBois, guessed that anthropology would suit me so well. My sojourn in Buenos Aires gave me a new family. I thank Consuelo Marsuzzi, Amado Luques, and Sonia Luques for welcoming me and letting me take Daniel with me. Andrea and Sofía make everything more fun. Finally, but by no means least, Daniel Luques, in addition to helping me with this book in all sorts of concrete ways, has taken up a life in the North, and with an academic, with such good grace and love that I cannot imagine how I would have survived without him. All these people tried to teach me in their various ways, but the responsibility for what I may not have learned is mine.

THE POLITICS OF THE PAST IN AN ARGENTINE WORKING-CLASS NEIGHBOURHOOD

Chapter 1

Introduction

The Argentine dictatorship of 1976 to 1983, known officially as the Process of National Reorganization (*el proceso*), set out to transform Argentine society. Employing every means at its disposal, from the rampant violation of human rights to union-busting to regressive economic policies, the dictatorship aimed to create its own particular kind of order, and in the process paved the way for a neoliberal economy. This book uses ethnography and oral history to explore the lasting impact of this project for some of the working-class people who lived through it. More specifically, it examines the politics of the past in a working-class housing project called José Ingenieros[1] in the Partido de la Matanza, a suburb of Buenos Aires.

As a subject of anthropological study, José Ingenieros is not, on the surface of things, a likely choice. It is distinguished from other neighbourhoods in the cosmopolitan city of Buenos Aires neither by the ethnicity of its inhabitants nor by their extreme poverty (thus differing from other sites of urban anthropology, see Guber 1991). What characterizes José Ingenieros is its particular relation to recent Argentine history.

The neighbourhood where I conducted fieldwork from May 1991 to December 1992 is made up of housing blocks that together contain roughly 2,500 two-, three-, and four-bedroom apartments (see maps 2.2 and 2.3). In the early 1990s most residents were self-employed, or worked as domestic labourers, semi-skilled construction workers, piece workers, or low-income wage earners. The total population was about 11,500 people, living on thirty-seven hectares (370,000 m²).[2]

José Ingenieros was a compelling location for my research in part because of its dramatic history. The still uncompleted, nearly empty neighbourhood had been populated in a massive squatter invasion, one of the many occupations that occurred during the early moments of the 1973 democratic period. In the almost revolutionary fervour that led up to Juan Perón's triumphal return, thousands of those living in substandard and overcrowded housing, in shanty towns and urban slums, occupied José Ingenieros and similar neighbourhoods. In the months and years that followed the squatters organized to complete construction, install services such as water, gas, and electricity, and gain title to the apartments. Vital community organizations sprang up in the process, including community administrations, mothers' cooperatives, health care and child care centres. Thus José Ingenieros was indelibly marked by the turmoil of the 1973 to 1976 period that is such an important part of the context for what came after.

By the time I arrived in José Ingenieros in 1991, it had the look and reputation of the housing projects of big North American cities. Its modernist concrete architecture was daunting; outsiders told me it was populated by delinquents who would prey on unsuspecting strangers. Even many of those I met there began conversations with an insistence that the neighbourhood was not a shanty town. The statement startled me; it had not occurred to me that it might be. This insistence reflected the principal concerns of residents at the time: crime, dirt, and the deterioration of the infrastructure and green spaces through vandalism and neglect. Most had become legal residents, having gained title to their apartments. Many lamented the apathy of their neighbours and decried the corruption of the local officials who were supposed to administer and maintain the four *complejos* (complexes) that make up the neighbourhood. At the same time, most supported President Carlos Menem, who rose to power as a Peronist and proceeded to champion neoliberal economic policies.

The contrast between these two moments, the squatter occupations and the early 1990s, presents a conundrum, producing its own set of questions. How did a militant Peronist working class become a Peronist working class without work, supporting a neoliberal Peronist presidency? More specifically, how did a collection of people once so active and radical that it could invade, occupy, and transform a housing project on this scale become a community where apathy and cynicism were the norm, where people turned inward, unable to look past their daily struggle to the ways in which they might address some of these problems together with their neighbours? These are the kinds of questions confronting those working in community organizations in José Ingenieros and places like it.

The answers to these questions begin with recognizing that both the militancy and the apathy are tied to larger processes: changes in class, national, and international conditions that make militancy more or less imaginable, plausible, or even possible. The explanation lies primarily in the neighbourhood's recent history. The Process of National Reorganization and the neoliberal economic policies that it implemented (and which continue) had lasting effects in José Ingenieros as throughout Argentina. This dictatorship's unprecedented human rights abuses are notorious; what is less obvious, but maybe even more important, is the way in which the policies of repression were part and parcel of a wider strategy aimed at, as the regime itself put it, 'reorganizing Argentina.'

As a militant working-class neighbourhood, José Ingenieros was subject to particular attention from this regime. The night of the coup on 24 March 1976 saw the first sweep of death squads through the complexes; community leaders and participants in the community council were targeted. Later, massive search and seizure operations were carried out. The neighbourhood was surrounded as so-called censuses were conducted, and apartments were searched for guns and subversive materials. In 1978 the neighbourhood was assigned a military administrator. In the early 1990s, with the economy in a state of perpetual crisis (from the point of view of workers, if not banks) people were increasingly focused on their practical familial problems. It is not accidental, then, that the neighbourhood seemed disorganized and unkempt. This state was the end result of a set of social processes which this book aims to describe.

The Argentine Context

Before I proceed, some general observations about contemporary Argentine culture may help orient readers unfamiliar with the country.

Visitors to Buenos Aires are often struck by the European style of the capital. They marvel at the elegant avenues, cafes, and plazas, not realizing, perhaps, how intentional is the Argentine capital's resemblance to European centres. Here an avenue resembles Paris, there Barcelona, reflecting the shifting gaze of architects and planners, as they modelled their capital on centres of power abroad. Buenos Aires, home to one-third of Argentina's thirty-seven million inhabitants, wears its history on its sleeve (Robert 1997).

Argentina's historic reliance on its export economy, particularly agricultural exports, is inscribed in the landscape: all roads, trains, and now air routes, lead to the capital's port. It is virtually impossible to travel from one region of the country to another without passing through Buenos Aires. The trains and the metropolitan subway run on the left although Argentines drive on the right, a vestige of Britain's historic economic dominance; as in much of Latin America, Argentine railroads were built by the British to facilitate export.

The country's agricultural and cultural history is also evident in diet. Most working-class Argentines I know abhor the spicy food often associated with Latin American cuisine. The ideal working-class Argentine diet is similar to the North American meat and potatoes standard, except for the Italian influence that adds fresh pasta to the mix. In the early 1990s many working-class people could no longer afford to eat beef twice a day, as they once had, but women often complained that their husbands insisted they had not really eaten if red meat did not make an appearance. One sometimes still sees workmen in the street cooking *bifes* (steaks) on gas burners for their lunch. Like the North American barbeque, the traditional Argentine *asado* is (in principle) a masculine domain, but it is much more serious business in Argentina, usually involving many kinds of meat served in courses over several hours. The country's importance as an exporter of the beef of which Argentines are so proud can also be seen in the continued passion for *chinchulines*, the bits and pieces which may have become prized as delicacies, in part because they were not so readily exported.

Another process shaping how Argentines see their place in the world is the country's relatively recent pauperization. Many of the markers of Argentine urbanity were no longer accessible to working-class people by the time I arrived in 1990. Going out for dinner or to the movies had become luxuries even for many middle-class families. People often read the state of the economy from the size of the crowds in the downtown bookstores and cafes. Residents of the nation's capital, *porteños*[3] as they are known, have long been proud of their Europeanness. Their confidence about their place as the most European of Latin American nations, and the arrogance this is supposed to convey to their neighbours, makes Argentines the butt of jokes across the continent.

The Argentine sense of difference is often thought of as cultural. I knew *porteños* who asserted that Argentina had no 'Indians'; instead they say, theirs is an immigrant culture akin to those of North America. Although there are certainly indigenous people and indigenous cultural influences, Argentina received a tremendous number of immigrants in the nineteenth and twentieth centuries who dramatically reshaped Argentine society and culture. As historian David Rock puts it, 'immigrants arrived in enormous droves: between 1871 and 1914 some 5.9 million newcomers, of whom 3.1 million stayed and settled. Altogether between 1830 and 1950 Argentina absorbed some 10 percent of the total number of emigrants from Europe to the Americas' (1985:141). About half of these immigrants were Italians, a quarter Spanish, the rest mainly Ottomans, Russians, French, and Portuguese. By the First World War, 'one third of the country's population was foreign-born, and around 80 percent of the population comprised immigrants and those descended from immigrants since 1850' (Rock 1985:166). Although the influence of this history of immigration is broad – apparent in the Spanish spoken by Argentines, in their names, in their diet – one place this syncretic immigrant culture is most vividly expressed is musical forms such as the tango and the *chamamé* (a polka-like music from Argentina's northeastern provinces).

One of the ways that Argentina, and especially Buenos Aires, is distinctive from other Latin American nations then, is in the particular configurations of race, ethnicity, and class. Although most Argentines I met deny that race has any relevance as a social category in their country, it is clearly considered a marker of class. In part, this denial points to the absence of any substantial population of African origin in Argentina, which, unlike Brazil, never had a plantation economy. In contemporary Argentina, darker skin and hair suggest origins in South American indigenous populations, either from the interior of the country (Argentines use the term to refer to anywhere outside the capital) or the poorer neighbouring countries, especially Bolivia and Paraguay. Argentines know about North American notions of race from watching television and enjoy pointing out their country's superiority on this count.

Despite denials that skin colour matters in Argentina, there are conspicuous patterns that suggest an association. Most famously, Eva Perón referred to her adoring working-class supporters as her *cabecitas negras* (little black heads), pointing to their humble origins. Employing a previously pejorative term which had been used to describe working-class people because they tended to be less 'white,' coming, as many did, from the interior, Evita symbolically inverted the relation between 'whiteness' and 'blackness.' This symbolic inversion remained important in Argentine culture in the 1990s, as evidenced by the way the term continued to be used with a marked sense of irony, evoking both its original meaning and its resignification. In the early 1990s I still met people, both working and middle class, who disdained *los negros*, meaning people from the popular sector. When I met with a class of seventh graders from the high school adjoining José Ingenieros one afternoon, they were eager to discover whether it was true that only *rubios* (fair people) could get into nightclubs in North America. There was much scandal at the time about *negros* (in the Argentine sense), being turned away at some of the most popular nightspots; they were amazed to discover that I too had been denied entrance to a club, despite the fact that I was conspicuously middle-class and fair (they were not sophisticated enough to recognize that I was insufficiently chic).

So although my sense is that Argentines underplay their importance, ideas about ethnicity and race play more crucial roles in organizing relations of inequality in other parts of Latin America. All racial and ethnic categories are social constructions (Wilmsen and McAllister 1996), but they are tremendously important in much of Latin America. John Gledhill describes how racial constructions become 'deeply sedimented in social practice' in Mexico (1995:78), structuring and seeming to explain systematic and historically constituted inequalities. For example, much of the political violence in Guatemala, and more recently in Chiapas, Mexico, has been organized as an assault on Mayans in those two countries (Green 1999, Gledhill 1997). Argentina, perhaps together with Uruguay and Chile, is distinctive in the lesser importance of race and ethnicity as explicit ideological markers of inequality. Although there are patterns of racism and racial discrimination, these are more readily thought of by Argentines in terms of class. The reverse is probably the case for much of Latin America where, as in the United States, class differences are often read as ethnic differences. This is not to argue that social relations are not racialized in Argentina, however. Galen Joseph persuasively argues the centrality of whiteness in *porteños'* understanding of their place 'in the national and transnational imaginary' (2000).

Perhaps more important to Argentines' sense of distinctiveness, though, was the country's economic strength. Members of the large, highly educated, cosmopolitan middle class felt themselves akin to the European middle classes and relatively distant from many of their Latin American neighbours. Thinking of what happened to Argentina in the 1960s, 1970s, and 1980s, observers from abroad probably focus on political turmoil. But for Argentines, this period is also a time of progressive, almost uninterrupted economic decline. This has affected their sense of their place in the world. They saw their position in the world change from one that in the Peronist 1950s seemed full of possibility – one comparable to that of Canada, Australia, or New Zealand – to an economy that was unquestionably mired in debt and dependence. An Argentine sense of difference has eroded as their country increasingly resembles other Latin American nations on the economic front. Be that as it may, one should note that Argentina is still relatively well off by measures of economic development, ranking first among Latin American countries (if only thirty-fourth overall) in the UNDP's Human Development Index for 2003 (United Nations Development Program). Part of what makes Argentines so indignant about their current economic plight, is that it is so recent. In chapter six I describe the processes of impoverishment associated with neoliberal restructuring. For now, it is important to note that this experience has made many Argentines feel more Latin American.

Some Issues Framing the Research

An Ethnographic Approach

Contemporary Argentine history, and particularly the era of the last dictatorship, has received a wealth of attention from journalists, political scientists, sociologists, and historians. There is also an important body of literature from and about human rights and human rights organizations as well as some gripping testimonial writing. This book draws on these literatures, but it also departs from them by starting in a specific community and placing the experiences and understandings of the people who live there at the centre of analysis. This vantage point cuts across and complicates some of the ways in which recent Argentine history has been understood.

For example, a history which has been characterized largely in terms of political regimes and forms of rule, bureaucratic authoritarianism and democracy among them, is not so neatly compartmentalized for the people in José Ingenieros. An ethnographic approach uncovers the ways in which the watershed dates of regime change are fuzzy, while some continuities between periods of democratic and military rule are clearer. This approach also reveals how people understand and evaluate these different periods against and through each other. I do not mean to undermine the careful and penetrating analyses that have considerably advanced our understandings of how institutions and structures of power work, but to suggest that beginning from a different angle illuminates other parts of these processes.

An ethnographic approach also raises questions about how these large processes thought to characterize recent Argentine history are played out for working people. It calls attention to how such processes intersect with individual lives, shaping, if not determining, how people see, think, and act. It moves our attention from the centre to the periphery, and to the particular connection between politics and culture.

Other anthropologists working in Latin America have discussed and analysed the quotidian consequence of processes like the ones described here, illuminating their effects on social relations. Gledhill (1995) and Lesley Gill (2000), for example, see the ethnographic approach as central to understanding fully what neoliberal economic restructuring is doing to societies and people. As Gledhill notes in his book on rural poverty in Michoacán, Mexico: 'Focus on qualitative social and political implications of recent developments will suggest the need to work with different measures of "success" and "failure" than those enshrined in conventional macro-economic indicators of economic performance' (1995:13).

Similarly, ethnographic studies of political violence and its aftermath get at some of its more insidious and lasting consequences. Linda Green's study of Mayan widows in Guatemala describes the powerful effects of fear on social life in a way that resonates with my own findings. She writes: 'Fear destabilizes social relations by driving a wedge of distrust between family members, neighbours, friends. Fear divides communities by creating suspicion and apprehension not only of strangers but of each other. Fear thrives on ambiguities' (1999:55). Steve Striffler, in turn, describes the long-term effects of political violence on patterns of cooperation and political organization for workers in the Ecuadorian banana industry (2002).

The specific location of this analysis also poses questions about the relation between individual experiences and social processes. This has to do with the problem of 'community' in José Ingenieros, to which I return in greater detail in the next chapter. For now, it is important to underline that there is no one way of thinking, acting, or being in this neighbourhood. This fact, obvious enough on its face, often forced me to move between levels not always linked in the literature, between individuals and small groups on one hand, and big structures and the state, on the other. This is not to argue that the level of community is irrelevant, but it does challenge views of 'the community' or 'the working class' as unitary actors.

Much recent writing on Argentina accepts that the dictatorship aimed to 'disarticulate social ties' (Villareal 1984, Acuña et al. 1995), that is, that the Process of National Reorganization effectively dismantled social relations in everyday life. Little attention has been paid, however, to how and why this happened. There has been a related inattention to how dictatorship affected various social groups in profoundly different ways.[4] This variety of experiences helps explain a problem facing human rights groups and their sympathizers. Some are perplexed by the apparent failure of their arguments to convince or mobilize large groups of working-class and poor people. In informal conversations some activists write this problem off to the 'inherent fascism' of the Argentine working class. Others believe in an impeccable working-class memory. By starting with the lives and understandings of a specific group of working-class people, I go beyond either stereotype, recognizing that individuals and groups within the working class feel and act in a variety of ways, and that they do so in social, political, and economic contexts that have sometimes imposed terrible constraints on their ability to act as they choose.

This study points to culture as a crucial location where processes such as dictatorship and democracy take place. As a wealth of writing on hegemony has pointed out (Gramsci 1971, Williams 1977, Roseberry 1994), many forms of domination work not only by controlling the state apparatus, but also by being able to shape people's sense of the desirable, the likely, and the possible in small as well as large ways, thus influencing decisions and actions.

Human Rights

My decision to look to working-class experience had its origins in questions about the place human rights discourses occupied in Argentine society when I arrived there in May 1990. Arriving after the famous human rights trials (see chapter five), I expected to find a country which had come to grips with its past, where people had heard and understood arguments for human rights and taken them as their own. So I was shocked when, shortly after taking up residence in Buenos Aires, the Ingeniero Santos vigilante case blanketed the media. Santos was an engineer (and it is interesting that this was considered an important enough fact to be perpetually attached to his name) who had shot and killed two young men as they stole his car radio. This was not the first time his radio had been stolen, so he had retaliated. What was striking about this case was the public reaction. There seemed to be a lot of support for the vigilante. Most notoriously, Bernardo Neustadt whose daily radio talk show and weekly television program had large audiences, was reported to have said that he would have done the same thing. What had happened to the new ethos of human rights and the rule of law in Argentina? What did this case say about the success or failure of the human rights discourse in reshaping how Argentines thought about justice?

These questions led me to reflect on the understanding of human rights expressed by the human rights organizations as they responded to the dictatorship. How had the particular constitution of the groups and the constraints under which they acted shaped the way human rights were understood in Argentina? As I argue in chapter four, for the middle class, and especially those members of the intellectual middle class who were direct or indirect victims, Argentina's last dictatorship was characterized by the violent repression of the most basic human rights – to life, to the integrity of the person, and to freedom of thought and speech. Members of this group tended to experience the repression as directed at politically active individuals. The perpetrators of violence went out of their way to convince witnesses and survivors that discussing what they knew was both counter-productive and dangerous. Because people rarely discussed the violence with others, it was often difficult to contextualize.

This liberal (in the philosophical sense) view became the dominant narrative for human rights groups.[5] Reasons for the prominence of the liberal view include strategic considerations in making the most persuasive case for international consumption and the constitution and leadership of these groups. I do not mean to criticize the unquestionable heroism of Argentine human rights activists, who after all had to work towards immediate and strategic goals. But I do see it as having had an unintended consequence for the ways in which human rights came to be understood in Argentine society. Las Madres de Plaza de Mayo, Linea Bonafini, the organization of mothers of the disappeared, is one group that has most obviously moved beyond this relatively narrow definition since the end of the *proceso*. It is important to note that this move has had negative effects for their image; Las Madres were subsequently marginalized in the main-stream Argentine press.

My sense that this decontextualization may have been particularly strong for the middle class led me to turn my attention to working-class Argentines.

Although my original focus was the experience and interpretation of the *proceso*, it soon became apparent that people recalled the dictatorship in the context of preceding and subsequent periods. I thus soon expanded my project to embrace the whole history of José Ingenieros from its formation and occupation through the end of the research in December 1992. An advantage of this expanded scope is that it forces one to confront the ways in which the dictatorship was and was not anomalous, and this, in turn suggests a qualitative difference between working- and middle-class experiences of the *proceso*. For example, from their social and geographic vantage point, people in José Ingenieros were particularly conscious of how the police continued to act with impunity in the years after the dictatorship.

Popular Memory

In starting from the point of view of the people of José Ingenieros, I place particular emphasis on the complicated ways in which this past is (and is not) discussed. I also attend to how the past comes through in present activity and in plans for the future. The theoretical frame of popular memory illuminates the processes through which people's politics, identity and activity are rooted in their experience, and importantly in the ways they interpret and understand that experience.

In this book, I use the notion of popular memory as a way of understanding how large structural processes – development, dictatorship, restructuring – translate into people's everyday experience. It suggests a complex relation between experience, memory and interpretation. I see popular memory not as the object of study itself, but as a way of interrogating categories and material.

The bundle of issues around memory, history, and identity have received considerable academic attention of late (Connerton 1989; Swedenburg 1991, 1995; Passerini 1992; Boyarin 1994; Gillis 1994; Rappaport 1994; Grant 1995; Malkki 1995; Daniel 1996; Antze and Lambek 1996; Trouillot 1996; Sider and Smith 1997; Cole 1998). Some authors have even begun to write about an emerging field of 'memory studies' (Confino 1997, Crane 1997, and James 1997a). From protracted debates around suppressed memory, to controversies over museums and monuments, something in the historical moment draws our attention to this set of questions. Some have suggested that these interests are a product of a climate of social dissolution (Antze and Lambek 1996:xiii). For others, the connection between memory, identity, and politics is part of the post-modern or post-structuralist turn (Marcus 1993). I agree that questioning master and authoritative narratives is part of what is at stake. I want to emphasize, though, that this need not be a move to an idealist discursive realm. If these questions matter, it is precisely because of their materiality.[6]

There is no longer anything surprising about the assertion that history is made and remembered in particular ways by particular people. The notion that historical accounts are constructed has become a truism. Nonetheless, the actual processes of their construction deserve considered attention because they can reveal much about how relations of power make themselves felt in culture. Historical accounts are among the most obvious contexts in which the things people take for granted in their social worlds become domains of struggle. People are seen to fight over understandings of how things have been, how they are, and how they should be (O'Brien and Roseberry 1991, Comaroff and Comaroff 1992).

It is not surprising then, that both popular and academic examinations of memory have often focused on troubling and contested historical periods; the most striking example of this is Holocaust studies.[7] For Argentina, the *proceso* has elicited similar attention. A significant subset of the literature on the dictatorship examines the problem of memory. Some authors consider how legislative and legal processes become domains for contesting the past, imposing their own rules on the debate (Osiel 1986, Kaufman 1991, Taylor 1993, 1994, Acuña et al. 1995). Others focus on the problem of how individuals and groups live with the past (Parelli 1994, Carlson 1996, Robben 1996, Verbitsky 1996, Isla 1998, Taylor 1997; and fictional accounts like Bonasso 1990).

A popular conception of history as contested and contestable terrain is older and closer to the surface in Argentina than in North America. The Argentines I know have a very clear sense of the political significance of historical narratives. This belief in the importance of history-writing led people in José Ingenieros to help me in my research (see especially chapter 6).

Just as the residents of José Ingenieros were sensitive to the politics of historical accounts in general, they were aware that the language they used to talk about the last dictatorship was thick with political implications. This fact asserted itself uncomfortably in the research for this book. In an interview which I discuss later, Don Fernando avoided using any labels at all rather than choose a word to describe the period variously known as 'the dirty war,' 'the dictatorship,' 'the military government,' 'the time of the military,' 'the defacto government,' 'the military process,' or 'the time of [General] Videla.' Any of these names carries a political load. Perhaps Don Fernando was reluctant to flag his own politics, or maybe his evasion was out of deference to me (unaware of my position, or unwilling to disagree). As a researcher, I generally tried to use the term employed by the people with whom I was speaking or else a term seen as relatively more neutral: *proceso* or *época de los militares* (time of the military). In writing this book, however, I have usually chosen Process of National Reorganization or *proceso* because the title that the armed forces chose for its reign emphasizes the extent to which they saw themselves as engaged in a project to remake the nation. The term calls attention to the convergence of political, economic, and social agendas.[8]

Popular memory is useful methodologically as well. The concept helps get beyond a previous tendency to rather naive readings of oral history, especially of working-class and oppressed people. Anthropologists and historians have become increasingly sophisticated about the particular limitations and richness of oral accounts. They acknowledge that early assumptions about the transparency of the stories people tell about the past were misguided. Memory is tricky in that it can be unfaithful in the literal sense. Neither can we assume that the meaning behind stories is transparent (cf. Frisch 1990:22). These realizations have led to a new subtlety in the way scholars work with such accounts, reading from them much more than the facts they seem to convey.

As writers have become increasingly conscious that they are looking at narratives about the past, at the traces produced for specific reasons at particular moments, they have also begun to pay more attention to the place the past plays in present social and cultural formations. This attention to what the Popular Memory Group calls 'the past-present relation' (1982) has suggested ways of thinking through these connections. Thus many have read particular historical narratives as written not just from, but also about the moments in which they are fashioned (Anderson 1991 [1983], Hobsbawm and Ranger 1983, Scott 1988, Frisch 1990, Comaroff and Comaroff 1992, O'Brien and Roseberry 1991, Wallace 1996). At the same time, those interested in the past have learned they must consciously read through the distortions of the present in attempting to recover the 'meaningful worlds' of people who lived in the past (Comaroff and Comaroff 1992:xi; James 1987, 1997b, 2000; Passerini 1987; Portelli 1991).

The past-present relation is important in a third way: specific experiences, both personal and collective, are sources of knowledge which may challenge the dominant political and cultural order by running counter to official histories. These histories shape how people understand, feel, and act in the present (Steedman 1987, Fraser 1984, Williams 1977, Striffler 2002). In José Ingenieros, for example, the troubled present structures people's understandings of the past. The preoccupations with dirt and danger at the time of my fieldwork provide the lens through which many evaluated previous eras. Questions of physical and social order figured prominently in the stories and understandings of people in José Ingenieros. The contrast between order and chaos of both varieties thus constitutes a central theme of the book as well.

Anthropology and History

This study is also informed by an anthropological tradition which takes history very seriously. The increasing anthropological and ethnographic attention to history dating from the 1980s has brought a previously unfashionable tradition of anthropological interest in history to the fore.[9] For anthropologists, history provides a way of looking at process, moving away from static notions of culture and society and from reading social and cultural forms as received or natural. The attention to process is more than just about acknowledging social change, however. It sets social life in motion, calling our attention to the dynamics and relations of power that constitute ever-shifting social terrains. How could one understand anything about José Ingenieros without such an approach? A less historical focus leaves out too much of what is crucial here. It makes all the difference in the world to understand that the physical and social disorder which observers see in José Ingenieros is not a result, as some would have it, of the inherent failings of its inhabitants but is, rather, socially produced.

Anthropology shares with social history a preoccupation with the specific. At their best, both disciplines strive to reconstruct the social worlds of people living in particular times and places. We try to understand how and why individuals act and are acted upon in myriad subtle (and less than subtle) ways. To understand the difficulty, the contradictions, and the costs of the recent past for people like those who live in José Ingenieros requires looking where analysts have not tended to look, and hearing stories social researchers have not often heard. It requires, I think, a degree of daily contact and intimacy I hope not to have abused.

These two traditions – popular memory and historical ethnography – are essential because without them characterizations of working-class people and working-class consciousness can too easily slip into romanticization. Alternatively they can take on an accusatory tone. I keep thinking of a woman in a graduate seminar in New York in the late 1980s. We were discussing Argentina's recent experience of dictatorship. The woman, clearly upset by the reality being described, broke her long silence, asking in frustrated befuddlement, 'Why can't these people just get it together?!' She was embarrassed, of course, but the sentiment is not uncommon. I have heard people in Argentina, and in José Ingenieros, say similar things. The answer, I think, is that there is a history to how people were systematically prevented from getting it together, and simultaneously that there is a surprising degree to which they do get it together, despite everything.

The State

In examining people's struggles, my aim in this book is ethnographic. I have tried to take as my central problem what the world looks like from the perspectives of a particular group of people. But one cannot hope to understand 'the native's point of view' (Geertz 1983, following Malinowski) by abstracting it from the larger social field in which 'the native' is enmeshed. The story of José Ingenieros and the perspectives of those who live there make no sense unless one tries to understand the state agents and state projects exercising their influence, not just as context, but as constitutive, in crucial ways, of everyday life. As even my brief opening sketch suggests, the state is a central character in the stories I am about to tell.

However, the term 'the state' is itself misleading; the state is neither monolithic nor unitary. As anyone who has ever been a state employee can attest, the state is a collection of people, agencies, and branches with diverse, and even conflicting agendas, projects, and interests. As Philip Abrams spelled out in an influential article (1988 [1970]), to reify the state is to risk radically misunderstanding the nature of politics and political power. The idea of the state serves to naturalize relations and practices of power, making them appear technocratic rather than political. Instead of reinforcing the illusion of the state, what Abrams calls 'the mask that prevents our seeing political practice as what it is' (1988:82), he suggests that we undertake to study the state system and the state idea. Abrams's critique is directed principally at the northern liberal democracies rather than at Latin America in the second half of the twentieth century, where, after all, the mask has slipped more often than not, revealing crude political interests for all to see. Also, as Gill notes, following Roseberry (1994) and Nugent (1997), 'such tightly organized, efficient, and interconnected state institutions are rare in Latin America' (Gill 2000:17).

Abrams's exhortation to resist reifying the state remains crucial, however. Echoing his assertion that 'the obvious escape from reification ... is historical' (1988:80), a number of scholars of Latin America have turned their attention to state formation (Joseph and Nugent 1994, Mallon 1995, Nugent 1997, Clark 1998). This approach examines how the state, like hegemony, is always a work in progress (Roseberry 1994). To write about state formation for these scholars is to emphasize the construction of the state system (the political and governmental institutions) and the state idea as historical processes. Such an undertaking for Argentina is beyond the scope of this book, but the work of these authors reminds us not to take the coherence of the state for granted, and to attend to the changing nature of the Argentine state apparatus and state idea over time.

Outline of the Book

In the next chapter I introduce the reader to the social and geographic location of the people who are my central concern. It describes José Ingenieros and my presence there as an anthropologist. The remainder of the book is divided in two parts, the first entitled 'Histories,' and the second, 'Memories.' In 'Histories,' I try to sketch the events and processes most important to people in José Ingenieros between about 1968 and 1992. Chapter 3 describes the constitution of the community, most importantly through the squatter invasion and its consolidation. Chapter 4 focuses on the violence of the Process of National Reorganization and some of its particular manifestations in José Ingenieros. Chapter 5 sketches some of the most important events in the political life of the country between 1982 and 1992. It goes on to describe not only the economic legacy of the *proceso* years, but also the effects of the ongoing neoliberal policies which continued to hold sway through the years of my fieldwork.

The history of José Ingenieros is, for many residents, a vertiginous roller-coaster of hopes conceived and dashed, of possibilities imagined, realized, closed off, revived. In the part of the book called 'Memories' I examine the presence of this past in the lives of people who live or work in José Ingenieros. I return here to the problem of popular memory, asking how people in José Ingenieros recall and make sense of this past. Chapter 6 thus examines the history workshops which I instigated and helped run. Chapter 7 focuses on narrative truths, the ways in which people actively make sense of their pasts and lives. The accounts described here underline the connection between identity, politics, and stories about the past. Because these identities are so profoundly influenced by the history of Peronism, I have included an appendix addressing these questions with respect to the constitution of working-class identities in Argentina.

Chapter 8 looks at how the past resurfaces in unexpected times and places in the ongoing flow of events. It demonstrates the material consequences of popular memories. By looking at two controversial community projects – one about policing and the other about health – launched while I was living in José Ingenieros in 1991 and 1992, I show how history intercedes in contemporary debates in unexpected but important ways.

The conclusion briefly reconsiders some of the book's central themes. An epilogue brings the reader up to date on some developments in Argentina and in José Ingenieros in the years since I left the neighbourhood in 1992. Finally, for the reader unfamiliar with recent Argentine political history, in addition to a short discussion of Peronist identities in Appendix A, I have included a brief chronology in Appendix B. A glossary listing abbreviations and Spanish words can be found at the back of the book.

Chapter 2

'This Is Not a Shanty Town'

The Setting

It took me a while to find my way to José Ingenieros. I had resolved to find a working-class location from which to examine the issues that puzzled me. This task proved more difficult than I anticipated, however. In retrospect, I believe part of the trouble arose precisely from the processes of social atomization that I seek to explore here. I was looking for a community organization that might provide a point of entry, but although I encountered several possible sites, my contacts felt the community groups were too fragile to receive me, and in fact at least one subsequently fell apart. After some time looking for a suitable location, in May 1991 I was given a name and address in José Ingenieros. Telephones were still a middle-class luxury in Buenos Aires at the time, so I had no choice but to try to decipher a route in the complex bus guide and make my way out to *rotonda* (roundabout) La Tablada, a journey of a little over an hour on city buses (see map 2.2). I ventured forth on a Sunday afternoon, thinking that Anahí, the woman I was to try to meet, was more likely to be home then.

By the time I made this trip, I had been living in Buenos Aires long enough to have absorbed some *porteño* prejudices about the qualitative difference between the capital and the *conurbano*, the formerly industrial and working-class ring around the city. On the surface the contrast is indeed striking. Heading out of the capital, crossing the General Paz, the beltway circumscribing the capital with its concentration of money, services, and power, one feels as if one has suddenly entered Latin America. Unexpectedly the patina of Europeanness is gone. The density of buildings decreases, while that of graffiti and potholes increases.

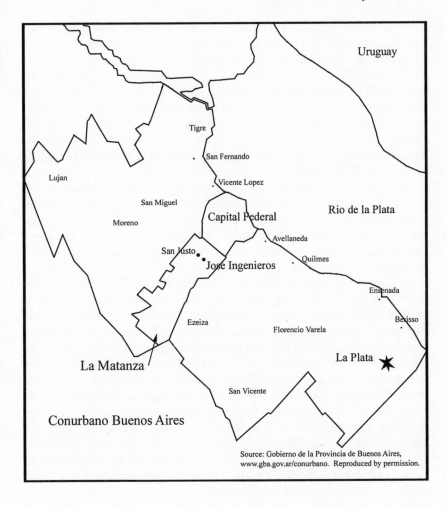

Map 2.1. Location of José Ingenieros in Gran Buenos Aires (Courtesy Gobierno de la Provincia de Buenos Aires)

I got off the bus and crossed the *rotonda* at the intersection of two major arteries, Camino de Cintura and Avenida Crovara. On first approach, the neighbourhood, known by people from adjoining areas as *los monoblocs* or *los complejos*, is a somewhat forbidding sight. Its weathered concrete, four stories high, sticks out. The physiognomy of the suburbs of Buenos Aires is characterized by the one- and two-storey houses built up gradually by the European immigrants who inhabited them. This same pattern is also followed in new neighbourhoods. The *villas*[1] (shanty towns) are more densely populated but little construction exceeds one storey.

The system of addresses in José Ingenieros is a bewildering combination of numbers and letters so when I saw someone, I asked for help. I stopped a woman heading out for that Sunday afternoon. As fate would have it, we soon discovered that she was Anahí,[2] the very person for whom I was looking. We agreed that I would see her at her apartment the next morning.

In her late thirties, Anahí had four children, three of whom lived with her. She is calm, centred, and self-possessed when one gets to know her, but also shy. Born in the northern province of Misiones, like her many brothers, sisters, and cousins, she moved to the capital in search of work. In this sense she resembled many of her neighbours. In 1991, 44.4 per cent of residents of José Ingenieros were from Argentine provinces other than Buenos Aires. Almost half were born in Buenos Aires (49.4 per cent) but if one looks at the number of children born after the *toma* (squatter occupation), the importance of internal migrants becomes clearer. Fully 42.2 per cent of the population was under twenty years old, therefore born after 1971, presumably many the children of migrants.[3] A small portion, 6.8 per cent, of residents were born in bordering countries, and only eighty-one people (including me, 0.7 per cent) from farther afield.

Anahí was living in a *villa* in 1973 and was part of the *toma*. Although a very young woman at the time, she participated in organizing her part of the neighbourhood between 1973 and 1976. She still lives in the *complejo*, as do a few of her relatives. Anahí speaks Guaraní, an indigenous language used in Paraguay and parts of northeastern Argentina. She expressed the importance of these roots in the Guaraní name she chose for herself as a pseudonym here. Anahí's character is also manifest in her refusal to let me do a full life history with her. She decided she wanted to write it herself. I do not think this is because she lacked confidence in my project (she always supported it in every other way); rather, she wanted to be fully the author of her story.

El Hornero Community Centre

It was through Anahí that I came to know the people in the Centro Comunitario El Hornero.[4] We agreed I should meet other members and seek their support the following Friday.

El Hornero occupied a one-storey building of the same vintage as the apartments (1970–3). According to many neighbours, it was originally to have been a daycare centre. This building spent several years as the home of a scout troop (coed), was abandoned for some time, and then came under the temporary authority of the federal Ministerio de Acción Social y Familia (Ministry of Social Action and Family). In this incarnation a community centre was established with one employee (originally a trained social worker and later a member of the community), and the participation of neighbours. The organization began offering sports and cultural activities, mainly for children, but for some adults also, usually free or for a low fee.

I first visited El Hornero on a winter night. The concrete construction and tile floors held the chill in the air. Perhaps one reason people were hanging around the office was its electric space heater working full blast. When I entered, people were chatting and drinking *mate*.[5] After Anahí introduced me, I explained who I was and that I was interested in studying the history of the neighbourhood. The Hornero members asked me questions: Why Argentina? Why them? Where had my funding come from and how I had gotten it? They were also curious about how Argentina was seen in North America. Pablo, a young man in his mid-twenties who taught at the centre, was particularly concerned about the negative image of Argentina conveyed in recent World Cup soccer matches. Pablo worried that the drug scandals surrounding Maradona[6] had sullied the national reputation. I was asked how North Americans (Argentines use the term *norteamericano*, by which they mean residents of the United States) saw Argentina. I had to concede that most were not well informed. When I noted that people in the United States did not know much about Canada either, they were slightly mollified.

Three hours later, after a wide-ranging discussion about the state of the world, Argentina, and José Ingenieros, punctuated by the comings and goings of children and adults, conversation returned to my project. People began planning to help me, offering to perform introductions, and generating a long list of those with whom I should speak. That day, as in the year and a half that followed, I was often struck by their openness. Despite the never-ending succession of local conflicts in which El Hornero and its members were embroiled, they told me to talk to people of all stripes, insisting I speak even with leaders who were opponents, and trusting me to make my own evaluations. At this first meeting, I was also warned that there were few if any useful documents. This turned out to be basically correct. Most government documents from the construction and early days of the neighbourhood had been lost in the shift from federal to provincial jurisdiction in 1978. No other likely repositories emerged.[7]

It was after ten when I left, the first of many evenings when someone would wait with me at the bus stop for a return trip to my apartment in the capital. At night buses were infrequent, but many trucks used this route taking cattle to slaughterhouses here and in the neighbouring Mataderos district in the capital. The *rotonda* that acted as an interchange for the intersecting highways was poorly lit; the dense fog generated by the subterranean Rio de la Matanza added to the eery effect.

I eventually became quite active in the centre, especially after I moved to the neighbourhood. At the request of other members I volunteered my services as an English teacher. My laptop became the typewriter of choice when letters had to be written and my camera came in handy when people wanted to document the sewage crisis. I also participated in a course for the training of community health agents and I increasingly spoke up in meetings. My association with the centre surely influenced my reputation in the neighbourhood, although my evident outsider status probably meant people permitted me a more liminal identity than they would have afforded a local. On the other hand, my residence and consequent knowledge of the day-to-day affairs of the neighbourhood surprised people, distinguishing me, I was told, from a long line of outsiders, especially social workers.

Conducting Research in José Ingenieros

It is tempting to present the research for this book as having been carefully and cleverly planned in advance, but the truth is that what changed most in the journey from graduate school in New York to fieldwork in José Ingenieros was the methodological approach that I would apply to the set of questions about Argentine culture and politics that I brought with me. As I have already noted, my attention shifted from human rights activists to a working-class community after I arrived in Buenos Aires. In the next section, I discuss some theoretical and pragmatic problems with the very notion of community when applied to José Ingenieros, but for now suffice it to say that a community study suggested particular methodological avenues including participant-observation, informal and formal interviews about the neighbourhood's present and past, and collecting documentation about the neighbourhood.

Many researchers from other disciplines find participant-observation, the ethnographer's workhorse, disturbingly vague. It is best understood as a strategy of cultural immersion. By living with a group of people over an extended period and participating in the life of a community, one hopes to learn about local life in its dailiness and about what the world looks like from a particular social and geographic perspective. This requires much hanging out, listening, pitching in, chatting (and in working-class Argentina, a lot of *mate*) and then writing down everything one can think of about what one has heard and seen and thought about during the process. In my case, my ethnographic gaze originates (although not exclusively) from El Hornero and its social field. In addition to participant-observation, I conducted formal and informal interviews with residents of José Ingenieros. Once people had agreed to speak with me – which not everyone did – I almost always found them generous and forthcoming. They inevitably offered me *mate* or coffee and a snack, which quite often they had prepared in advance. I had to be careful not to arrive too close to meal time, or people might invite me to eat with them, even if they could not really afford an extra plate at the table. I encountered this expansive friendliness and generosity throughout my time in José Ingenieros. I also spoke with non-residents who had particular kinds of knowledge and experience of the neighbourhood, including social workers, former residents, school teachers, administrators, and politicians.

Although the past-present relation emerged from these methods usually associated with synchronic[8] ethnographic research to a remarkable degree, this work also benefits from a method borrowed from social history: the community history workshop. History workshops are occasions for the collective thinking through of the past. Most successful when they move away from conventional narrative forms, they can be highly evocative, produce enlightening debates among participants, and reveal much about the processes of recalling the past. Chapter 6 discusses the history workshops I conducted in José Ingenieros in detail. For now, however, a brief description is in order, since these workshops are a key source of my knowledge about the local past.

I was involved in two distinct history workshops in José Ingenieros, with from four to thirty participants. The first emerged almost by accident through conversations with participants in El Hornero; it mostly entailed group discussions about the local past. The second, more successful, attempt was organized with the director of a local preschool. Participants were mostly drawn from the preschool community, parents or grandparents of the children there as well as teachers, a custodian and some neighbours who sometimes volunteered their services. This second attempt incorporated much more varied activities, including dramatizations, focused discussions, and the production of a neighbourhood mural. These workshops produced a lot of helpful information about the particular events and processes that shaped José Ingenieros, especially for the period from the *toma* through the *proceso*. As I discuss in chapters 6 and 7, though, they were even more interesting as sites for examining how the past was recalled.

José Ingenieros as *Barrio*

Most anthropologists now accept the critique of bounded and static notions of community; Eric Wolf's billiard ball image (1982:6) is one of the most evocative. In fact, when I set out to do fieldwork on the politics of memory in Argentina, I thought I would avoid this trap by locating myself in Buenos Aires, a city of twelve million. That soon changed. A year later I found myself profoundly relieved to be situated in a working-class neighbourhood that, if not bounded, was at least clearly discernable.

When anthropologists and social scientists have taken an interest in urban neighbourhoods in big cities like Buenos Aires, it has often been shanty towns on which their attention has settled. Perhaps they are drawn by the superficially self-contained nature of such settlements – an assumption Perlman soundly lays to rest in her study of Brazilian *favelas* (1976) – perhaps because the *villas* and the *villeros* that occupy them are often the most desperate, evoking empathy and solidarity from researchers. I have wondered if residents' insistence that José Ingenieros was not a shanty town was not also a question about my own interest in the neighbourhood. This book considers a group of people who are poor, but in general not desperately so. They have decent housing, relatively clean water, most of the children go to school, and so on. In this respect, the lives of residents of José Ingenieros are lives not terribly different from those of many urban working-class Argentines.

The move to José Ingenieros solved a range of methodological problems; I now had a location from which to work and a group of people from whose points of view I could try to understand history, memory, politics, and the state. Retreating to the anthropological tradition of a village-like setting for my work, though, did not solve the epistemological part of the dilemma. Residents of José Ingenieros call it a *barrio*, but what do they mean? Is this place just a neighbourhood (that is spatially defined) or also a community or communities (socially defined)? José Ingenieros has an evident spatial identity; it looks like a distinct place and is seen as one by outsiders. From inside, the neighbourhood's status is more complex.

Each of the four *complejos* which make up José Ingenieros (officially Nucleos Habitacionales Definitivos 4-5-6, 17, 18, and 19) has a singular building design with distinctive physiognomy and internal organization, and a specific identity as well. All the buildings are four stories high, and are interspersed with public and green space. Systems of stairways organize the apartments vertically. The architects had learned from the mistakes of apartment blocks of the 1950s and 1960s when the scale had made public spaces too impersonal and anonymous. There are no long hallways; rather, stairways service eight or sixteen apartments (either two or four per floor).

This decision turns out to be important since stairways became the basic social and political unit of the neighbourhood. Especially in the early days, close neighbours looked out for one another and shared basic domestic tasks, such as cooking, child care, and guard duty. When decisions had to be made there were meetings with representatives from each stairway. This is one of the most striking manners in which the organization of space in the complexes can be seen to shape social relations there.

Some stairways had made improvements, installing tile flooring or windows in the larger hall spaces, or a locked front door with a buzzer. Other groups of neighbours were unable even to maintain stairways clean and painted. Depending on the inhabitants and the norms of the building, the hallway can become a place where children meet, play, and hang out, fortifying a sense of community and sometimes engendering conflict.

The neighbourhood's planners also designed public spaces that play important roles. Because of the squatter occupation, some were interrupted before completion (although many wonder whether a sophisticated sports centre was ever really in the cards) but others, like the two pedestrian malls and the educational centre, are essential to a sense of community.

José Ingenieros may stand out for its architectural style, but there is nothing bounded about it. People go outside the neighbourhood for work, study, and entertainment. In fact, one thing people valued was José Ingenieros' location at a major intersection with many bus routes. This means relatively convenient access to the capital, La Plata (the provincial capital, sixty kilometres away), San Justo (the administrative centre of La Matanza) and to other work sites throughout Gran Buenos Aires. Buses, frequent during commuting hours, were fewer in the evening. Late at night residents were suddenly isolated; few residents had cars and many taxis refused to enter.[9]

Location is important in other ways as well. On the northeast corner of the *rotonda* and bordering the neighbourhood on its north side along Camino de Cintura, the manicured lawn of the Army's Third Armoured Regiment, Regimiento La Tablada, faced the neighbourhood. Horses grazing peacefully gave the regiment a bucolic air, belying the violent and confused events of its 1988 armed takeover by members of Movimiento Todos por la Patria (MTP), a political organization which the name La Tablada now evokes for many Argentines.

On the northwest corner of this intersection is a gas station, a café, and a few stores. Facing the neighbourhood on the west, along Avenida Crovara, is an enormous natural gas processing plant. Until 1991 the plant shared its green landscaping with the neighbourhood, but now a large wall cuts the street off from what lies behind. When it was erected, presenting its clean white expanse to the world, neighbours waited with bemusement to see how long it would take for the wall to be covered with the messages of local Peronist groups; it took about a week. The smell of gas sometimes pervades apartments downwind of the plant. To the south, the side of José Ingenieros facing away from the *rotonda*, the neighbourhood adjoins Ciudad Evita, a large attractive neighbourhood built as worker housing during Juan Domingo Perón's first presidency in the 1940s. The neat white bungalows with their red tile roofs and green yards present a stark reminder of the difference twenty years makes in the character and quality of housing for the poor. One of the rumours that circulated about Ciudad Evita is that the Onganía regime intentionally situated José Ingenieros between the Peronist development and the road to block the view of the model workers' neighbourhood from the view of the highway.

Can this collection of *monoblocs* be described as a community, though? Outsiders see José Ingenieros as a clearly defined place with a bad reputation: poor, crime-ridden, and unkempt. This view assigns a negative image to the neighbourhood's residents; they might be expected to distance themselves from it.[10] The question of identity is even more complicated from the inside. It is striking that, despite the bureaucratic ring, the *complejos* are still known by the numbers that originally denoted their place in a national housing plan. The sectors look different from each other, and each functions as a distinct administrative unit. Some residents were at pains to differentiate the complexes. Claudia told me that she had moved to José Ingenieros as a child, but was fifteen before she dared even visit the adjoining complex. The distinctive identities of the four *complejos* may just be a question of segmentation, of groups within groups and nesting identities, however.

José Ingenieros provides a sense of place and shared history. People in José Ingenieros have lived through twenty years together; they have neighbours with whom they have worked, or fought (or both) for two decades, through different political regimes. Common experiences such as the *allanamientos* (search and seizure operations) of the last dictatorship are events about which people have dramatically different opinions and memories, but which are considered central by all. The neighbourhood, seen as suspicious by the state, was the target of these activities. Common experiences were spatially determined.

Gavin Smith has pointed out that contention can be as generative of community as cooperation (1991). Disagreement, often born of social and political divisions, is the stuff of everyday life in José Ingenieros. Fights over resources, struggles over how to deal with crime, and arguments over who should negotiate with municipal authorities, all show that the residents of José Ingenieros are connected to each other in important ways. José Ingenieros is a community, but like all communities, it is manufactured.

Life in José Ingenieros

Despite its reputation, José Ingenieros is a lively place with an active economic and social life. The neighbourhood's at first bewildering system of roads and concrete walkways carries little car traffic and no buses; the streets are dominated by people. When the weather permits (Buenos Aires has a temperate climate) children play in what green spaces they can find and in the parking lots. The most common diversion is soccer, but children engage in all the usual pastimes requiring little equipment: hopscotch, string games, and jump-rope among them. Teenagers perch on small constructions (housing electrical or hydraulic equipment), while their elders are more likely to chat in doorways, in the shade of a tree, or while shopping.

Soon after I began visiting José Ingenieros and El Hornero, I expressed my interest in living there. This was greeted with some surprise. My new friends were not optimistic but assured me that they would see what they could find. Renting is uncommon in the neighbourhood; most people own their apartments or are paying them off. According to the 1991 census only 1.9 per cent of the apartments were rented, while 89 per cent of household heads said they owned their own apartments. I was extraordinarily lucky, then, when Marisa, one of those most active in El Hornero, was able to offer me a room in her apartment. This was possible because her mother and brothers had gone to try their luck living in a little house in a different neighbourhood. A university student in her early twenties at the time, Marisa is extremely bright, articulate, and committed. She had been a child when the family participated in the *toma*, so had lived in José Ingenieros most of her life. My home was in a three-bedroom ground floor apartment in *complejo* 4-5-6. I lived there from July of 1991 until I left Argentina in December 1992. In many ways my point of view in this book emanates from this apartment and from among Marisa's, and also Anahí's, networks and neighbours.

Although Marisa was unusual in pursuing post-secondary education, she was not alone in the community. The Argentine university system was essentially free with an open admission policy. By virtue of living in a poor neighbourhood, Marisa received a small subsidy to help pay for transportation and materials. Graduating was far more difficult than entering the university, however. According to the 1991 census, 158 residents (1.3 per cent) had at least some university education, and ninety-six were currently enrolled in a university, but only twenty-two were recorded as having graduated from university.[11] It was especially hard for people like Marisa who had to work to support themselves at low-wage jobs. Although few residents had post-secondary education, most residents in José Ingenieros were literate, although those raised either in the interior (anywhere outside Buenos Aires) or in neighbouring countries were less likely to be so.[12] The relative scarcity of books, magazines, and newspapers in José Ingenieros was a function of their cost rather than lack of interest. The newspapers I regularly bought circulated among friends.

Complejo 4-5-6 borders Avenida Crovara (see map 2.2). It was the first constructed, and the simplest in design. Eight hundred and thirty-two apartments in twenty-six identical and symmetrical apartment blocks are differentiated only by the blue, red, or yellow shutters and window frames.[13] One enters Marisa's apartment off one of the building's two stairways into a living-dining room with a table, chairs, and a storage cabinet. The television had been stolen (a neighbour was believed to have been the culprit). The ancient black and white I brought with me when I moved rarely worked. Because most apartments were occupied before they were appropriately finished, residents were responsible for any amenities their apartments might have. Marisa's had tile floor only in the most public part of her home. Elsewhere the floor was simply the original cement. Ahead to the right was a galley-style kitchen. The gas *calefón* heated the water for the kitchen sink and the shower in the bathroom on the other side of the wall. Over the stove was a kitchen window looking onto the garden; Marisa's cat used it as her private entrance. At the end of the kitchen was a *lavadero*, a washing area with its own deep sink, prized by some residents as an advantage of the apartments of *complejo* 4-5-6.

Across from the *lavadero*, a doorway had been cut to provide access to the garden which Marisa's mother Carmen cultivated over the years. In nice weather, we drank our morning *mate* or ate a meal on a bench there. Marisa's dogs spent much of their day in the garden. If a soccer ball should stray into their domain, the owner was hard-pressed to retrieve it. This usually brought cries of, '*Doña! Doña!* Could you get us the ball?' Marisa or I would wrest it from its captors. Although they were pets, the dogs were also seen as protection.

Returning to the front door, a long straight corridor lay directly ahead. Some shallow closets lined the wall on the left. A bathroom and two bedrooms opened off the hallway to the right; a third bedroom lay at its end. The bathroom had a window to the kitchen, bringing in light and air. It had the basics: a shower, but no bathtub.

The first of the bedrooms, which was larger than the second, was set up as Marisa's work room. It held a professional sewing machine, a

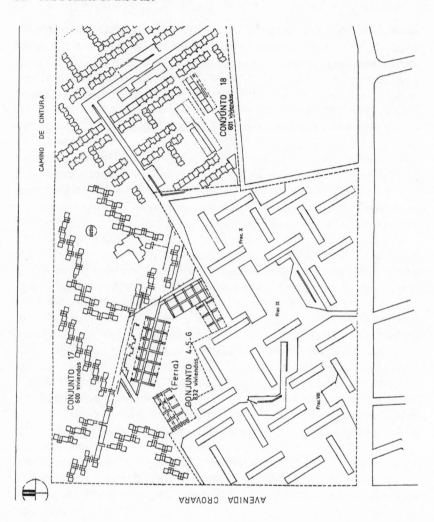

Map 2.2. Plan of José Ingenieros, NHD 4-5-6, 17, and 18

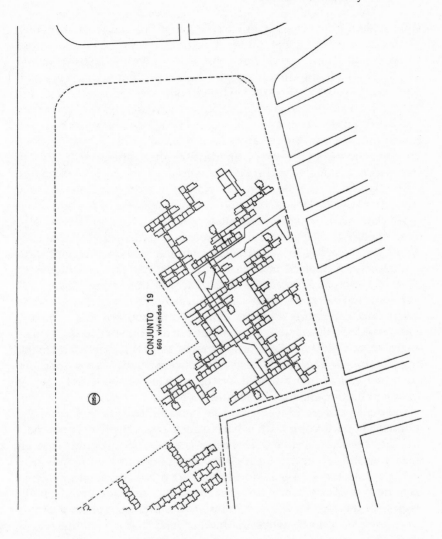

Map 2.3. Location of José Ingenieros, NHD 19

work table covered in cut fabric or a stack of finished work for which Marisa was paid by the piece. A radio always played as Marisa worked, talk shows more often than music. Like the large shuttered window in the living-dining area, the bedroom window had bars on it to protect against theft. The next bedroom was the one I used, big enough for a single bed, a small desk, and a dresser. Marisa's bedroom was a little larger, but not spacious. She had a large armoire, a bed, and a chair in her room. Almost all the apartments in the *complejo* have the same layout, although corner apartments are a little bigger. Variety comes from the degree and style in which they have been fixed up.

The buildings of 4-5-6 were the plainest, and to the outsider they may seem inferior, lacking the more complex massing of the other *complejos*. Although barren of balconies or terraces, this sector was also more open. The plazas were once green, and some had even had children's play sets, but they had fallen victim, neighbours recounted, to vandalism and neglect. In contrast, the buildings and apartments of NHD 17 were more varied. At the corner near the *rotonda, complejo* 17 had six hundred two-, three-, and four-bedroom apartments. These apartments had more spacious living rooms and terraces complete with outside grills suitable for the traditional Argentine *asado*, or barbecue. Many had enclosed these terraces to provide an extra room. Most stairways in NHD 17 also had four apartments to a floor, but some had half as many with doors opening off one side only. Fewer separate buildings had multiple entries.

The density of José Ingenieros has increased over time. Part of the unfinished sports complex has been turned into a lively covered market, the *feria municipal*. The U-shaped *feria* had recently replaced an open-air market that had been established in one of the many underused parking lots of 4-5-6. Housed in part of what was originally to have been a sports centre, in plan the structure made about ninety degrees of the arc of a circle, split into two buildings. The back of this form faces *complejo* 17, while the muddy field that it surrounds faces 4-5-6. The police office, object of the vociferous debate described in chapter 8, is located here as well.

Here, as elsewhere in José Ingenieros, skeletal structures had been filled in and occupied by a more recent wave of squatters. Throughout, people had taken advantage of their ground-floor locations to start businesses using capital that often came from the severance pay from layoffs. The progressive deindustrialization of the Argentine economy has pushed ever more residents (and the working class in general) into this type of relatively insecure employment. There are take-out joints, and kiosks selling candy, cigarettes, and soda. Some people have encroached on public space to build additions. Also characteristic were the many local Peronist party offices (*unidades básicas*).

People usually shopped daily and on foot, the ubiquitous plastic weave shopping bag over the arm. Small stores were scattered throughout the neighbourhood, but the three main shopping areas housed greengrocers, bakeries, butchers, dry-goods stores, and ice cream parlours (in summer), and fewer beauty-supply, clothing, and gift shops.[14] Notable by their absence were grocery stores, drug stores, liquor stores (although both wine and beer were available), cafés, and bars. Residents said these types of businesses made attractive targets for thieves. A few places offered take-out food, but this was less common than in the capital. Shopping at these stands generally meant short waits at most stops. Crossing paths with friends and neighbours, one stopped to chat with merchants and fellow shoppers. The public phone, one of the few in the neighbourhood in the early 1990s, usually had a line. Except for the bakeries that opened at 8:00 a.m., most stores opened in the late morning, closed at about 1:00 p.m. and opened again from around 5:00 to 9:00. Peak hours were noon hour and early evening.

Also bordering the *feria* was NHD 18. This *complejo* looked different from its neighbours in that its stairways were on the outside of the structures. Pairs of long buildings are tied together by common stairs accessing sixteen apartments each. Instead of terraces, these apartments had balconies. As in *complejo* 17, many had been enclosed to make an extra room. NHD 18 includes a few semi-detached two-storey houses. A busy pedestrian mall has trees down the centre and is lined with shops. A health clinic and the sector's administration lie at one end of the mall where it meets an internal road.

Complejo 19 (see map 2.3), bordered by open fields to the north and east, is the farthest from the *rotonda*. Its 660 two-, three-, and four-bedroom apartments were organized into strips running parallel and perpendicular to the L-shaped internal road. The perpendicular sections cross the road at the third storey. These relatively varied apartments have balconies. The architecture of the shopping area contrasts with that of the apartments; separate one- or two-storey buildings have large corrugated zinc roofs.

Although far from isolated, José Ingenieros was remarkably self-sufficient; almost any service was available. These included hair salons, manicurists, plumbers, carpenters, electricians, locksmiths, all types of repair people, and even a few doctors. Many, like Marisa, did piece-work of various kinds at home or in a 'workshop' in a neighbour's house.

Although drugs were seen as a social rather than economic concern, they were part of an underground economy. When I lived in the neighbourhood there seemed to be few major drug dealers operating within the neighbourhood, although drug use was clearly a problem.[15] One way the drug trade made itself felt economically was through theft and resale. Stolen goods, from the neighbourhood or from farther afield, were resold at low prices.

Neighbours had also established schools and health services that they convinced the state to fund. The schools appeared in the architects' original plans. There were two primary schools inside José Ingenieros, one in NHD 4-5-6 and the other in NHD 18, but many parents chose to send their children out of the neighbourhood to semi-private secular and religious schools.[16] A provincially run preschool (ages three to six) faced the primary school in NHD 18. The Centro de Acción Familiar (CAF, Family Action Centre), also public, was in NHD 19. Although there were no secondary schools in the neighbourhood, one was nearby in Ciudad Evita, across a field from *complejo* 4-5-6.

As is the norm in Argentina, children attended school morning (8:00 a.m. to noon) or afternoon (1:00 to 5:00 p.m.). Because the neighbourhood was considered needy (*carenciado*) children could attend the Centro Educativo Complementario (CEC, Complimentary Educational Centre) when not in school. This was the third part of the educational enclave in NHD 18. All three institutions were housed in airy, but also leaky, buildings. Staffed by teachers who supervised various activities and helped with homework, the CEC also provided lunch and a snack. Three municipally funded and staffed[17] health clinics in NHDs 17, 18, and 19 provided low-technology services to those who otherwise sought their health care in distant and crowded public hospitals.

After a long and complicated history between José Ingenieros and various levels of government, and once it became obvious that residents of José Ingenieros were not going anywhere, the government extended mortgages to occupants through the Banco Hipotecario Nacional (the National Mortgage Bank). In the early 1990s authorities viewed José Ingenieros as private property belonging collectively to those who had cancelled their debts on their apartments. These owners were subject to the same regulation as those in co-op apartment buildings. Consequently, in theory, various services were provided only as far as the border of the neighbourhood. As the reader will discover, the reality was more complex.

Several institutions aimed to fill the gap between individual households and public services. Each *complejo* should have an administration collecting expenses from every household for maintenance and repairs. In most *complejos* this system was only partially successful, but in 4-5-6 it did not exist at all at the time I was conducting fieldwork. The relation between cause and effect here is unclear since those who did not pay their quotas justified their decisions by pointing to the lack of service. Those who were supposed to provide services, on the other hand, argued they could not afford them because of the many who did not pay. There was criticism and distrust on both sides but the result was a depressingly run-down environment. The original infrastructure had many problems; the most obvious was the sewage system that broke down at regular intervals, sending raw sewage into the streets and even into people's apartments. There was also a problem with garbage collection. Litter was strewn throughout the neighbourhood by dogs because it was collected infrequently and containers were inadequate.

Unofficial organizations tried to provide private services to pick up the slack. The Asociación Vecinal José Ingenieros was a new organization that charged a fee for emergency ambulance transportation and medical attention to its members. Although located in the *chalets* (the local name for the Ciudad Evita bungalows), the office was in a house that directly abutted the neighbourhood. The association focused its recruitment efforts on the *monoblocs*. The services provided by the association can be seen either as complementary to or competing with those of the municipally funded health clinics. With ties to a private health plan, the municipality, and to the Peronist Party, its presence had implications for local politics. Another service was provided by a postal station located in the administration's former office in NHD 4-5-6. Mail was delivered to the station while door-to-door delivery was provided for a monthly fee.

Surprisingly, the church was not a particularly important institution in the neighbourhood.[18] Like the majority of Argentines, most residents are nominally Roman Catholic, but there was no local church or chapel, although catechism classes were offered in the CEC. A space on the mall of NHD 18 was used for funerals. Many went outside the neighbourhood, especially for life-cycle rituals. There was also a growing Protestant evangelical presence in the neighbourhood, most evident in its amplified outdoor summer meetings.[19] These took place in the open field behind the *feria* and reverberated throughout the neighbourhood.

Local Politics

To understand working-class Argentine culture, one needs to start from an appreciation of the crucial role Peronism has played in the country's recent history. Peronist ways of being and doing are hegemonic in the working class; they are important elements of common sense and are intrinsic to a nationalist working-class identity. During Perón's first and second presidencies (1946–55), Peronism came to represent not only the ideology but also the practices of the beneficent modern welfare state. Juan Domingo Perón, and his famous second wife Eva Duarte de Perón, imbued that state with a personalism that legitimized a politics of patronage and mediated between this modern, bureaucratic state and its subjects. I explore this process in greater detail in the first appendix. For now, it is important to note how deeply and thoroughly Peronist most Argentine working-class people have been. La Matanza and José Ingenieros were more Peronist still. I want to underline that this is not merely, or even chiefly, a political affiliation. It is an identity that, for those who share it, has become almost synonymous with what is good and noble in being a working-class person. It is also an identity so strong that it could muster support for neoliberal politicians if they effectively invoked and spoke through a Peronist idiom.

This Peronism came through in two related aspects of everyday life in José Ingenieros. First, the Partido Justicialista's control of the state at all levels during the time of my fieldwork shaped local relations to the state. The dominant mode of dealing with the state apparatus was through patronage, not confrontation. The traditional funnel for patronage, the *unidad básica*, the local political office, was ubiquitous.[20] Political operators, *punteros políticos*, usually controlled an *unidad básica*. Because Peronism was so hegemonic, local political struggles were generally about internal factional disputes and their fates hinged on leaders' abilities to mobilize local support for one or another of these factions. The number, location, and membership of the *unidades básicas* changed depending on the fortunes of the various factions of Peronism. These locales burst into a flurry of activity at election time, with as many as a dozen offices operating at once. The physical presence of these organizations was evident in the storefront offices which, when possible, inhabited central locations like the pedestrian mall of NHD 18. Their presence was also announced by the *pintadas* or political graffiti that were such a notable part of Argentina's urban landscape.

That El Hornero, the community centre I worked with, was conspicuously not Peronist, and thus not a reliable player in the local political game, made it suspect. The building it occupied was always a bone of contention as well. The same structure housed a mothers' club and soup kitchen run by a *puntera* and funded by the municipal government. As with many local organizations, there was an overlap between party activists and the people running social welfare programs. Various municipal social programs usually operated through these political networks. The lines between party organization and public service became blurred or disappeared as patronage flowed through municipal programs. There was also a long tradition of giveaways at election time, often directly associated with participation in rallies or other political events where the political *unidades básicas* were expected to produce support.[21] When competition between different political operators was fierce, as it sometimes was between the different factions in José Ingenieros, forms of patronage could be glaring, even shocking.

Sara, a neighbour living in *complejo* 4-5-6 who was not a particularly active Peronist, indignantly recounted a tale of clientelism. When her husband lost his job and she found herself without enough food for her children, the mother of four went to the state-funded soup kitchen to ask for powdered milk. To get it, she was told, she would have to go out that evening and post flyers supporting a specific list in the upcoming Peronist primaries. In telling the story, Sara expressed her dissent. Incidents of this sort were important mechanisms by which the party and the state-apparatus cooperated to produce the special kind of order I describe here.

Women, Community, and the Valiant Ladies

Women constitute a powerful, often a dominant, presence in the social world described in this book.[22] Their presence is so striking that I was startled to discover, when I later gained access to census data, that the proportion of men to women in José Ingenieros was essentially balanced.[23] I did not set out to write about gender and community in my study of José Ingenieros. I began this work convinced that gender, like class, was an important social category marking and organizing social life, and also an important cultural idiom (Scott 1988, Pratt 1990) but in this particular case, I did not choose it as an object of study. Nonetheless, the particular character of the female presence calls for some explanation. The prominent place of women in the account that follows is tied to the gendered division of labour in José Ingenieros, to disillusionment with old ways of doing politics, and to my own placement in the neighbourhood as a woman.

The ideal gendered division of labour for working-class Argentines places men in the workforce and women at home engaged in the multiple tasks of social reproduction. Although such a pattern is often not possible – given deindustrialization, shifting patterns of employment, and increasingly precarious employment – changing economic circumstances have not yet undermined the sense that the home and the community are the proper feminine domains. Although some writers have seen policies of economic restructuring as potentially strengthening the hands of women because new forms of employment give women greater economic power, McClenaghan (1997) points out that this has not tended to be the case in Latin America. In general, women are being incorporated into the workforce at the bottom of the labour process, in contexts of insecure work and desperation. Secondly, greater participation in the paid workforce may not translate into a reduction in household responsibilities.

One way these assumptions about the division of labour are made material for women is in the organization of the school day. As noted above, Argentine children attend school either in the morning or in the afternoon. These shifts allow twice as many children to use the facilities, but they are predicated on someone being available to care for children for half the day.[24] The state apparatus is thus instrumental in structuring domestic labour.

When women worked for pay, as many did in the neighbourhood, they often attempted to organize their work to allow them to continue to bear the brunt of child care and other reproductive responsibilities. Many women, for example, preferred to do piecework, despite the low wages and high stress such work usually entailed, because it allowed them to retain some control over the timing of their daily activities. Cleaning houses was another preferred form of employment (generally the homes of middle-class families, where women also worked outside the home) because it, too, allowed some flexibility. Thus women seemed to be more present in José Ingenieros than men because they were. That is, although there were no more women than men resident in the neighbourhood, they spent more of their time in the actual space of the community.

Having noted these gendered distinctions in community participation, I must concede that for a long time I hesitated to highlight this apparent pattern of feminine responsibilities. For one thing, women in José Ingenieros rarely called attention to them. I also feared that describing these distinctions would overdraw them. Despite the gender ideology and the gendered division of labour – both of which I think are significant – none of this is very rigid. Women and men, and especially younger men and women, often took on roles considered atypical: I knew a young man who sewed with his mother at home; male and female *punteros políticos*, the neighbourhood representatives of the Peronist party, often held similar positions and acted in similar ways. There were households, generally where the couples were younger, in which men did a significant portion of the housework and child-rearing.

The predominance of women in local-level organizing points to a gendered politics, I think, but certainly not a feminist one. During my stay in José Ingenieros I encountered many stories of 'valiant ladies.' I take the phrase from an especially feisty and headstrong woman I call Doña Inés who used it to describe her neighbours (see chapter 3). This formulation, *las señoras valientes*, at once ironic and proud, describes how women of José Ingenieros portrayed themselves as they faced a series of challenges and dangers. These women would never call themselves feminists, but they saw themselves as willing to do what must be done. This is not simply a question of labels, although the understanding of feminism I encountered was narrowly conceived (often highlighting lesbianism). If we take some sort of explicit questioning of men's and women's roles – either inside or outside the home – as a basic tenet connecting many feminisms, then this sort of question was largely absent among the women I knew in José Ingenieros. Note that Doña Inés chose the word *señoras* (ladies/wives) not *mujeres* (women). In this sense, women in José Ingenieros seem different from their counterparts in Chile, where Schild (1998) describes a history of feminist activism in poor and working-class neighbourhoods. This activism, though redirected since the democratic transition, seems to have transformed the ways that women in such neighbourhoods understood themselves and their place. As Schild describes it, Chilean women have come to see themselves as political actors in their own rights. In

José Ingenieros in the early 1990s, on the other hand, many women continued to be seen, by both themselves and the state, primarily in relation to their familial roles.

In using the notion of valiant ladies, I am not asserting that these particular women are especially brave or that they are braver than their male neighbours, although they may be. Rather, I mean to highlight the ways in which women described themselves and their own actions in some of the stories that follow in this book. In these accounts, their ferocity, framed by them as a defence of their children, their families, and their community, seemed almost to startle them; they laugh and joke about it. Valiant ladies do not particularly seek to overturn gender roles, but they do stretch them. Some of these stories are of considerable daring: they defy their husbands by participating in the squatter occupation; they arm themselves to defend their new homes preparing kettles of boiling oil; they send up a hue and cry when death squads come to take their doctor away; they cajole, berate, and otherwise press their neighbours to do their parts. In general, the idea of the valiant ladies is not explicitly articulated in the accounts of women in José Ingenieros. It is, however, my description of the particularly gendered logic they impute to their own actions.

This pattern of feminine resistance has a more famous manifestation in Argentina: Las Madres de Plaza de Mayo.[25] Las Madres captured national and then world attention through their persistent and public quest for their children who had been disappeared (as the Argentines put it) in the dictatorship. At a time when there was very little organized dissent, when unauthorized meetings of any kind were illegal, the women who encountered each other in the round of government and military offices, hospitals, and even morgues, in a ceaseless search for their missing children, began to march weekly in front of the presidential palace. Unlike other human rights groups in the country, they explicitly excluded men. In a classically counter-hegemonic move, they chose to use the military's patriarchal ideology against it. They were only mothers they said, looking for their children as any good mother should. Las Madres became icons of loss; they carried placards with their children's photographs (enlarged snapshots); they demanded their children's safe return, and they demanded justice.

Finally, the prominence of women in the account that follows has also to be understood in the context of my own place in the neighbourhood. As a relatively young, originally single, woman, friendships with women came more easily.[26] It was also easier and less complicated to talk with women in their homes, or wherever we happened to be, often drinking *mate* together. I did have friends and acquaintances who were men, but several of these were attached to the women I knew. If they were not, I was more likely to feel constrained to maintain some kind of professional air to avoid any mistaken impression.

Sometimes valiant, sometimes less so, the women and men of José Ingenieros cast light on history-writing in both senses, as shapers of their social world and as tellers of stories about it. At times they have been buffeted by events beyond their control, at others they are more clearly the authors of their individual and collective fates. They are both the subjects and objects of history, as will become clear in the chapters that follow.

HISTORIES

Chapter 3

The *Toma*, Its Origins, and the Early Years, 1968–1976

Most residents of José Ingenieros begin the tale of their neighbourhood with the squatter invasion, or the *toma*, as it is known locally. In the early days of the 1973 democratic period, thousands of predominantly shanty town dwellers took possession of the nearly empty housing. Often seen as the neighbourhood's proudest moment, the *toma* serves as a dramatic origin story particular to the community, but it also represents a point of contact with national history. Through the *toma*, residents of José Ingenieros can see themselves as active participants in processes of national political importance. On prompting, they saw it as the kind of event in which a foreigner like myself might sensibly be interested. Recalling these events, people expressed wonder at their daring. They were proud to have won homes for themselves and their families. The *toma* is thus a central marker of local identity. It affected the social configuration of the neighbourhood in other significant ways as well. The processes encapsulated in the *toma* influence how and where people live, and how they relate to each other both personally and collectively. These processes also substantially affected the ways José Ingenieros has been seen by people from neighbouring communities and by state officials and agencies.

Doña Inés's Story

Doña Inés, a formidable woman, about forty years old at the time I spoke to her in 1991, conveyed something of the excitement associated with *toma* stories in one of my earliest formal interviews in José Ingenieros. In 1973 she was married and had two small children. I asked about her first impressions of the neighbourhood.

Inés: Look, it was marvellous! An impression that will never be erased. For me, a home and a roof is fundamental. When you have a husband, the home is the fundamental thing.

LD: Where were you living before?

Inés: I rented, you see, in Lanús but it was no luxury rental, more modest, because my husband is a worker. It had only one room, a shared bathroom, not a private apartment. So when my neighbour brought me here ... I didn't know what a squatter occupation was because I had never lived one. So when a man opened the door for me [to enter the apartment she would occupy] ... How can I tell you? What an impression, something so marvellous! Everything illuminated, large. I'm reliving it! And I said, 'my God, it's beautiful! But I'm not going to be able to pay for this with only a worker's salary!' ...

LD: Were you there alone long?

Inés: I was alone for one day. But I was desperate. I had to leave to tell my children. I had left the baby with a woman I knew, but not well enough to leave the baby all day. I don't know, a mother worries. So I tried to leave, bribing the conscripts, but they didn't want it. Finally one man let me out.

So I called my sister-in-law and told her I had a house, but I couldn't tell her where it was because I didn't know the place. Then the man in the store said, 'Señora, it's at Ciudad Evita.' So I told my husband to bring mattresses and blankets. After that the problem was to get back in. So I went in, crawling (I wasn't fat like I am now). When I look like this [looking over her shoulder], I see a pair of boots. I lift my head and I see a soldier standing there. He asks me, 'Señora, where are you going?!' And I say, 'nowhere. I'm just looking for a coin I lost.' After that I got in. At night my husband arrives, but furious! What had I done? Where had I been? They didn't let him in. But after we talked and talked, I said that we had little kids. Finally he came in.

I tell you, it was hard. We slept on the floor, on the inside doors that we had taken down because they wouldn't let us bring anything in, not clothes, nothing. We spent a week like that. There were very sick people, kids who died of the cold. *Ojo*, the soldiers treated us well, truly. They brought us *café con leche*.

The hardship the squatters endured is part of what makes the story of the *toma* compelling and dramatic. For many, heroism and sacrifice are important elements of their history.

Just as important though, is the collective effort that turned this partly finished and somewhat anarchically occupied housing project into a good place to live. Inés goes on to describe the emergence of local organization.

> *Inés*: There was a man here in the *barrio* who said he was a delegate. I am a teacher, so I joined him. I did the census of this whole neighbourhood [she means her sector, complex 4-5-6, with 832 apartments], house by house. Day and night. We ate an *alfajor* [cookie] a day. It was three or four in the morning, and we were censusing the people. We tried to organize.
> *LD*: When was this?
> *Inés*: In the first weeks. We tried to unite, to organize. There were people who I later realized had come because of their politics. ... We set ourselves to organize. I could feel it in my bones [*mi necesidad se hizo carne*]. That is, I suffered, suffered because I didn't have a home. This was marvellous. Well, after the army ended the siege, we made a treaty in my apartment.

Inés is now uneasy about the politics of the *toma;* she even told me that she now thinks they should not have participated, although she is one of only two people who told me they regretted participating. Occupations were the order of the day during the tumultuous period leading up to the return of Perón, but the occupied neighbourhoods are among the only sites not quickly dismantled shortly afterwards. In that sense, they are important vestiges of that almost revolutionary moment. This fact, and the efficient and militant community organizations that arose from the neighbourhood, help to explain the severity of the attacks after 1976. Not only were most of the experienced organizers abducted or forced to flee, but the message that such activity is inherently dangerous is hard to shake to this day.

The Plan for the Eradication of Shanty Towns

The *toma* is taken as José Ingenieros's origin, but as is usually the case with such tales, the story begins some years earlier, with the creation of the conditions which produced it. The neighbourhood now known as José Ingenieros was built as part of PEVE, the Plan for the Eradication of Shanty Towns in the Capital and Gran Buenos Aires under the Social Welfare Ministry of the Onganía military government, known as the Gobierno de la Revolución Argentina. The plan arose in response to severe housing shortages: although 2 per cent of the population of Gran Buenos Aires and the Capital lived in *villas de emergencia* (shanty towns) in 1960, this number had tripled to 6 per cent in 1970

(Yujnovsky 1984:334–64).[1] The generalized housing crisis had been further exacerbated by flooding in 1967 that had displaced many people, especially from the shanty towns in the low areas of the Reconquista and Matanza rivers (Davolos, Jabbaz, and Molina 1987:23).

In keeping with the big projects of the developmentalist strategies of the 1950s and 1960s (Torrado 1992), the plan was enormous. It called for the total elimination of the *villas* of Buenos Aires (Ministerio de Bienestar Social 1968).[2] According to the government, these had an estimated population of seventy thousand families. Assuming that 20 per cent of these families would find their own solutions to their housing needs after the elimination of the *villas*, the plan called for the construction of fifty-six thousand units over seven years, and of an additional eight thousand temporary dwellings (*Nucleos Habitacionales Transitorios, NHTs*).

The PEVE project proved both ill-planned and over-ambitious. First, it drastically underestimated the number of people involved: the plan identifies 280,000 *villeros* (people who live in *villas*), but a 1968 census carried out by the same Ministerio de Bienestar Social counted 526,043 *villeros* in metropolitan Buenos Aires. Furthermore, the plan did not even come close to meeting its own goals: in the first three years (January 1968 to April 1971) it removed only 35,692 people from *villas* (instead of 96,000 people), of which 25,052 were in transitional housing (Yujnovsky 1984:164–7). Organizational and political problems within and between the two responsible agencies – Ministerio de Bienestar Social representing the federal government and the Comisión Municipal de la Vivienda for the government of the city of Buenos Aires[3] – contributed to the plan's failure, as did finance problems and an extremely optimistic construction schedule (Yujnovsky 1984:191-5, Davolos et al. 1987).

Meanwhile, PEVE met with strong resistance from the *villeros'* organizations. The plan required an unrealistic level of control of these traditionally autonomous settlements, especially given the government's refusal even to recognize the organizations functioning within the *villas* unless these were directly controlled by the state (Yujnovsky 1984:164). The political opening of the early 1970s further galvanized the organizations of *villeros*, the most important of which was the largely Peronist Frente Villero de la Liberación Nacional.[4] The autonomy of the *villeros* must have been particularly alarming to the military men who saw the *villas* as naturally anarchic.[5]

One technical difficulty inherent in PEVE was how to identify who was to be moved. People were enrolled in the plan based on a census conducted in the *villas*, but the impoverished population was highly mobile; many people moved frequently in search of the best solution to their housing problems.[6] One former resident recounted how his family relocated to a *villa* earmarked for the plan so as to qualify for it.

Although the plan called for the relocation of all *villeros*, there was, in fact, a selection process. Participants had to qualify for the program. Social workers describe a hierarchy, 'according to certain criteria,' but are not forthcoming about what those criteria might have been.[7] Once participants were enrolled, social workers set about normalizing their legal statuses, especially with respect to documentation: foreign immigrants needed the appropriate papers, children had to be officially registered so they could go to school, and so on. This process served to disrupt existing community ties. Not only were many people excluded from the plan, but people who had lived as neighbours in the *villas* were moved to different complexes. A study of one particular case in the capital argues that administrators were especially careful to disperse local leaders (Davolos et al. 1987:23).

The *Barrios Transitorios*

One of the most revealing aspects of the PEVE was its system of transitional housing. Participants were required to spend time in temporary dwellings before moving to their allotted apartments. The proposal calls for eight thousand such units, calculating that one-seventh of the participating families would be relocated each year, thus leaving the transitional housing empty for the next group. At the end of the plan, the *viviendas transitorias* were to be dismantled. Memories of the conditions and rules applied to residents of transitional housing suggest that these would have increased resistance by *villeros*. The original documentation expresses, albeit awkwardly, the civilizing agenda behind the transitory housing phase, and thus the ministry's analysis of the *villero* problem:

It is worth underlining the reasons justifying the construction of the housing meant for temporary residence.

The principal objective that these locales must fulfill, besides better housing, [is] to serve as centres of adaptation to facilitate and accelerate the process of change for these families.

This change, adaptation to the urban industrial environment, can, theoretically, come about in the shanty towns with or without help; but [without help] – according to our experience – the cost is too high, and the time excessively long ...

Family groups living in the shanty towns are, in fact, really barren islands and no man's lands [sic]. As squatters, [the residents] are subject neither to the control nor the protection that socio-political organisms give all citizens. The result is certain interests or, on the other hand, violations that are not conducive to human dignity.

This abnormal situation impedes the normal development of the family and of citizens since they cannot rely on the natural support of the institutions of any organized community. (Ministerio de Bienestar Social 1968:10–11)

Undoubtedly the *villas* were, and continue to be, terribly inadequate living environments, but the government's overwhelming interest seems to have been in social order, and only secondarily in social welfare. People who passed through this transitional housing tell stories about the ways in which this civilizing function was made quite explicit. Many of the *villeros* were poor migrants from the rural areas, especially northern Argentina or bordering countries, who had moved to Buenos Aires in search of work. There was a perception that they had to be taught to live properly. Rules of conduct were stapled to their housing contracts. These rules included prohibitions against pets, making noise, decorating the outsides of the houses (Ministerio de Bienestar Social 1968:78–80), and some say they included curfews.

Don Fernando, an *adjudicado* (the local term for someone assigned an apartment through PEVE) who participated in the plan, tells how, when army trucks moved groups of people and their belongings from the *villa* to the *barrios transitorios*, both he and his possessions were fumigated. Anything left behind was flattened along with the old dwellings when bulldozers tried to ensure the shanties would have no new tenants (Davolos et al. 1987:23).

One evening, in a lively group interview at El Hornero in José Ingenieros, residents remembered these attitudes with marked irony:

Elena: ... those neighbourhoods that they made to be transitional are really big.
Gloria (ironically): They take you out of the *villa* and you go to this neighbourhood, and you learn to live like people.
Marisa: Right, you use the toilet, for example.

Elena: ... that's why there is this problem here of living together, because there were people who jumped over that, and went straight to the apartments. ...
Marisa (continuing): ... so that you don't use the door frames to make a barbeque, understand?
Gloria: Right, there you learned to live.

Although the plan stipulated that participants would live in the *barrios transitorios* for one year, the waiting period later grew to five. This helps to explain why so few of the apartments were finally occupied through the plan.[8] People who gave up the wait were replaced by new candidates who were added to the bottom of the list. Though this transitional housing was supposed to be destroyed at the end of the plan, much of it was still standing twenty years later. This is no doubt partly explained by the fact that those living in the *barrios transitorios* never moved onto the *Núcleos Habitacionales Definitivos* because of the *toma*.

Few of the residents of José Ingenieros are *adjudicados* (assigned residents), and these were given apartments in NHD 4-5-6, the first of the four *complejos* to be completed. For some reason the process of assigning people to their apartments seems to have been very slow until the Ministerio de Bienestar Social discovered the illegal occupation of neighbourhoods. With this news, according to social workers involved at the time, the process was accelerated and bureaucratic steps were overlooked, but even with this rush effort, *adjudicados* ended up constituting only a small fraction of those living in NHD 4-5-6. The social workers insist that they managed to place many people there. When asked about this apparent contradiction, residents suggest that some *adjudicados* may have refused to move into their assigned apartments given the volatile, even violent context into which they were being asked to relocate.

The Social Organization of Space

An important consequence of the historical moment in which José Ingenieros was constructed is its architecture. The neighbourhood may have been conceived as part of a state plan to rehouse and reform shanty town dwellers, but it was designed by progressive modernist architects. These architects stood between the government plan and its realization. Although, in the abstract, the PEVE was the expression of a particular social agenda, the buildings themselves were designed and built by people who had no special commitment to this project. At least some PEVE contracts were awarded to architectural firms that embraced the ideals of the social architecture movement of the late 1960s.[9] Surely economic constraints played an important role, but these apartment blocks were also designed in a style consonant with the international trends of the time.

Although the architects of José Ingenieros may have attempted to build in a way that fortified community, they did so without the participation of future residents. An alternative model is suggested by a neighbourhood in the capital known as Villa 7. Undertaken as a cooperative effort between *villeros* and progressive members of the Municipal Housing Commission, this project grew up in reaction to PEVE during the Lanusse presidency (March 1971 to May 1973). The fact that *villeros* were actively involved in its planning and execution led to some fundamental differences between it and PEVE. The results emphasize the important link between process and product.[10]

Although the PEVE process was interrupted, even overrun, in the rush of subsequent events, it constituted the physical, and to some extent the social, space of the neighbourhood. For example, the clearly discernable form of the neighbourhood is a key part of its significance for outsiders and, in a more subtle way, for its inhabitants.

The Political-Economic Context of the *Toma*

It is hardly coincidental that José Ingenieros should have been taken over in a squatter occupation in May and June of 1973.[11] The timing is tied to the transition to democracy and the legalization of Peronism; *intrusos* are explicit on this point. Period newspapers convey a sense of almost revolutionary political turmoil. This climate had been building for some time and was both realized and intensified in the wave of popular occupations taking place across the country.

The excitement of the moment can only be understood, however, in the context of the accumulated frustrations and dissatisfaction of the previous decades. These included: shifting economic strategies, declining standards of living for the working class – and some segments of the middle class – and political exclusion, especially the aggressive prohibition of Peronism.

In her authoritative history *Estructura social de la Argentina: 1945–1983*, Susana Torrado divides the Argentine postwar economy into three broad periods: the Peronist Strategy (1945–55),[12] the Developmentalist Strategy (1958–72), and the *Aperturista* (opening) Strategy (1976–83).[13] The period leading up to the *toma* was one where *desarrollista* (developmentalist) policy dominated. This strategy differed from Peronist import substitution[14] in that it concentrated on medium and heavy industry and no longer targeted working-class consumers. It also aimed to attract more international investment, especially from U.S.-based multinational corporations (Torrado 1992:51; Rock 1987: 328). Although the industrial sector led the economy in growth, it generated little or no increased employment. For Torrado, developmentalism was successful in producing overall economic growth and the modernization of economic structures, but 'both elements are achieved at the cost of marginalizing a considerable section of the population from the achievements of economic development' (1992:430).

The period beginning with the exile of Perón and ending with his return, although one of overall growth in the economy, also saw increasing economic and social inequalities. Despite a 10 per cent increase in real wages overall, the interval was characterized by the 'increase in the self-employed working class, increase in precarious employment for both middle and working classes, and the frank deterioration of the well-being of the most modest social groups' (Torrado 1992:429–30). While the 10 per cent improvement in real wages represented only a small percentage of increased productivity, social spending with respect to GNP decreased by about one-third and social spending per capita fell about 10 per cent. The progressive and uninterrupted deterioration of public services had its biggest impact on the poor. This, in turn, produced a general deterioration in social well-being as shown by decreases in life expectancy and levels of primary school education (Torrado 1992:422–9). Although the welfare state still worked, dissatisfaction with respect to social services grew.

Onganía

Lieutenant-General Juan Carlos Onganía acceded to the presidency in a bloodless coup on 28 June 1966, removing the Radical Party's President Illia from office. Unlike previous coups which had declared themselves 'provisional,' Onganía's Revolución Argentina was to be in power indefinitely. His implicit model was the Brazilian military regime established in 1964; 'Onganía sought to create a modernizing autocracy that would change society from above, with or without popular backing' (Rock 1987:346). Repression was employed early and often in order to impose 'social peace.'

In his attempt to impose peace through force, historians Juan Carlos Torre and Liliana Riz argue, 'Inevitably, a dangerous rift [opened] up between the forces of civilian society and a state power that was becoming increasingly remote and authoritarian' (1993:304). Furthermore, by closing all the usual political channels, popular leaders lost authority and were unable to direct and control disaffection or rebellion. Onganía's autocratic practices even extended to the military; he alienated his colleagues as well.

Onganía's problems were not only political. Economic difficulties also fanned the flames of opposition: real wages fell in part thanks to repressive practices, and the government was plagued by a recurrent crisis in the balance of payments (Torrado 1992:58–62).

Peronism Underground

Although Onganía's rule was especially devoid of political legitimacy for most Argentines, the legitimacy problem was not created by it. One central factor in the political volatility of the late 1960s and early 1970s in Argentina was the continued exclusion of Peronism and its large (but not exclusively) working-class constituency.

Although Peronism was exiled from power in the coup that removed Juan Domingo Perón from office on 19 September 1955, its importance hardly waned. On 6 April 1956 the military took the remarkable step of passing a decree warning Peronist opposition members that they would be judged by military tribunals. All forms of Peronist proselytizing were prohibited as was the mention of the very word Perón. Suddenly photographs and Peronist songs sung at home were punishable by imprisonment. As historian Daniel James notes, such actions overshadowed class differences within the Peronist movement. Instead, the military divided Argentina into two broad groups: Peronists and anti-Peronists. They may have even inadvertently strengthened Perón's symbolic importance. James writes: 'If a worker could be arrested for going to work on a bicycle with a picture of Evita stuck on it, then it was hardly surprising that the figure of Perón and his return to power should serve as a focus for his rebellion. A clear cutting across class lines was implied' (1988:95).

The formal exclusion of Peronism led to a kind of millenarian faith in the return of Perón. This faith became one of the unchanging elements of resistance to the succession of four military and five civilian presidents who ruled for the almost eighteen years Peronism was prohibited. As one worker put it, 'For us the return of Perón meant so many things; the return of dignity and decency for those who worked, getting the boss off our backs, the return of happiness, the end of so much sadness and bitterness in the hearts of ordinary men, and the end of persecution' (anonymous, in James 1988:88). This kind of hope fed the Peronist Resistance.[15] It became a rallying cry for anti-government forces, and eventually grew so strong that Perón's return was widely recognized as the only way to achieve a government with legitimacy.

The Demise of the Military and the Return of Perón: *El Cordobazo* to Ezeiza

Thinking on political unrest and violence in this period of Argentine history is often exemplified in, and framed by, two events that mark Argentine memory: *El Cordobazo*, that began the process that would eventually bring Perón back to Argentina, and Ezeiza, that foregrounded the conflict within Peronism that persisted throughout the Peronist interregnum.

In political and social terms, *El Cordobazo* on 29 and 30 May 1969 is often seen as the first important sign that the end was near for military rule. Unrest had been building for some time, but events in Cordoba would change people's sense of the possible. Students and workers joined in a rebellion that took control of the city of Cordoba for several hours and 'surpassed all popular demonstrations during the past generation' (Rock 1987:349). The mobilization was put down when troops occupied the city. Despite repression, an example was set. The *Cordobazo* demonstrated the fragility of the social peace Onganía had promised.

Waves of uprisings in other cities in the interior, wildcat strikes, student militancy, and the emergence of guerrilla organizations combined to convince the military that the only hope was to hand power back to civilians. Notwithstanding various attempts to keep Perón from returning to power, the most anti-Peronist voices eventually lost out to those who saw Perón as the only person who might hold sufficient authority and legitimacy to reign in the 'unruly' populace.

For the first time in almost ten years, general elections were held across the country on 11 March 1973. Hector Cámpora won 49.6 per cent of the vote for the Frente Justicialista de la Liberacíon, the Peronist Coalition. Oscar Eduardo Balbín was a distant second with 21.3 per cent of the vote for the Unión Civica Radical (Graham-Yooll 1989:249). Cámpora assumed the presidential mantle on 25 May 1973.

Soon after the return of Peronism came the long-awaited return of Perón. He had been in the country briefly before the elections, when his reception had been jubilant.[16] In retrospect, the events surrounding Perón's return on 20 June 1973 seem to have been grisly harbingers of the coming period.

Both Peronist and non-Peronist guerilla organizations had been forming throughout the 1960s.[17] Most guerrillas, and especially the Peronist Montoneros, were middle-class youth for whom more radical classist organizations (such as Peronismo de Base which focused on participation in working-class struggles) were not really a practical option (Gillespie 1982:75).

Perón was to have arrived at Ezeiza, Buenos Aires's international airport, on flag day, 20 June 1973. Perhaps as many as three million ardent Peronists awaited him, among them both *adjudicados* and *intrusos* from José Ingenieros. Shortly before the plane was to land, shots broke out. At least twenty people were killed and another four hundred injured (*New York Times* report, cited in Andersen 1993:86–7). In the days that followed, both left- and right-wing Peronist groups blamed each other for the massacre, although it is now clear that the right engineered the violence. The events foreshadowed the intensity and ferocity of the struggle for dominance between Peronist factions once their common goal, the return of Perón, had been achieved. When Cámpora was chosen as Perón's proxy (Perón would assume the presidency himself on 12 October), the move was read as a sign that Perón was favouring the left. But Perón had always played a complex game, setting different factions against each other in order to retain ultimate control.

Meanwhile the plethora of groups that had formed and participated in the struggle to return the country to democracy and Peronism continued to act as if they were making a revolution. Reading Argentine newspapers from 1973, one is struck by the character of the historical moment: Nixon was on the verge of impeachment, the United States was losing ground in Vietnam, and Allende was hanging on in Chile. Alongside this international news are reports of popular occupations (*copamientos*) in all spheres of life, all over the country.

The popular occupation of José Ingenieros was part of this movement, which also included the occupations of factories, hospitals, schools, radio stations, government offices, housing, and land in the countryside. With the return of Perón, there was a belief that social justice, as one of Peronism's pre-eminent values, would carry the day. People from José Ingenieros, for example, say that the political transition, and especially the return of Peronism, led them to believe that the illegal occupation would be tolerated by the authorities. Hector Cámpora, the interim president who was known as el Tío (Uncle) Cámpora, was seen as a benevolent leader who would be sympathetic to the needs of the poor.

Many of these occupations were sustained by workers who then attempted forms of collective management.[18] They were also often instigated or encouraged by competing political groups vying for position and influence in the new Peronist era. In general the *copamientos* were short-lived, however. The institutions were restored to their original management once Perón's new government was in place. Thus neighbourhoods like José Ingenieros are among the only locations where these attempts were not interrupted in their initial moments.

The *Toma*

It is hard to untangle precisely how the *toma* came about. Conflicting scenarios circulate in José Ingenieros, even among people who personally participated in the occupation of apartments. Various participants and witnesses tell substantially different stories. The illegality of the *toma* helps to explain some of the difficulty in reconstructing it accurately. If it was organized, and this is probable, it would have been organized clandestinely. Groups would not have advertised their roles widely. The public position of the squatters was that they were exercising their right to decent housing; they would not want to be seen as making a political gesture. Although significant political capital would accrue to organizations which redistributed apartments to their constituencies, the notion that the *toma* was essentially political would also have undermined its legitimacy.

Finding many of those most active on the left so that they might tell their stories becomes difficult, especially because of the intervening years, including seven years of dictatorship, and because many fell victim to repression. Those on the right may wish to downplay their roles although perhaps for different reasons.

One way to make sense of the varying accounts that follow is to recognize that the process was complex. Although almost everyone speaks of the *toma* in the singular, there seems to have been a series of occupations which may have spanned as much as a year. There is good documentation for occupations beginning roughly 1 May 1973 and ending more or less with Perón's return to Argentina on 20 June that same year.[19] However, other people say they arrived in José Ingenieros as much as twelve months earlier, some time in May 1972.[20]

Residents describe the occupation of the four sectors as occurring from different points and in waves, as one after another building or sector was claimed. Some buildings were less desirable because they were farther from completion, so were passed over and then occupied by the last to arrive. The earliest incidents seem to have been on a small scale; some suggest that these were carried out by point men, sent out in advance by various groups to pave the way for subsequent, more massive occupations.

Newspaper accounts place the occupation of the neighbourhood (then known as Barrio General Belgrano, and occasionally as José Ingenieros)[21] at about 1 May 1973; these occupations did not capture the attention of the press until about two weeks later. When the squatter invasions finally did make it to the newspapers, the images were dramatic, and the coverage largely sympathetic to the new occupants, especially in newspapers with largely working-class readerships. For example, on 17 May the Buenos Aires paper *Crónica* published a large front-page photograph and the headline 'Army and Police Evict a Neighbourhood.' The story, on pages eleven and twelve reads:

> People in the General Belgrano neighbourhood in La Matanza are living a tense and dramatic climate in the face of possible evictions from illegally and prematurely occupied dwellings, according to a communique from the Commander of the Emergency Zone[22] today. General Belgrano neighbourhood has been taken over by the Security Forces. Last night there were confrontations and new occupations, and some apartment doors had been broken. There was heightened anticipation amid the attention of security forces, which included soldiers. Doctor Cámpora's intervention will be requested ...
>
> Anguished by the lack of a roof, families evicted from shanty towns without alternative housing, and, according to affected families, an apparent lack of coordination in the delivery of apartments constructed there, have created a climate that resulted in violence last night and that has required the presence of security forces, since this morning, including the police and troops from the Regiment based at Tablada ...

Fifteen days ago, the neighbourhood's apartment blocks still incomplete, numerous families entered the apartments. Everything indicates [that they did this] with the corresponding order from the Comisión Municipal de la Vivienda.

[Yesterday evening] after noisy demonstrations with many families arriving [at the neighbourhood] affirming that those living inside were 'intruders,' there was a new takeover where the other 60 percent of the neighbourhood was 'taken by storm,' as one neighbour put it this morning. Present were women with babes in arms, angry men, old people: all the makings of a true assembly of desperate families. Keys in hand, showing receipts for the sum of 4,700 pesos of the national currency paid to the Municipality [as the first instalment on the apartments], they entered the apartments for which they were destined, when the incredible fact that they were occupied emerged ...

At some point [that night] there were confrontations between groups armed with clubs. There is no information on injuries ... At press time there had been no evictions. (*Crónica* 1973e:1)

By the next day, the papers were reporting evictions in language sympathetic to the affected families who spent the night 'at the mercy of the elements.' On 27 May *Crónica* reported that these same families had occupied a housing project in the capital unimpeded by police (1973b).

On 30 May the tone of the reporting changed notably as the journalist pointed out:

But it is also clear that this is not the way to get housing; one should not discredit the rights of legitimate occupants of the houses, taking them by storm and evicting them by force, or occupying the apartments of people to whom they have been legitimately assigned, but who have not yet occupied them. This situation within the occupied perimeter has generated what has been called a 'no man's land.' On one hand, those who defend, even with arms, their legitimate rights; on the other, those who imagine a possibility and defend it, also with arms. (*Crónica* 1973g:5)

At least some of these early *intrusos* were astute enough to send a delegation to *Crónica* to argue their case. This group said that of the twenty-seven apartment buildings in José Ingenieros, only four had been assigned to *adjudicados*. They went out of their way to represent themselves as 'respectable,' saying that they were, 'families that did not come from *villas*, but need decent housing like any human being.

They add that they are all working people, not delinquents, and that they are Argentines, but that nobody listens to them. They ask, "Must we be foreigners from the bordering countries for the authorities to pay attention to us and solve our problems?"' (*Crónica* 1973g:5). The effort on the part of these *intrusos* to distance themselves from foreigners and *villeros* contradicts the image more commonly painted by residents and observers. The idiosyncrasy here suggests that the particular group which spoke to *Crónica* may have constituted a specific faction.

Although newspaper stories continued in June and July, the *tomas* are given much less attention, and José Ingenieros drops from sight. This does not mean, however, that the wave of occupations subsided. Oral accounts suggest that most *intrusos* who continue to live in the neighbourhood moved in at the very end of May and the first half of June. It may be that many of the earlier *intrusos* had been evicted as reported in the press.[23]

How People Came to Participate in the *Toma*

A few people, all politically active at the time of the *toma*, believe that the operation was spearheaded by some kind of political organization. I was told that specific people were selected to participate as point men. The fact that some *intrusos* are reported to have visited the neighbourhood before the *toma* occurred supports this argument. Likewise the testimony of a professional Peronist and union activist, who recounts being sent to the area to participate in the *toma*. Beto, a charismatic man in his fifties when I spoke to him in 1992 recalls:

> I was working in the Union in San Miguel. I had a position there called 'political opening' 'round about 1971. There was a general idea that there would be a political opening, but they didn't know what year it would happen ... [My position] wasn't that necessary in the area where I had been working in San Miguel, but it was necessary in La Matanza. So they inform me that there will be a squatter occupation, and that I have to prepare to work there ... They tell me this work is coming in '73, so I come here. I arrived like anyone else, I suffered the same wants, which in reality weren't so bad since one had come to take an apartment for free ... I contacted the Union, and we began to plan the whole thing. What should happen, what was happening, and how we should prepare politically.

When I asked whether he felt the whole project was planned ahead of time, Beto replied: 'Yes. They already knew about this. That is, the people who ran this knew when it would happen. And well, it happened. It happened just as had been planned. I wasn't part of the planning system. The only thing they told me was "such and such will happen" so I have to be there or not.'

On the other hand, and as we saw in Inés's story, the vast majority of *intrusos* tell a remarkably different story. The kind of organization described by activists seems to have gone largely unremarked by those who arrived by a different route. Occasionally they mention groups of people (extended families, a group from the same *villa*) arriving together, but a more personal tale is more common. People describe accidentally discovering, either directly or through an acquaintance, that apartments were being occupied. They recount having seen the activity first hand, or having heard it by word of mouth or on the radio. Often the source of information was a close relative, often the sibling of a household member.

Susana's account is typical. The political activist explains why her family decided to occupy an apartment in José Ingenieros' *complejo* 18.

LD: When did you move to the neighbourhood?

Susana: We arrived in 1973.

LD: In the *toma*, or afterward?

Susana: In the *toma*. We had a house in another neighbourhood where we had bought a plot of land and built a house.[24] We had been living there for three years. I didn't like the place at all, because when we left work at night it was very unlikely that the buses would enter. So rain or shine, we took a bus that left us eleven blocks from home. There were still dirt roads, not asphalt. So, one day when I got to work a girl [*chica*] told us, she said: 'Did you know that in Ciudad Evita, in those apartments, there are people moving in?' I sort of didn't believe her. 'What do you mean moving in? I thought there were guards, police ...' Yes, there were, but they were people from the [construction] company. And well, when they saw that people were starting to move in from all over, well ...

LD: It was a little difficult to control ...

Susana: It was difficult to control. But they weren't that interested in looking after [the property], because in reality the thinking was (I spoke with the engineer) ... He understood the position of many people who didn't have a decent place to live.[25] Decent, not that I mean that the other place wasn't decent, but here, certainly, there were many more comforts – water, natural gas, electricity, there was a water pump. It wasn't the same living on asphalt. We had small children. I wanted a secure roof [over our heads].

LD: You had three children?

Susana: Four. Right. So one night I decided. I say: 'I'm going to check it out.' This was how [it was: there were] people who were going in [*metiendose*]; another [person] wanted another [apartment], another wanted another ... So we opened an apartment that was on the third floor. It was small for us, very small ... We stayed there that night. Meanwhile, I went to find my younger brother and his wife and asked them if they wanted to come because they were renting somewhere else. [My sister-in-law] said yes. So that night she came and stayed with us. I tell her that it's because we are going to try to get a ground floor apartment, and a bigger one, because our family is bigger. The next morning my husband went down to talk to the boss, the man in charge of the site. The man came with the key and everything, opened this door [of the apartment in which we were speaking], and said 'Stay here.'

LD: There was collaboration from the construction site, then?

Susana: Yes. There was collaboration. Because, in reality, we were in a period in which many things were about to return to the country – General Juan Domingo Perón. And this is a neighbourhood, the part of the *chalets*, [which] was built by order of General Perón and of Eva Perón.

Once a family had learned of the *toma*, a decision had to be made about whether or not to risk participating in the occupation. Although eventually successful for most people, it was hard to predict what would happen. Whenever possible the family would split up leaving some members in the old dwelling to protect it and its contents. Usually one person was sent 'just to have a look,' and ended up taking an apartment. People already installed let the newcomers know which apartments were available, and some shuffling occurred as people attempted to choose the best apartment for their needs.

Many current residents say that had it not been for the squatter invasion the housing would have gone to military men and police. Alejandro, an *intruso* who says he was involved in the initial planning of the *toma*, both in José Ingenieros and in other similar neighbourhoods, recounts how a friend in the military came to him with information that the PEVE apartments were to be allotted to the gendarmery, the police, and the army, even supplying specifics on how many apartments would go to each of these groups.[26] This, he says, forced them to organize the *toma* to ensure that the housing would go to those for whom it was intended.

In interviews, social workers from the Ministerio de Bienestar Social who had been responsible for placing *adjudicados* insist that this was never the case. There is probably no way of knowing which of these versions is true. Nevertheless, even the notion that public housing would go to military and the police instead of the *villeros* for whom it had ostensibly been built, was a powerful justification for the squatters' actions.

There is some disagreement about the significance of economic speculation as a motive for some who occupied apartments. The main group of people accused of speculating are the residents of the relatively better-off *chalets* of neighbouring Ciudad Evita. Many residents recount how there were instances when a large household object like a refrigerator was placed in an apartment to stake a claim. In telling this story speakers suggest that such speculation was illegitimate for two reasons: first, because people with extra refrigerators were too wealthy to make a justifiable claim to an apartment, and second, because those not actually present avoided the hardships and risks entailed in physical occupation.

Until the early 1990s the apartments in José Ingenieros could not be sold legally, but, in fact, people had been buying and selling them from the very beginning.[27] The illegality of these transactions meant that buyers were taking considerable risks and that the selling prices were low. The state bureaucracy eventually recognized most inhabitants as long as they paid the required instalments, however. In practice, I seldom heard of anyone who illegally purchased an apartment who was not eventually able to gain official recognition of their property rights. The important exceptions here occurred during the *proceso* when military administrators used a much heavier hand.

The early sellers are usually divided into two groups. The wealthier *intrusos* are thought to have sold off apartments at the first opportunity, seeking profit, while the poor (or foolish) are said to have sold their apartments for very low sums – a television, a few hundred dollars – returning to the *villa*. Over the intervening years, many apartments have changed hands, but these exchanges do not seem to represent economic speculation. The low prestige of the neighbourhood has meant that the market value of the apartments is artificially low compared to comparable housing in other areas.[28]

The Participation of Political Organizations

As I have noted, the character and extent of participation by organized political groups in the occupation of José Ingenieros is difficult to sort out. Likewise, details of their subsequent involvement in the neigh-bourhood remain unclear. This set of issues represents one of the obvi-ous connections between local and national processes, however. It may be precisely this connection, and the ambivalence residents of José Ingenieros feel about it, that makes it a troubling topic of conversation. In the discussion that follows I describe what I know or can surmise about such connections.

Describing his role in the initial planning phase of the *toma*, Alejan-dro says that participating political groups went so far as to divide up the terrain, allotting different sectors to different activist organiza-tions. Given the political capital inherent in distributing housing, it makes sense that such a role would have been hotly contested by organizations trying to create or fortify their connections to the urban working class – a traditionally important source of power in Argen-tine politics – as everyone scrambled to take advantage of the demo-cratic opening.

A number of neighbours attempted to explain the complexity of the *toma* to me in a group discussion at El Hornero. This particular exchange began when I asked about how information about the *toma* circulated.

Pablo: There was organization.

Gloria: There were people who came in groups.

Pablo: There was organization at the political level. Each delegate, in each zone ...

Gloria: Yes, the activists [*militantes*] ...

Pablo: It was their job to bring people here. And everything, I believe, had to do with the moment which we were living: the elections, the return of democracy. There was a situation here, let's say in support of Peronism, that organized everything. You know what I mean? It was a political situation.

Many: Yes.

LD: I've heard that it also had to do with an internal struggle.

Someone: More than anything it was internal.

[Everyone talks at once.]

Pablo: ... Comando de Organización more than anything.

Elena: The *Montos* [Montoneros] were here, ERP [Ejercito Revolucionario del Pueblo] was here...

LD: Really?

Gloria: ... so the problem in the neighbourhood was really between them.

Pablo: Right.

Marisa: People also came of their own accord.
Gloria: We came with a lot of people who were organized, in trucks.
LD: Those groups that came already organized, did they stay together?
Did they act as a group?
Everyone: No.
Roberto: It seems to me that they didn't. A place was found for them, and
ciao.

It was during this discussion that I first became aware of the importance of the political organizations in the *toma*. The *toma* occurred at precisely the moment when various Peronist, and even some non-Peronist, organizations were vying for position on the ground. It was a moment when the name of the game was mobilization, especially for those who did not have large institutional bases of support. This process began well before the democratic opening, but carried on into, and to a lesser extent throughout, the entire period up to the 1976 coup.[29]

In an account of the Peronist Youth, Juventud Peronista, Jorge Rulli gives a taste of the climate. As part of an account of his experience organizing in La Matanza from the end of 1971, Rulli describes attempting to build an organization from the bottom up, neighbourhood by neighbourhood. This tactic, he says, brought his group into conflict with more 'verticalist' tendencies, such as the left-Peronist Montoneros. Local culture made it difficult to organize into cells, which was the operative model; people in the communities where he worked refused to be left out of actions and were suspicious of secrets. As a result, Rulli's group engaged in less dangerous activities in which everyone could participate: setting up barricades, burning tires, and painting walls, for example.

> We had a terribly insurrectionalist posture; little by little we managed to mix together the military with the political until we moved in semi-liberated neighbourhoods, where everybody knew what we were doing. Sometimes they even consulted us about problems of cohabitation or they consulted the leaders of the *unidades básicas* ... We controlled the security of the neighbourhood; we distributed medicines; people drank *mate*; sometimes they even cooked; advice was given; women knitted. That is, our *unidades básicas* were like community centres. (Anzorena 1989:183)

Rulli goes on to complain that the Montoneros – whom he describes as young and middle class – then captured the neighbourhoods where he and his people had been working, thanks to their greater financial resources. One of the things that becomes clear from Rulli's account is the degree to which neighbourhoods were political spaces to be fought over, and that the competition was ferocious, even potentially deadly.[30]

Some of the organizations which had members working in José Inge-nieros were the Comando de Organización (known as CdeO) which was an important faction within the right wing of Peronism; the Per-onist Youth (Juventud Peronista – JP)/Montoneros,[31] the Maoist Revo-lutionary Communist Party (Partido Comunista Revolucionario – PCR), the Communist Party (Partido Comunista – PC) and People's Revolutionary Army (Ejercito Revolucionario del Pueblo – ERP).[32]

La Matanza, and especially this part of it, had been traditional CdeO territory. One of the central phenomena of the moment, how-ever, was the explosive growth of the Juventud Peronista, which became the strongest left-Peronist faction. The JP was recognized as the legitimate arm of the guerilla organization, the Montoneros. Although many residents told me of JP and Montonero presences, especially in *complejo* 18, no more details were forthcoming. This is probably because members of these organizations were among the principle targets of subsequent military repression.

At least two organized groups seem to have taken leadership or bro-kership roles in José Ingenieros. They assigned apartments or removed people from them, often by force, based on their own criteria. One of these was the Comando de Organización, and the other became central in organizing NHD 17. There are indications that the Montoneros and/ or the Juventud Peronista were dominant in at least parts of NHDs 18 and 19, but I have very little data on what their participation was like.

José is probably a CdeO sympathizer. About forty when he spoke to me in 1992, he remained politically active, and continued to live in *complejo* 18. He described the process through which apartments were allotted. They were assigned, he told me,

> according to when people arrived, and according to need. There were people who signed others up. When people came to visit, or when a rela-tive came ... someone took down [the newcomer's] document number, where they lived, tried to confirm that they really didn't have [housing], that they lived where they said, or that they rented, and that they didn't have their own plot of land. When [the broker] came and found an apart-ment in good condition [he] called the guy, showed him the apartment and said: 'You can have this apartment. Is it OK?' 'Yes.' And there it is.

It has to be registered. Just like that. And things got better for people. The ones here had all been living precariously.[33]

From this account, CdeO seems to have been one of the major organizers of the *intrusos*. It seems somewhat ironic, then, that they also appear to have been active in the defence of legally assigned apartments. *Adjudicados* recount how CdeO helped them to organize patrols in NHD 4-5-6 to defend themselves against *intrusos*. No doubt the organization saw itself as maintaining order in both cases.

It is important to note that there was considerable variation between, perhaps even within, *complejos*. According to José, CdeO had a 'general secretary' in each of the four *complejos*, but its power varied considerably depending on whether other groups existed and how strong these other groups were.

Those associated with CdeO's main rivals argue that the CdeO (unlike their own organizations, they say) was more interested in building a power base than in absolute criteria of necessity. The group is reported to have assigned apartments based on the politics of the would-be occupants. Gloria, an *intrusa* from NHD 17, was a member of the Communist Party at the time of the *toma*. She said it was evident to her at the time that one needed at least to claim allegiance to Peronism. 'The neighbours who came in to take a house had to stay neutral, say that you were Peronist. At least that's how it was in my neighbourhood. If you weren't Peronist, at night they'd come and take your stuff and throw it out the window. So you had to go around mute: you didn't know anything, you didn't see anything' (from Hornero group interview). Note that the neighbourhood was so overwhelmingly Peronist that she equates Peronism with neutrality.

The CdeO was an armed organization, famous for its militarism and internal discipline; it is quite likely that members would have been threatening when it served their purpose. In contrast to CdeO, which may have ejected non-Peronists, or even Peronists of the wrong stripe, people in rival groups say that they considered speculators and single people, especially single men, undeserving.[34] It is worth noting the patriarchal ideology expressed in this policy. The argument that women and children came first was understood to demonstrate that the CdeO's opponents took the moral high ground. It bears repeating that such an understanding was as taken for granted at the time I heard the story, in the early 1990s, as when the policy was (supposed to have been) exercised twenty years earlier.

Although I have first-hand confirmation of PCR activity, their presence is less well-known than others. As Maoists, people in PCR would have been loathe to identify themselves, especially given the overwhelmingly Peronist nature of the Argentine working class in this specific time and place. PCR activists also had ideological reasons for not advertising their affiliation: their position was that the working class was not yet ready for revolutionary action. In contrast, despite the presence of individual members in the *toma*, the Communist Party itself does not seem to have had any significant organized participation.

Finally, the fluidity and flexibility of this situation should be underlined. Although armed and unarmed political organizations had important presences, and sometimes effectively imposed discipline on their members, the physical and social construction of a community in the years following the *toma* took on a life of its own. Even when the larger political project of these organizations might have set them against each other, participants on the ground often found reasons to cooperate, despite orders from above.

Life in the Early Days in José Ingenieros

The *toma* was essentially over by the time Perón returned to Argentina on 20 June 1973. Once the wave of occupations had subsided, José Ingenieros was left with inhabitants who could be divided into two broad categories: a small number of *adjudicados* who were legally assigned apartments by the federal housing authority in NHD 4-5-6, and, the vast majority who were *intrusos*. Five classes of *intrusos* are delineated by residents: people enrolled in PEVE but who despaired of ever getting their apartments through legitimate channels; people from the *villas*; people living in urban tenements downtown; the younger generation from overcrowded households in the bungalows of neighbouring Ciudad Evita; and speculators.

Although some may have hoped to make money out of the *toma*, it seems unlikely that there was much to be made. Occupying an apartment required work and sacrifice. It required constant vigilance; some people gave up jobs because apartments could not be left alone for fear others would take them. Second, living conditions were rustic. *Complejo* 4-5-6 was the only sector that had water. Some portions of the neighbourhood had been completed, but others were far from finished. (This, after all, is the reason that they were empty and vulnerable to squatters in the first place.) The *toma* took place in winter (May and June) and cold figures prominently in most of the stories people tell about those early days.[35]

Of the four, *complejo* 17 was the furthest from completion. Some buildings were essentially finished, lacking only interior details like flooring, but sections of NHD 17 were far from habitable. Some apartments had no interior walls to divide rooms or even apartments. Unfinished stairs made the setting treacherous, especially for children. There were apartments without windows and even doors, exposing squatters to the wind, rain, and cold of the Buenos Aires winter.

When the site was overrun, the construction companies abdicated responsibility for finishing the project. Many residents say that employees, or perhaps even the companies themselves, took advantage of the situation by selling off construction materials stored on the site. Residents report seeing loaded trucks leaving José Ingenieros sometime not long after the *toma*. Contraband is said to have included kitchen and bathroom fixtures, water heaters, and tiles.

Most people lived without light and heat because the gas and electricity lines had not been connected. Cooking was relegated to portable gas burners. Those in *complejos* 17, 18, and 19 spent months without running water; they depended on their neighbours in 4-5-6 or went outside José Ingenieros altogether to collect it.[36] Living without water meant living without bathrooms. Latrines were built, but many tell comic stories about the hazards of walking through the neighbourhood in the early morning hours when someone, too lazy to carry it downstairs, tossed the night's waste from a window.

Community and Organization

When people talk about life in the new community they helped to create, their own accomplishment figures first and foremost: a home for themselves and their families. For virtually all adults who had participated in the *toma* almost twenty years earlier, the story of the occupation was about the risk they had undertaken and the hardship they had endured to get a decent home for their families.

Part of this achievement was the squatters' ability to band together and form a community out of a large and diverse group of people. There is a powerful element of nostalgia in the way people talk about the early period. Ernesto, who lived in *complejo* 17, recalled how squatters came from all over: from the provinces, from Paraguay and

Bolivia, from the villas and the urban tenements, with very different customs. 'We had to come to an agreement, work together, and we did. It was a very good moment when people were united. We lost that over time.' Don Eduardo, a man in his sixties in 1992, from NHD 19 had similarly warm memories. He recalled planting gardens: 'The neighbourhood was very attractive at that time. It had a kind of splendour.'

In the early period, the four sectors seem to have organized separately and in their distinct ways, but the leadership in all sectors managed to coordinate their activities around such issues as official recognition and the provision of basic services. NHD 4-5-6 is often seen as somewhat different from the other three *complejos* because of the presence of *adjudicados*. To this day, there are residents of 4-5-6 who feel this fact entitles them to a privileged relationship to the state. Both social workers who had been involved in overseeing the neighbourhood and some of the older residents of 4-5-6 mark this distinction by sometimes calling NHD 4-5-6 'the PEVE neighbourhood.'

The chief response of the squatters to the many threats facing them was organization. Despite the complex underlying forces and the apparent chaos of the early days, residents seem to have got organized quite quickly. The first common problem that brought the new residents together was fear for their own safety. Two distinct security problems presented themselves in José Ingenieros: squatters feared that the military or police would remove them, and they worried that other *intrusos* would supplant them.

A strong state security presence was in place for some time trying to curb the influx of new people into the area. José Ingenieros was circumscribed by a mesh fence which had originally been used to protect the construction site. (This is the fence Inés described crawling under.) In order to enter or leave the area one needed to provide documentation, such as a receipt from the Instituto de la Vivienda.

Things were more complicated for *intrusos*. Except at the very beginning of the *toma*, however, authorities allowed them to remain in the apartments. For *intrusos* the front door handle came to serve the double purposes of identification as an official squatter, on one hand, as key, on the other.[37]

Despite their fears to the contrary, it appears that *adjudicados* were not normally in danger of losing their apartments to *intrusos*. Serious prior claims were generally accepted. One *adjudicado* explained:

Roberto: There were cases where an *adjudicado* arrived and discovered that his apartment was occupied by an *intruso*. So, with papers in hand, he would show them and say: 'Look, you're going to have to leave because I have been allotted this apartment and here are the papers.' And they would more or less come to an agreement. The other person would realize that the [*adjudicado*] was right and, well, leave. I know that there was a neighbour who came, and showed all the papers, and said: 'Look, this is my apartment. I am supposed to be here. The military even brought us.'
LD: The army?
Another neighbour: Did they intervene if the apartment was occupied?
Roberto: I don't remember. It seems to me that with the fact that the soldiers came, that they brought us, people just left. It seems to me that maybe people came to an agreement more rapidly.

This story also shows that the Ministerio de Bienestar Social was still having *adjudicados* brought to NHD 4-5-6 after *intrusos* had started to take apartments, that the installation of *intrusos* and *adjudicados* were simultaneous processes.

Doña Inés, who continues to play an important role in dealing with state institutions, tells of negotiating with authorities. She says that a bargain was struck: they would honour any legitimate title holder's claim to an apartment by moving out and relocating to an empty apartment. Interestingly, the deadline for the arrival and accommodation of *adjudicados* was 20 June, the day Perón was scheduled to return to Argentina.

Originally *adjudicados* were suspicious of *intrusos*, but the two groups soon learned to work together in the interest of normalizing the situations of all residents. One of the greatest fears shared by occupants, *intrusos* and *adjudicados* alike, was that *villeros* would come to displace them. The irony here is usually apparent to those recalling this anxiety: many *adjudicados* and *intrusos* had been *villeros* only a short time earlier. But rumours of impending invasions were perpetually circulating and all four sectors established armed patrols to protect against them.

Doña Inés, who we have already seen has a flair for the dramatic, tells an especially evocative story about the lengths to which neighbours went in defending themselves, the real fear that underlay their preparations, and how some of these conflicts were resolved. Her complex but vivid account is worth citing at some length here.

Later [after the *intrusos* had moved in] other shanty towns wanted to
come and take homes. There we had to arm ourselves, or rather, the
whole neighbourhood armed to defend what we had. In my case, my husband [didn't want to]. 'I'm not going to kill kids over something crazy!'
But I said to him, 'I'm staying here!' I don't know how people do things
like that but, 'I'm staying,' I said.

'Go if you want, but I'm not leaving.' So my husband stayed, you see?
He's no coward. He thought, and its only logical, he thought that in a confrontation ... We didn't know ... Many people could come and kill. Imagine, they could kill your child. 'There is nothing like a human life,' my
husband says. But in that moment, I got the idea in my head not to
[leave].

In our building most of us were women. There was an old man [too]. So
I organized. One man gave me a Molotov cocktail [laughing a little],
armed me. I didn't know what a Molotov cocktail was. And I say, 'What
do I do? I light it and throw it?'

'No!!' he says, 'how could you do that?! You have to go up high and
throw it behind you. And throw it far because where it lands, it kills
someone.'

'*Ay!*' I say, 'if I don't kill him first he will come up here and kill me!' You
see? I was capable of anything at that moment.

So, we organized ourselves like in the English Invasions[38] ... You know
how we have a landing? So we get doors, wire, we gather pots of hot
water. Of course in our building we were all women. So suddenly someone says, 'Here they come!' And all the valiant ladies – one fainted,
another started to cry [chuckling]. Whatever. But we had stones as well.
Of course there were people who were armed. Not us. We were working
people. There was never a gun in my house.

So, what happened? Those of us who were column delegates at that
moment arranged a meeting to go talk to those people, because it would
have been a massacre. So we went and talked. Over the years I've continued seeing that man, who at that time was a youngster, he was from
Juventud Peronista de Base.[39] We held a meeting in one of the rooms of
my house. We told them the truth. 'And if you have empty apartments?'
he asked. The man was right, but honestly we had censused the people
and everything was occupied. I say, 'We'll give you any empty apartment
you can find.' So a few families come in without any problems. We reasoned, you see. So we took them around and there were a few empty
apartments. They went and occupied them. In other neighbourhoods
there were shoot-outs and everything. But here, thank God, the part that I

experienced, (and I was here involved in everything at that time – day and night, afternoon and morning) [nothing happened]. We worked more it seemed because we had to keep guard and all that. Until we did the census, anyway.

Doña Inés particularly relishes the image of the 'valiant ladies' here (who also faint). To emphasize her point, she lets the men fall out of her story as she proceeds. Although Inés assumes that women are less prepared to defend themselves, she is happy to portray herself as breaking the mould. Inés has a particularly forceful personality, but she is not the only woman to emphasize the relative quiescence of her man in stories of the *toma*. Many of the *intrusas* I spoke with told tales that, like this one, explicitly acknowledged but refuted images of feminine passivity. Women in particular emphasized how the difficulties and the sacrifices they made were for their children.

Some residents suggest that the image of marauding hordes may have been a ploy on the part of the CdeO to justify their hegemony. Be that as it may, these patrols came to represent one of the most important ways in which neighbours worked together to further their common interests in the neighbourhood's earliest moments. Most who talk about this early period speak of guard duty and their participation in it. The specifics may have been different in the neighbourhood's various sectors, but the fact of guard duty appears to have been universal. José is passionate in describing the cooperative spirit of the time.

Do you know what that guard duty was like? Guard duty: women at night, putting themselves in the man's role doing guard duty, just like a soldier. But [they did this] not because it was required; they volunteered. They shared *maté cocido*[40] at night; they shared sandwiches. In the morning people would share what they had, because there were many with little income. We were few, so we lived with a greater sense of community. One lived in an organized way. One felt more companionship. As the whole thing grew, it evolved, it changed. And the people changed: for the better individually, but for the worse as far as everything else was concerned.

Here, note again the way that women's presence in supposedly masculine roles is considered, this time by a man, a particular indicator of their sacrifice and commitment.

Susana also describes the early days of the occupation, although in less nostalgic terms: 'It was a little complicated at the beginning because they said that people were coming in trucks from other places – people even poorer than us – to kick us out, or to try to take every apartment that they could. And in this moment, neighbours' councils [*comisiones vecinales*] were formed by those who were already neighbours – because we had been living here for almost a month – and they established guard duty. My husband had to do guard duty every night, from corner to corner, from one block to the next, looking out for strangers, because we already knew each other here.' When guard duty or other business meant that children would have been left unsupervised at home, they would be brought together in an apartment under the care of a teenager.

The stories underline how the galvanizing force was fear of other poor people. Neighbours spent countless nights patrolling, not out of fear of the state, but to protect against people much like themselves. Under the circumstances, they seem to have felt there was little room for class solidarity broadly conceived. The sense of community thus fostered was not at all abstract. It was very much the product of shared concerns, necessities, experiences, and objectives. On one hand, this sense of common purpose sometimes meant setting themselves against their fellows outside José Ingenieros in disturbing acts of poor-on-poor violence. On the other hand, this same practically constituted community allowed them to bridge divisions that, in the early 1970s, in Argentina at least, might have seemed insurmountable. Despite the very real conflicts between groups of differing political and ideological stripes (about which, more below), there was also a remarkable degree of cooperation on the ground.

Soon systems of political representation were set up. In NHDs 17 and 4-5-6, for example, each stairway elected a delegate to go to community meetings. Doña Inés referred to these as 'column delegates' in her account. Depending on the architectural layout of the housing block, stairs had anywhere from four to sixteen apartments on them, so the representation was quite direct. The system was described in a group interview. My question arises from a comment made by one of the participants.

LD: Was that common, organizing by stairway?
Gloria: By building.
LD: And this started right away [after the *toma*]?
Roberto: Yes.

LD: And what did they do?

Gloria: The neighbours in our stairway were democratic, because we were only four [households]. So somebody raised their hand and said, 'I'm it.' It was one at a time.

LD: And what did you do as delegates?

Gloria: We had to go to the neighbourhood commission, which at that time was in Cañete's house, who was in [Comando de] Organización. And they had the meetings there. That's where they organized the guard duties, you see, because you had to look after the apartments; everyone had to do it. The delegate had to organize the guard duty. For example, one person had to do it one night, another person another night, different hours, and all that.

Anahí: [The delegates] tell people about the decisions made in the meetings. (Hornero interview)

People on the same stairway would often meet informally in the evenings to discuss what was going on.

Like José, many speak nostalgically of the meals shared among neighbours. When supplies were scarce people would contribute what they could. Shops, especially greengrocers and dry goods stores, soon sprang up. People remembered these stalls as a considerable asset given that the neighbourhood was isolated and often semi-besieged. The Hornero group also described the climate in José Ingenieros in a discussion sparked by a question about the prices at the local shops that appeared soon after the neighbourhood was occupied:

Anahí: They didn't take unfair advantage with the prices. We were pretty united.

LD: And was there a climate of solidarity?

Everyone at once: Yes! Yes. Totally. Always.

Gloria: What's more, in the stair meetings, sometimes you went downstairs and everybody was talking together. In our stairway, at least, we sometimes all ate there together.

Pablo: I think that this was pretty common.

Anahí: There was even the New Year's Eve party. It was celebrated downstairs here. Everyone in the building joined in to have one big party. We danced. We dined.[41]

This spirit of community seems to have continued in much the same tenor until the coup, on 24 March 1976.

Politics and Violence

In contrast to tales of struggle, fortitude, and solidarity, stand other events of the early years. These are not accompanied by the same rosy glow. For most people, memories of local political struggles and violence are held at a distance. This is partly because they are much more problematic in the light of intervening history. A right-wing Peronist, probably a former member of the paramilitary Comando de Organización, tried to convey why it was impossible for him to explain this past in terms of the present: '"Pity" had another meaning then,' he told me.

Given the volatility of the moment, the inevitable conflict which emerged in the new neighbourhood often turned violent. This was very much a sign of the times. Many of the national political organizations present in the neighbourhood were armed organizations or had militarized factions. The guard duty so often mentioned was an armed militia. Many, perhaps most, of the households had some kind of gun.[42]

The experience of national political organizations in José Ingenieros shows something of how these struggles were played out on the ground. Most groups (Peronist and non-Peronist alike) were deeply vertical in their organizational structures partly because they came out of years of clandestine activity. The ability to mobilize people has long been a source of power in popular politics in Argentina, but the verticality of these organizations often placed important limits on local leaders. Part of what appears to have happened in the Cámpora period is that those constraints had seemed to disappear with the optimism of the initial moments of the democratic opening. The flurry of activity on the ground out-paced the organizations' abilities to direct and contain this activity. Discipline (the obedience to higher authorities) returned, however, although sooner for some groups than others.

Beto, the Peronist unionist quoted earlier, was an *intruso* but his political work lay elsewhere. He described what life was like in those days: 'At that time one was young, one "accepted positions" as we said. They sent us to a certain place, and we accepted it, precisely to defend ideological principles. Today, perhaps, I wouldn't do it. It depends. Now I'm fifty, as you might imagine. So we started to work. The occupations came. Here the political part went to work, they had their tasks.' Later in the interview he returned to this theme, this time with a note of bitterness, saying: 'I repeat: everyone who acted here [in the *toma*] – the people who acted weren't those who thought things up and made plans – the people who acted here responded to a pre-established plan. And we were the guinea pigs. That is, we went to the slaughter for idealism. We didn't know what we were doing.'

One armed conflict was documented in the left–Peronist magazine *Noticias del País* because it led to a protest in which a thousand residents blocked Camino de Cintura and Crovara, the two major arteries which run along the north and west borders of José Ingenieros. This impressive demonstration was the culmination of a struggle for control between two political groups in NHD 17. Auriliano Araujo had displaced Lalo Cañete (the leader from Comando de Organización mentioned by Gloria, above) as the president of the Neighbourhood Council in the *complejo*.[43] Araujo had been voted in and Cañete displaced at an open outdoor meeting. The article describes the conflict and its outcome in some detail. I quote it at length here because it conveys some sense of the climate at the time.

Last night residents of Ciudad Evita at Camino de Cintura and Crovara, San Justo, stopped vehicular traffic in these arteries. More than one thousand people present placed themselves in the intersection with signs calling for the liberty of Auriliano Araujo, President of the Neighbourhood Council, detained yesterday, Monday, at 9 p.m., as he returned from school after having received his primary school diploma.

[The article briefly explains the *toma* six months earlier.] Residents recount how dating from the occupation of the housing, a Coordinating Commission was formed and presided over by Rodolfo Santos Cañete. 'He revealed his intentions right away,' they said, 'forcibly evicting inhabitants in order to give the place to the highest bidder, converting these families' dramas into a dirty business. After that,' added one woman, 'they set themselves to collecting protection money from the businesses. They beat the baker and the coal seller [*carbonero*]. One rainy night they threw a family with four children into the street in order to replace them with another that had paid. At night they walked around the neighbourhood armed ...'

Don Eduardo, 58, speaks with clenched fists: 'They say that it's the Juventud Peronista, from the Federal Movement.[44] This Cañete has been denounced, but he goes in one door of the police station and out the other. We know that he is, or was until recently, from the Federal police. Firpo, Cristaldo and Cosquián are also in the gang.'[45]

Alcarón, the vice-president of the Neighbourhood Council, recalls how the inhabitants of the neighbourhood finally started to organize to defend themselves, 'which infuriated Cañete and his people.' 'For two months we have been meeting in the home of one of three families who have been threatened. At night seven stood guard because people were really scared at the beginning. At about three in the morning something extraordinary happened: all of a sudden they started bombarding us. They had reflectors, flares, tear gas, and shotguns. It was like a war.'

People accompany the journalist from *Noticias* to the house. There he sees impact marks and blood stains on the wall. The owner, who has several children, adds: 'They came in shooting and said they were going to kill us all. Two men were hurt and they tortured them [leaning them] against the wall. That's why there are stains. They are in critical condition. We also had to check some kids affected by the gasses into the hospital.'

'We aren't involved in politics,' [Alarcón continues], 'we are workers, we fight for decent housing. That's our only objective. We support the popular government because we are workers, but we don't understand how they tolerate this thing that has happened. Because you don't buy gas, flares, and machine guns at the corner store. Who is responsible? Why do they take Araujo prisoner when he is only an honest worker who fights for his people?'

Araujo is 36, has a son, and is married to Cirila Benítez. Cirila is overwhelmed in the middle of Camino de Cintura with her son in her arms. The thousand people present surround her as if protecting her. She speaks tiredly: 'He was coming from night school in the 97 [bus] when 'coincidentally' in front of the Güemes station a man says that they have stolen his wallet. Auriliano was carrying a small revolver because he has received many death threats. They take only him. The next day, after a brutal beating and interrogation about a Neighbourhood Council document which he had, they let him go. About an hour after he got home two policemen come to take him away because of some unimportant paperwork, they said. He is still a prisoner. When we all went to the police station, they said he was incommunicado.'

The document given to the press by the Council states: 'The delegates have called an alert and call an assembly in order to mobilize until we obtain the release of *compañero* Araujo.'

In other moments residents have marched in front of the provincial government and the Social Welfare Ministry, where they have gotten them to conduct a census and to semi-legalize the status of the occupation. In this last instance, some say they have seen Cañete enter the Ministry as if it were his home. (14 December 1973, p. 6.)

Araujo was subsequently released and continued to work as the president of the Neighbourhood Council until the coup three years later.

Estela, from *complejo* 18, described another armed confrontation which she witnessed in January 1975. The battle took place in the open field behind her apartment. She says she saw a truck arrive with a bunch of men on it who then distributed guns. What followed was a ferocious battle between this group, from CdeO, and a group of Montoneros, who were dominant in *complejo* 18. One man from CdeO was killed; today a *unidad básica* is named after him: Darwin Passaparte.

The Neighbourhood Council of NHD 17

Because it is neither documented nor widely discussed, the information that I have on the specific events and activities of these early years in José Ingenieros is partial and spotty.[46] For this period, the *complejo* that I heard most about was 17, in part, because the Neighbourhood Council of 17 became the most active of the four. This sector was furthest from completion at the time of the *toma*, but the council extended its objectives beyond finishing construction and getting utilities on line. In the less than three years that it was in place, the Council flourished through hard work and creativity. Not only was construction completed, but a health centre, a child care cooperative, and festivals to raise money for the community were organized.

The first order of business was the completion of construction of housing and infrastructure. Construction had halted with the occupation, so leaders negotiated with the construction company to complete the unfinished work. Neighbours worked together with outside construction workers to make the job go faster. When work was stopped because of a conflict between workers and management, leaders from NHD 17 stepped in as intermediaries to help settle the dispute. One resident illustrated the remarkable efficiency of the community organization with an anecdote about a 1974 census. The Ministry of Housing wanted information on the residents of the NHD 17. By using stair delegates, the commission was able to produce an accurate census in forty-eight hours. The people in the government could not believe it, Ricardo recalled with enjoyment. They did not think a group of *negros* could be so capable.

One of the consequences of lack of infrastructure in general, and lack of water in particular, was health problems. The Council built a small structure to house a health clinic where volunteer doctors tended people for free. To this day, residents remember these doctors with affection. They were so well liked that they were invited to move to the neighbourhood with their families, which they did. What no one says is that some of the doctors were activists, perhaps because most residents do not know about their political affiliations. On the other hand, when people marvel at their availability to all, day or night, they imply surprise that a patient's politics were irrelevant. This suggests that people knew or suspected, but did not much mind that their doctors' interests may have gone beyond medicine. Shortly before the coup, the doctors set up a course in community health promotion to train local people to look after their neighbours throughout José Ingenieros.

The other half of the structure built to house the clinic was a child care centre, established by a mothers' cooperative. There was also a small chapel. These projects were supported with funds raised through community festivals, some with benefit performances by well-known folk singers. In retrospect, the most notable is the concert given by the future star of Argentina's *Rock Nacional*, Charly García.

The details of the vital history of community organizing in NHD 17 between 1973 and 1976 seem to have been largely forgotten, but perhaps they are only not discussed. A few people who were intimately involved in the work speak of it, but even they are often reluctant to talk about this past. It has become too complicated to think about in light of the events of the subsequent *proceso*. Those most active in these projects became the targets of repression. Several – including Araujo, the president of the council, Benítez, the head of the women's cooperative (and the president's wife), and the doctors who worked in the health clinic – were among the disappeared; in other words, they were illegally detained and tortured by security forces for long periods of time. Strikingly, many residents of José Ingenieros do not even know that some of these former neighbours are alive today. Many never returned to the neighbourhood after their release from detention several years later. Most of those I heard of were living elsewhere in the capital. Two women were forced into exile abroad.

Official Recognition

The government eventually recognized the squatters. This was a slow and partial process, the fruit of persistent lobbying on the part of community leaders. The means of official recognition varied from one *com-*

plejo to another. The formal recognition of inhabitants' rights to live in José Ingenieros would probably have been completed in relatively short order had the process not been interrupted by the coup. Further complications arose when the neighbourhood passed from federal to provincial jurisdiction in 1978.

Two decades later there were still people in the neighbourhood who did not have title to their apartments. In general this process has involved the granting of mortgages through the Banco Hipotecario de la Nación (the National Mortgage Bank). Payment plans were very reasonable, and here the remarkable Argentine inflation rates have worked in the residents' favour. Many people have been able to pay for their apartments, and now own them. In her book on the political thinking of poor people in the Argentine capital, Nancy Powers underlines how 'a home makes all the difference' (2001:50). She notes that the significance of owning housing goes beyond the security of a roof over one's head: it shapes quality of life, becomes implicated in one's identity, and can translate into credit, which in turn can finance entrepreneurial initiatives, a key factor in years when a large percentage of poor people are self-employed (2001).

Conclusions

The early history of José Ingenieros is dizzyingly complex precisely because it is part and parcel of one of those historic moments when things seem accelerated. Years of enforced quiet, 'social peace,' seem to have exploded into its antithesis. Only a few years later, the lid was put back on in no uncertain terms. Argentines seem to remember the rebellion and violence of the early 1970s more readily than the creativity and sense of possibility. José Ingenieros is one of the places where the creative forces had an upper hand for a while.

Because they were tied to struggles taking place on a national scale, the actions of *intrusos* in the squatter occupation of José Ingenieros carry a broader significance. Despite their initial protestations of inconsequence, it made sense to the people I spoke with that someone, even a North American, should see their history as important. The reactions and memories of residents are complicated and contradictory, however, for the same reasons that those of many other Argentines are. Their particular experiences give them a distinctive point of view, but these perspectives are also influenced by other discourses about the past.

The coexistence of creativity and violence is one of the main reasons that the early 1970s are so difficult to think about. Does that history imply that the two are linked? Certainly that was the argument of the military regime behind the Process of National Reorganization, and to a great extent of the democratic governments that succeeded it. This issue becomes all the more troubling because the violence is often born of conflict between groups of poor people: *adjudicado* against *intruso*, *intruso* against potential *intruso*, or one political faction against another. No one in Argentina thinks of the early 1970s without seeing that time through the lens of the intervening history. It is to this history that we now turn.

Chapter 4

Repression and Reorganization, 1976–1982

When we think of the last Argentine dictatorship, certain images come to mind: unmarked green Ford Falcons occupied by sinister plain-clothed military men; the kerchiefed mothers of the disappeared walking in silent vigil around the Plaza de Mayo; the 1978 World Cup soccer tournament, perhaps, and the rumours of human rights violations that circulated throughout it; a pointless war in the South Atlantic. These images are accurate enough, but they are also partial. They fall short of describing the quality and character of life under the regime known as the Process of National Reorganization. The activities these pictures conjure up occur in the cosmopolitan capital, for one thing. Women march in the plaza in front of the presidential palace and the national cathedral; for some reason we see the disappearances occurring in elegant neighbourhoods, or off the busy streets of the shopping or business districts. What did the years of dictatorship look like on the other side of the General Paz beltway that separates capital from province? How did they feel from within the working-class neighbourhoods, apartment blocks, and shanty towns? We know less about this.

This chapter attempts to address these questions. As I have already argued, the regime which called itself the Process of National Reorganization was quite successful at reorganizing: that is, ripping apart the social fabric, forcing people to turn inward, to abandon social ties, and seek personal and economic survival in a game with a new set of rules. It is clear that these processes were also economic, but violence and the threat of violence were central mechanisms of the *proceso*, and I focus on them here. By looking at how repression played out and is remembered in José Ingenieros, I hope to get past what we know in general and to gain greater understanding of the regime's more intimate processes.

The Coup

Although the coup of 24 March 1976 officially began the Process of National Reorganization, it was neither unexpected nor abrupt. Things changed with the coup, but there were continuities as well. When Juan Perón died on 1 July 1974, he was succeeded by his wife María Estela (known as Isabel or Isabelita) who was ill-prepared to rule: the economy became unmanageable; the military was increasingly active, and political violence escalated. Meanwhile her government moved steadily to the right. The cumulative effect of these processes was so untenable as to make a military alternative appealing to many (Cavarozzi 1992:59; Timerman 1981:45–6).

The military regime that seized power on 24 March, and which ran Argentina until December 1983, can be seen as continuing and building on the logic and practices of previous military regimes.[1] Political activity was prohibited, the press censored, labour leaders arrested, and unions taken over. In addition, and in a move that explicitly undermined the role of civil society, it became illegal for groups larger than three people to meet, except in the home, school, church, or workplace, or with express permission of the authorities.

The military men who took control of Argentina presented themselves as problem-solvers. They belonged to an institution that had thrown itself into the breach created by the economic, political, and social chaos of the democratic period. The ideological position of the leaders of the *proceso* fits squarely within the National Security doctrine. That is, the military leaders understood domestic politics within the context of the Cold War. They thus allied themselves with the United States and interpreted all dissenters as the enemy in a much larger battle.[2]

Like similar regimes before, the military justified its ascension to power in terms of the need for a technocratic government to rid the state of politics and inefficiency. The military leaders believed they had a particular aptitude for running the country because they could impart order in the multiple senses of the word. But they also aimed for more profound change; they were trying to make a New Argentina and New Citizens. Although they did not always have a very clear sense of what the New Argentina and New Argentinean looked like, they knew what they were not. Take for example Secret Directive 504, from President Videla. Dated 1977, it starts by proclaiming victory in the 'application of the National Countersubversion Strategy,' trumpeting not only the defeat of armed opponents but also 'the normalization' of the key areas of industry, education, and religion. It then goes on to point out the importance of the World Cup soccer championship to be held in Argentina in 1978 and, chillingly, sets out a plan 'to increase security measures to ensure [Argentina's] normal development.' Part of this plan was to 'increment military action in support of normalizing the industrial, educational, religious, territorial, and neighbourhood spheres as a way of preventing or neutralizing any attempt at infiltration, capture [*captación*] or activation of the masses in a way that might interfere with the progress of the Process of National Reorganization' (*El Diario del Juicio* 1985d:530).

It is abundantly clear, then, that the targets for repression were not simply the armed guerrillas, as earlier public assertions held. In fact, the military had long recognized that its enemy was often unarmed. In a 1978 press conference, for example, President Videla declared: 'A terrorist is not just someone with a gun or a bomb but also someone who spreads ideas that are contrary to Western Civilization' (quoted in Fagen 1992:43).

Terror

In practice, these policies translated into an elaborate and vicious repressive apparatus which acted on a scale previously unknown in Argentina. The regime was responsible for anywhere from ten to thirty thousand disappearances and probably another eighty to one hundred thousand detentions.[3] Other statistics – of people killed in 'confrontations' or of people driven into internal or international exile – are harder to come by, but these processes also had chilling effects.[4]

More than 340 secret detention centres were operated by the three branches of the armed forces and the police. These centres were not just jails; they also made it possible for torture to be carried out systematically and over prolonged periods of time.[5] State terrorism, as human rights activists came to call the repression, was both planned by the highest authorities and idiosyncratic in its realization. The system was based on work groups (*grupos de tarrea*) which operated somewhat independently. Some seem to have been especially barbarous or venal. However, *Nunca Más*, the Report of the Commission of the Disappeared, outlines remarkable consistency in their practices (CONADEP 1986). More importantly, the overall logic of their activity and their senses of impunity clearly came from above.

Juan Corradi's discussion of the aims and functions of state terror is helpful here. Following Walter (1969), he points out that there are three actors with roles to play: 'a source of punishment, a victim, and a target. The victim perished or "disappeared" but the target reacted to that destruction with some manner of submission or accommodation, initially by inhibiting his or her potential resistance' (1985:119). This helps to explain why the security forces' imprecision in identifying their victims was relatively unimportant to them. The target was the larger society. Corradi continues:

> Punishment could be ordered by the highest authorities or left to the judgement of autonomous paramilitary groups; the selection of victims could be random or according to specific categories – e.g. members of subversive organizations, their relatives, potential political opponents, professional categories, socio-economic strata, residential and ethnic groups. They were regularly selected and dispatched with variable rates of destruction. The terror process was applied continuously from the installation of the military regime in 1976 through 1979; from 1979 on, it went through phases of varying intensity, with the victims selected by specialized services or sometimes by other potential victims. In many instances, the population was made into an accomplice to the very acts perpetrated against it. (1985:119)

Corradi goes on to identify the functions that the campaign of terror served from the point of view of the regime. These were: to eliminate active or suspected opponents of the regime; to act as a deterrent by intimidating other opponents; to attempt to destroy 'institutional alternatives' and postpone 'the reintegration of the disorganized groups'; to act as a 'prophylactic' against potential opponents; to indirectly help military bureaucracies expand across the national territory; and to strengthen the regime's control over the economy, allowing for aggressive 'streamlining' and denationalization (1985:120).

The *proceso* targeted many groups of opponents. If it was more about remaking Argentine society than about putting an end to guerrilla activity, then the regime's outright attack on labour made sense. Among the first acts of the new government were the suspension of union activities and the military intervention in the national labour congress (CGT) and the most important unions through the imposition of military administrators.[6] Other moves against labour included: the interventions of the union-run social services (*obras sociales*[7]), the prohibition of any kind of collective action, and modification of legislation concerning labour contracts so as to leave ample room for arbitrary dismissals. Crushing labour was central because the most important political threat to the regime came from unions. As Rock argues, the state used its repressive apparatus to 'amputate the labour movement at its apex and crush a vast web of lower-level associations. The military did not want to risk a reprise of the labour riots and mass demonstrations that erupted during the *cordobazo*' (Rock 1987:376; also Munck 1998).

The regime's assault on labour was early and fierce. At dawn on 24 March 1976 the armed forces and the police occupied the main industrial plants. Some managers had planned ahead, sending telegrams of dismissal to workers, but in other factories workers were taken away in military trucks. The forces targeted leaders, delegates, and internal commissions. For example, almost all members of the three first internal commissions of Ford Argentina's General Pacheo plant were among the disappeared (Vázquez 1985:60). Once again, it is important to note that as early as March 1976 the security forces were working with an extended definition of 'subversive' that clearly went beyond the guerrillas.

Other incidents were somewhat less violent, but still effective. One labour activist told me of a strategy employed against his fellow workers in the metal worker's union (UOM) in Quilmes, Province of Buenos Aires. Workers were detained in clandestine detention centres for a week or two. Upon their release they tried to return to their jobs, but found they had been fired for absenteeism. When they protested that they had been detained illegally through no fault of their own, employers feigned disbelief and demanded proof. They lost their jobs and blacklists often ensured that they found no other work in the industry.

Disappeared from José Ingenieros

A broad definition of subversion and subversives helps to explain one early assault on José Ingenieros. On the night of the coup, a group of people connected to the Neighbourhood Council of NHD 17, the most elaborately and perhaps most democratically organized *complejo*, were targeted for 'disappearance.'[8]

Norberto Liwski,[9] a physician who later became a prominent human rights activist, was living in *complejo* 17 and working with the Neighbourhood Commission there. He described the initial moments of the *proceso* in a 1990 interview at the Centro de Estudios de Estado y Sociedad (CEDES), a research centre in Buenos Aires.[10] In response to a question about how he became involved in human rights, he describes José Ingenieros at the time of the coup:

> The dictatorship had a particular mode of violence toward this neighbourhood: a neighbourhood which had clearly opposed the coup, that participated actively in political expression, and which had an internal democratic life that articulated with other popular organizations in the area. This made it appear to be a neighbourhood with a certain capacity to mobilize, and which rejected – obviously – the *golpista* [pro-coup] situation which had been insinuating itself almost from the death of Perón. (CEDES 1990:2)

The night of the coup[11] security forces entered NHD 17 looking for 'subversives.' Thanks to the warnings of their neighbours, many activists escaped harm, but others did not.[12] Liwski continues:

> The neighbourhood is occupied at dawn on the 24th of March by plain clothes forces; they search a number of houses of leaders and delegates. Many of us thought that we shouldn't be in our homes at that moment, but we weren't far, just in other buildings. The cost of that first night is very terrible. They kidnap two people: one is Cirila Benítez, who was the president of the neighbourhood Mothers' Commission, and who was in charge of the day care centre, as well as the buildings where the day care, the health centre, and the chapel were located; and Mario Portales, a building delegate, a man of some fifty years who was a municipal employee of La Matanza, a street sweeper, who appears the next day in the middle of the street with five gunshot wounds, dead.
>
> Among the homes searched is my own. It is also sacked and burned. This whole situation occurs on the night of the coup, a night which the neighbours still haven't been able to remove from the zone of terror. It is very difficult to talk about today in the neighbourhood. It's a topic which continues being discussed only among the older people; the kids don't find out about it. (CEDES 1990:2–3)[13]

Those activists who escaped this particular sweep went into hiding. For the next six months, according to Liwski, the neighbourhood was under siege by the army, and the clinic that had been established by the Neighbourhood Council of NHD 17 was occupied (CEDES 1990:3).

Liwski recounts stories of community resistance. The clinic was reopened with a mass on Christmas Day 1977. Even more daring was another mass, this time for Cirila Benítez. Benítez had been disappeared to the Detective Squad Headquarters (*Brigada*) of San Justo.[14] She had then been *blanqueada* (normalized), that is she reappeared in the legal system under the *Poder Ejecutivo Nacional* (PEN), a special legal status that puts prisoners under the discretionary power of the executive branch of government. Benítez was scheduled for expulsion to her native Paraguay, a fate which would have been very dangerous, perhaps deadly.[15] In response, the UN High Commission for Refugees arranged an alternative exile to the Netherlands. This seemed too strange and faraway a place; Benítez's husband, although still in hiding, lived in Buenos Aires, as did her children (CEDES 1990:5).

In order that Benítez be allowed to stay in Argentina, signatures were collected, officials were seen, and a mass officiated by Bishop Bufano was organized in the Cathedral of San Justo. The mass was attended by many neighbours as well as by leaders from other working class neighbourhoods in the area.[16] Liwski comments: 'Surely at that time there had been no rally or meeting – we are speaking here of March of '78 – no human rights rally of this scale' (CEDES 1990:5).

The military clearly saw the event as a challenge; about forty people were kidnapped as they left the mass. There were searches in the neighbourhood, mostly in the homes of leaders, during that night and continuing the next day. Doctors who had worked in the clinic were also kidnapped at this time. Although they no longer lived in the neighbourhood, Norma Ereñú, Liwski's wife, was abducted at 9:30 a.m. one or two days after the mass from an ambulance belonging to the Hospital Gallegos, where she was working as a physician (*Buenos Aires Herald* 1978c:11). Liwski was kidnapped that evening as he returned home from work. Auriliano Araujo, community leader and Benítez's husband, was abducted at about the same time, as was his teenage sister, and other doctors who had worked in the clinic: Jorge Eduardo Heuman, and Francisco Manuel García Fernández.[17]

Those disappeared in this sweep seem to have been taken, like Benítez, to the Detective Squad Headquarters in San Justo where twelve of the original group of forty or fifty victims remained in illegal captivity for some time (CEDES 1990:7; CONADEP 1986:25).[18] In describing these events, Liwski makes a telling comment. He recounts how, when he went to report the detention of groups of people, human rights activists had a hard time understanding what he was saying. Their experience was of individual disappearances of specific people, not of groups of people at a time, such as seemed to be occurring in poor neighbourhoods. When he was kidnapped, he notes:

> I had come that night from meeting with some leaders from the area [in La Matanza] that were still free, trying to get some things going. I had been in the *Asemblea* [APDH – the Permanent Assembly of Human Rights] in the morning.
>
> But I also want to recognize that it was very difficult to transmit in the context of the formal organizations what was happening in the area, on the scene. There was another dynamic in the human rights organizations which persisted in all the years that followed, which was a more individual perception of human rights violations: to the right to life, kidnapping, disappearance, and so on. This also created a certain difficulty in understanding that we were faced with something gigantic. In any case they did a number of things, telegrams went everywhere. (CEDES 1990:6)

This point is important for the present discussion. People in José Ingenieros were targeted for their activity there, and were picked up there. The experiences of their families were thus somewhat different from those of other victims. As I noted in the introduction, the associations which brought victims under the gaze of the state may have been obscured for many middle-class families. In José Ingenieros, however, victims were often targeted *because of* residence and activism in the neighbourhood. People were thus more likely to witness and understand the patterns of repression. Consequently, residents' reading of the nature and aims of the repressive apparatus may have been different from that of people living in other kinds of neighbourhoods.

In retrospect, it is evident that security forces targeted groups of people for repression. At the time, however, this fact was generally much less clear to the relatives of the victims. Middle-class victims were more likely to appear to be targeted as individuals, in part because they were often picked up at home, at work, or on the street in a way that obscured the connection between the reasons they were targeted and their kidnappings. People were warned not to discuss kidnappings, so reporting was minimized and communication limited. Also, especially where activists were concerned, relatives of victims may have been unaware of the relevant social networks.

One should not underplay the insidious effectiveness of the pattern of fear and guilt by association sown by the practice of disappearance. One of the most striking findings of my research was a silence; I was unable to discover how many people from José Ingenieros disappeared because these matters are not often discussed. For example, there are several cases about which I heard very little, perhaps because the victims did not survive, or perhaps simply because I was not privy to their stories.

A terse account of one such case was reported to me by a neighbour who was not especially close to the family involved. A resident of NHD 18 told me the victim was a young woman of fifteen or sixteen. Her boyfriend, known as *El Zurdo* (Lefty) was also kidnapped. The teenager was seen being carried from her apartment one night rolled in a blanket. A neighbour saw the blanket move. The girl's father was from the Coast Guard. Two years later he appeared dead, floating in the river. His wife was left with a nervous illness.[19]

The personal costs of both illegal and legal detentions for the victims are probably indescribable although a number of attempts have been made.[20] But what were the effects of these repressive practices on the families and communities out of which victims were snatched? The story of the mass already gives a better glimpse than usual of the nature and character of part of the community reaction to such events. It also points to the very real danger to people who attempted to act in solidarity with victims of repression.

One afternoon in October 1992 the subject came up in the neighbourhood *taller de memoria* (history workshop). Claudia, a resident of José Ingenieros, recalled the 1978 abduction of Dr Jorge (as he was known). Alejandra, who did not live in José Ingenieros, remembered that she happened to be visiting a friend in the neighbourhood at the same time. She recalled the commotion which neighbourhood women made as Jorge was hustled out of his apartment. There were about a hundred women, she remembered, including some who were pregnant, trying to keep the military men from taking their doctor away. The shouts were terrible. They hit the women; some collapsed. Mounted police arrived. People threw things from the rooftops. Alejandra, who understood the gravity of the situation, was especially amazed that, after the security forces had taken Dr Jorge away, a group of women went to demand his release at the nearby Regiment.[21] Everyone in the *taller* remarked that it was an incredible story – one most had never heard. Here, as in stories about the *toma*, women seem to be using an image of fierce maternal protectiveness. Perhaps they also manipulated, as did the Madres de la Plaza de Mayo more famously, the patriarchal ideology which saw them as 'only women' and therefore less threatening than men.

Part of what makes this story so remarkable is the unbridled courage it displays. It is important, however, not to exaggerate the extent and scope of community resistance. Given what we know about the pre-existing conflicts in the community, it is not surprising that some neighbours may have been on the side of the security forces, at least in particular instances. In chapter three, we saw how the group in power in *complejo* 17 by 1973 had been in direct conflict with members of the right-wing Comando de Organización, for example. As throughout Argentina, there were people on both sides of the divide in this community. A significant number of residents were employed in the security forces, as police or prison guards, for example. At least one former neighbour (deceased of natural causes by the time I heard the story) was known to have worked as a torturer.

In general, people had to live through situations that were considerably more painfully ambiguous than the heroic incidents above suggest. Another story about the aftermath of the mass is more personal. Anahí's brother had been kidnapped. He had been living with Anahí, her husband, and their two small children in semi-hiding since the coup. After her brother was disappeared she decided to move back to José Ingenieros to stay with a sister there for a while, to try to find her brother, and to organize his release. Deciding to take an active role on behalf of her brother brought conflict with her husband who was afraid of the consequences. Anahí felt she had no choice. One day and with no warning her husband took their youngest child and vanished.

It was a terrible blow. Anahí was now absorbed in looking for both her brother and her son. After a series of legal proceedings, a judge agreed that she had a right to try to find her son and get him back. She looked for the boy and his father in the provinces where she thought they might have fled, but to no effect. When I heard this story, I asked Anahí when she saw her son again. She told me her estranged husband had appeared on her doorstep unannounced five years later, having brought the child for a visit. 'With the return of democracy?' I asked. She had never thought of it that way, but yes.

For me, this story is about the kind of binds the *proceso* placed people in. Was the husband wrong to be afraid? or the wife to try to help her brother? Others had been picked up for less. Lives had been spared by less. Both made their choices with full knowledge of what might lie in store. They had been present when a group of relatives had been terrorized, tortured, and some abducted, bearing the brunt of violent frustration when agents had found them in the missing man's apartment, but not the man himself. At a time when the military occupation of society was virtually complete, the family was supposed to be a safe place. For Anahí and her husband, however, even the family had become a site fraught with danger, fragmented by betrayal, fear, and loss.

The Short-lived Commission of NHD 18

Once these repressive practices had become a normal part of the functioning of the state, they could be called upon for reasons and in contexts that had little to do with so-called subversion. One such incident was described by Doña Teresa, a local small businesswoman living in *complejo* 19. When I knew her in 1992, she lamented the sad state of affairs in the neighbourhood but said that she would never again involve herself in community politics because they were too corrupt. She had turned her attention to the Catholic church where she was volunteering her services. When we sat down to a taped interview one October afternoon, Doña Teresa had a clear sense of the story she wanted to tell.

Sometime in early 1978, José Ingenieros was passed from federal to provincial jurisdiction as the federal government devolved responsibility for housing to the provincial level. José Ingenieros, in particular, was seen as an intractable problem of which the federal agency was more than willing to wash its hands.[22]

Doña Teresa explained how, with the encouragement of social workers who began to come to the neighbourhood after the transition, she participated in an attempt to form a neighbourhood commission in NHD 18. The story she was really eager to tell was of the project's failure:

We took over the neighbourhood on 11 June 1973. And we lived like that, in the air, until '78, when the social workers started coming here.
LD: When the neighbourhood passed over to provincial responsibility?

Teresa: Right ... Because we took the neighbourhood, we were in a bad situation. So the social workers began to come and they wanted the neighbourhood to form an administrative commission, to pay the expenses. So we formed a commission, choosing a representative from every stairway.

LD: In *complejo* 18?

Teresa: Yes, only here. So we made various slates of neighbours; I think there were three slates. We had elections and our slate won; I ran as treasurer. That's why I know all about the story. This commission lasted only a short while.

One of the commission's clauses was that it was always *ad honorem*; nobody got a cent. We were also required to have a bank account at the Banco de la Provincia. [She describes the structure of the commission.] The list of officials was approved by the Instituto. It turns out that the president and vice-president, as soon as they take their positions, they want to run a scam [*estafa*].

Since the neighbourhood had long received only a small part of its water supply from the municipal water mains, there were perpetual problems with wells and the electric pumps used to draw the water from them. According to Doña Teresa, the scam had to do with pretending to need to drill a new bigger well and buy a bigger pump. The people in the commission would get kickbacks. In order for the plan to work, members of the commission, and especially the treasurer, had to approve the estimate. In the commission's next meeting, the president and vice-president tried to persuade the others to approve the estimate although it was, in Teresa's words, an 'unpayable sum.' Teresa describes how the secretary realized that the document was prepared in such a way that it might be altered after being signed:

So [the secretary] looks at me and says, 'Teresa look at what it says here.' And I say, 'I won't sign this.' We got into a real [argument]. Because if I didn't sign ... I was the treasurer ... They wanted to kill me.

Well, the next day the vice-president asks me which side I'm on. 'I'm on the side of order.'

Once again, it is striking that the dissidents here were women. This particular instance suggests that these women were less incorporated than their male counterparts into the politics of patronage. They thus were shocked to discover some kind of under-the-table deal in the offing. Teresa continues:

> They call a meeting the next day, February 25th. We had a meeting of the commission, and there were people from 4-5-6 there, people who had come to make trouble.
>
> When he tells me about the meeting, the vice-president says to me, 'Look, tonight I am going to say a lot of things, but they're not about you.' [At the meeting] the first thing he says is: 'There are three traitors here, la señora Teresa, la señora Dorita ...' Things got difficult! ...
>
> Then I left because of the people from 4-5-6 and 17 who had no reason to be there with us, so I got up and said, 'I have to go,' and went home ... They wanted to make us sign that night. They didn't want to give us any time because they said, 'Tomorrow we need to take it to La Plata. This has to be signed today!' [Teresa bangs the table.] But when we said no ... Well! So that night I left ... Then the secretary came to my house, and another woman as well.
>
> Can you believe, Lindsay – a little while later we agreed to go outside and see what was happening. Everything was dark, the neighbours told us: 'There's a huge mess [*un lio barbaro*]. They're beating them with sticks.' I don't know ... It turns out they started to get out the Falcons.[23] All the lights were out. I was at home. Cars started to arrive and they put them in the trunks. People were looking out their windows: 'Inside! Close up! Lights out!' they yelled.
>
> I didn't see all this, they told me. I'd gone home, thank God. They started to take people away. They took the president, but it was he who sent them. He himself says, 'No, they didn't beat me.' People started in: 'They took my husband!' 'They took someone else.' They looked for everyone. They were coming to my place. We had been drinking coffee, and then we left to go see what was happening, and there is this whole mess. [So we all went home. One woman] arrived home ... and saw the president of the commission with the police. He accompanied them to show them where she lived. This woman was so upset that she went into the bathroom. They went into the bathroom to get her. Her husband works for LADE, the state airline. He takes out his ID and says, 'No. You aren't going to grab my wife.' They left.
>
> They took away a man who lived in stairway 10[24] ... They took him away. They took another man ... That is, they were all marked. But not me. They already had the list of who they were going to take away. They

didn't take me because one of the guys that brought the police knew me from before, when we lived in the other neighbourhood. And he said, 'No. This lady, no.' They all asked, 'How can it be? Why didn't they take you, the treasurer?' Because I was the one who refused. Well. Later that same person told me, 'Doña Teresa, do you know why they didn't take you away? Because there was someone who knew you very well.' Well.

The women, the wives of those men, spent the whole night searching. 'They've taken my husband!' All night. At six in the morning they appeared, barefoot and tortured. You have no idea!

LD: All men, or women also?

Teresa: They didn't take women from the commission. But after they took the commission, I-don't-know-who pointed out a woman from stair 8 whose brother is disappeared. He was disappeared from before. They went to look for her. They tortured her. They gave electric shocks to her breasts and everything. Well [Teresa clears her throat and continues quickly] this woman had nothing to do with the commission, but they took her anyway. It seems that when they took them they asked questions. They had accused those of us in the commission of being communists.

Later a man who they had taken away told us. He said that they tortured him and they said, 'So you're a lefty [*zurdo*]! What are you? What are you doing in that commission?' And he said, 'I don't have anything to do with anything. I don't belong to any party. I'm not ... I'm just in the commission.'

They reappeared at six in the morning. When I went to see, the social workers were here. I am never going to forget that in my whole life, Lindsay. He lifted his t-shirt like this, and from here to here [Teresa indicates her torso] there were boot marks on his back. He said that they kicked him. 'I'm busted up,' [*revantado*] he tells me.

Two days later, I think it was, there was a census.[25] He got up, he walked around and he said to me, 'Look Teresa, I'm busted up, but I don't want them to see how I am,' and he walked. 'I hope the guy who did this sees that I'm walking around.'

Teresa next tells how one of the social workers assigned to the neighbourhood came to them saying that someone from the army in Ciudadela had sent a message; he would be willing to talk to the people from the commission at a place of their choosing.

That's how we ended up at the army there in Ciudadela. Captain Alonso and Lieutenant Colonel Fichera received us. They asked us some things. Afterwards a guy we knew who was a lawyer said he would find out for us. Being there, I tell you, we didn't realize where we were! We had walked into the lion's den and we didn't know. We didn't know anything.
LD: Did you know that it was the military that had taken the people away, or wasn't it clear?
Teresa: No! At that time, no! We didn't know at the time, or we would never have gone. Afterwards the secretary and I agreed it was a miracle we survived.

Even after this saga, there were people who still wanted to form a commission. The president was removed by the social workers on the grounds that he had violated a rule requiring three price estimates per expenditure. A new president was selected. Teresa concludes, 'And that's how we continued. If the neighbourhood needed something to maintain order, we got things done until the intervention came.'

Teresa's story underlines several points that deserve further consideration. Teresa's language and tone (and what I know of her) suggest that she is not highly politicized, although she is active. We might note her admittedly retrospective reconstruction of what she did and did not know about the repressive apparatus of the state in 1978. Certainly she knew to be afraid, but she was shocked to see that her fellow council member had been beaten, and even knowing this, she did not seem to realize that the military might be behind it. Teresa's adherence to the ideal of 'order' also comes through clearly in her account. Her use of the term suggests how the concept is both malleable and persuasive.

This case also skates the line between local corruption and ideologically motivated repression. Was the president of the commission merely using his connections to get his way? Were the people who questioned the council members really afraid that they were communists, or were such categories just part of their standard battery of questions? The confusion here may be typical of the time and place. Regardless of the intentions of the man who denounced the commission, or even of those who interrogated them, the incident clearly accomplished some of the goals outlined by Corradi. Despite the fact that Teresa and her allies resolved to carry on at the bidding of the social workers, it was now clear to them how dangerous such a course might be. It was dangerous despite the fact that the kind of neighbourhood commission they had in mind differed significantly from the commissions which had functioned only a few years earlier. These former commissions had been much more political bodies which often served as advocates for neighbours rather than just collecting their dues.

The role of the social workers in this story is striking. They seem blissfully ignorant of what they might be getting people into. When I interviewed one of them, since retired, she lamented the apathy and sorry state of organization in José Ingenieros in the late 1970s. She seemed not to remember that she had worked in José Ingenieros in the dictatorship years, much less that delegates had actually been targeted for their participation in neighbourhood councils. Indeed this story illustrates the essential rationality of neighbours' non-participation.

Note also that this event was followed in short order by other repressive acts: first, the abduction and torture of the woman whose brother was disappeared, and second, a neighbourhood search. Although this action may have begun as a strategic move in a local political struggle, it seems to have taken on a life of its own – perhaps just by reminding security forces that José Ingenieros was there and potentially breeding organization. Finally, this incident was followed by the official intervention of the neighbourhood; a military man was placed in the role of administrator of all four *complejos*. The military state was thus better positioned to keep an eye on things.

Authoritarian Bureaucratization

Since the neighbourhood was under governmental jurisdiction, residents of José Ingenieros were especially vulnerable to surveillance and control. As we have seen, shortly after the neighbourhood became a provincial responsibility, social workers tried to convince neighbours to form commissions. When this strategy failed, an intervener was appointed to administer the four *complejos*. The shift to a military administrator meant a harder line on tenancy in the still illegally occupied apartments.

Although it had seemed *intrusos* were on the verge of gaining official recognition of their rights to the apartments under the Peronist government, the process was halted with the coup. In interviews, social workers employed by the Instituto de la Vivienda say they inherited a program already in place. The Instituto was interested in one thing:

'regularizing' the situation – order again. Social workers say that they were personally primarily interested in 'social promotion,' but that such concerns generally had to be addressed around the edges of more administrative duties. They tried to work with existing groups and to spend as much time as possible actually in the neighbourhood.

However, a set of rules came down from the Instituto regulating norms of cohabitation, organization, and administration. People under suspicion were required to document their continuous residence in the neighbourhood from the time of the *toma* in order to be considered legitimate. Social workers argue that their criteria were objective and fair. Those who were threatened with eviction believe otherwise; some read a political subtext in the revision process. In either case, by certifying the rights of at least most residents, this state agency legitimized the *toma*.

One woman whose squatters' rights were questioned described being called to an interview one day at eight in the morning together with about a dozen others. The social workers' mistake, she bemusedly told me, was keeping the residents waiting so long that they had time to formulate a collective plan. Everyone was to feign ignorance and disorganization. Since it was moderately difficult to prove continuous residence – no one received personalized utility bills, for example – one should say that one had some kind of document at home and promise to bring it in soon. Their bet that the matter would be dropped proved correct. None of those in this group who stalled were evicted. Perhaps the social workers were just as happy not to have to undertake evictions; this possibility reminds us of the imperfect fit between the plans of various state actors and their execution by those elsewhere in the process.

According to Teresa, a relatively conservative observer, the first military administrators were quite efficient.[26] With the appointment of the intervener, Teresa recalls, '[T]hings got working. Through the time when Alsina was here we were in good shape. The truth is, the neighbourhood was managed normally. But when he left and *Teniente Coronel* Coronel [his last name] came ... It was a disaster! A disaster!'

Teresa says Coronel was on the take. Some of those who operated little shops did not have title to them; Coronel said he would 'take care of things.' All the while the merchants gave him 'presents.' Finally, in December of 1980, an order came from the Instituto de la Vivienda saying that the administration of the neighbourhood would be handed back to local residents' commissions. Teresa recalls: 'On the very day they handed the administration over to us, [Coronel] was already threatening us. He called [the new council] to a meeting and said: "I don't want to find out that people are walking around saying things about me. Nobody touches my honour!" Because he knew I was against him.' The intervener tried to persuade the new commission to keep him around to facilitate things – paying his 'gas money' of course. There were also threats. Finally the *complejos*[27] got together and agreed that they would not work with the colonel. If there was to be a community-run administration, he would not be involved.

Refuge in NHD 19

In marked contrast to most of the people whose experiences are described above, José Ingenieros represented refuge for Katerina and her family. As a nurse active in her union, Katerina had been abducted from the hospital where she worked. Upon her release, her family secretly fled their middle-class neighbourhood in the night. With no time to sell their house and buy another, the family ended up in *complejo* 19 in 1976. Katerina remembered arriving with her husband one night in the dark:

> The next day, I went out onto the balcony, and it gave me a beautiful impression. I felt something warm. I saw the little windows with lights. I felt accompanied, and I was moved. For reasons that are obvious we stayed inside a lot. I liked to sit next to the window and listen to music, *chamamé* [a style of folk music popular in the northern provinces]. It was new for me. And right away, there was the solidarity of the people. They would ring the bell, '*Hola*, how are you?' The first face that I saw was Pichín, '*Hola*, I'm Pichín. Do you need anything?' That was something very supportive [*solidario*]. Something else struck me as funny; the next day the numbers runner [*el quinilero*] rang my bell to ask if I played.[28] This totally opened my eyes because, although I spent my whole life in politics, I was very [sheltered]. [My ex-husband and] I knew politics only from a very closed political party, where everyone knew how to read and write. But I didn't have experience like this – of the masses.

As a middle-class professional on the left, Katerina was struck by the friendliness of her new neighbours which contrasted sharply with what she was used to. Perhaps her impressions are somewhat romantic, but they are also memories overlaid with fifteen years of residence in the neighbourhood.

Although Katerina had fled to José Ingenieros, she did not keep a low profile for long. Out of work, she focused her efforts on the neighbourhood. She called a meeting, filling her apartment with people who wanted 'to discuss' and 'to bring ideas together.' Soon an organization emerged with treasurer, secretary, and so on. They arranged for a nurse and a doctor to tend to neighbours. The residents of NHD 19 had also worked to improve the public spaces of the *complejo*, making pathways where such work had been abandoned with the *toma*. Surprised, I asked Katerina if these activities had happened soon after her arrival in 1976. They had. Katerina does not see the support of such projects as a personal endorsement: 'Even today,' she points out, 'they've never accepted us or the kids.' These projects just seemed like a good idea to her neighbours.

Like Doña Teresa, Katerina was involved in a bid to organize a commission. Of the six hundred families in NHD 19, five hundred were on their side, she recalled. It was a tremendous amount of work, but the people wanted to establish a cooperative to run the *complejo*. The attempt ran into problems like those in NHD 18: a violent confrontation with opponents. In this case, the conflict 'got so bad that they tried to run us over with their cars.' These opponents belonged to CdeO. In recounting violent confrontations, Katerina is at pains to point our that she is now friends with some of her former antagonists whom she describes as 'excellent people' who 'couldn't find a different way.'

Katerina and her neighbours finally took over the commission. The victory was short-lived, however, lasting about a year. During that time there were *allanamientos*. Katerina recalled that people thought the censuses meant they were about to get titles to their apartments. A delegation was dispatched to the provincial capital in La Plata, but nothing came of it. People grew tired. By the end of that year there were only two or three people working in the commission until it was closed by the intervention.

Perhaps because Katerina arrived in José Ingenieros in 1976, the rapid changes in the tenor of social life in the neighbourhood during the *proceso* were especially apparent to her. She was surprised and gratified by the warm reception she and her family received, although it was clear to her that they have never been fully integrated into social life there because of class differences. In recounting these early experiences in the neighbourhood, Katerina quickly moved to a discussion of the neighbourhood's state in 1992, implicitly contrasting the two periods. 'Afterwards the *barrio* fell apart. [Before] it didn't look like a *villa*.'[29] In this last comment, Katerina, like others I had met in José Ingenieros, underlined the neighbourhood's deterioration.

Thinking about how such a transformation came to pass, she mused: 'It's not accidental that the people [*la gente*] don't want to do anything in the context of today's Argentina, no? They are disillusioned. There's nothing.' As an example, Katerina described a recent attempt to build a baseball diamond in one of the local open spaces. People wanted to do it for the kids, she pointed out, 'But there is always someone who blocks your plans.' Katerina's final analysis is bleak. She says: 'The possibilities were many, but what happened is that we never were able to concretize them. Very nice projects start well, people join in, but after they get worn out [*se gasta*], no? But we never arrived at such an abandoned state. Neighbours get into conflicts over any idiocy. Before the doors were open, "lend me your iron, *che*."[30] "*Che*, can you pick up some flour for me?" Because we lived together [*había una convivencia*]! It was nice. All day: *che* do you have flour? Do you have this? Do you have a bullion cube? Because we lived together.' Katerina laments the loss of the energy and ability to work together which characterized the early days of the neighbourhood, and which, it is worth noting, she still saw there after the beginning of the dictatorship. What seems to pain her most, though, is the loss of something much more mundane: a culture of everyday cooperation and sharing. The connection she makes points to the embeddedness of the more explicitly political endeavours in culture.

Los Allanamientos

Few people in José Ingenieros have much to say about the dictatorship period, but the story of the *allanamientos* is one tale told by almost everyone who begins to speak of those years. While disappearances and other acts of repression were selective – albeit, as Corradi explains, intended to sow fear more widely – the *allanamientos* affected each and every resident of José Ingenieros. Carried out several times during the early years of military rule, the operation always began very early in the morning, 4:00 or 5:00 a.m. The entire neighbourhood was surrounded and sealed by troops. Those going to work or school were told to return to their apartments, while people unlucky enough to have left the house without their identification documents might be held in a tent set up for this purpose. The troops, mostly conscripts, then performed house-to-house searches of the approximately twenty-four hundred apartments. In the searches, also known as censuses, household heads were required to identify and account for all family members, while conscripts looked for firearms, political pamphlets and other materials, as well as for 'subversives.'

After the searches were completed, male residents were instructed to leave their apartments in order to clean the corridors, stairs, walkways, and streets of the neighbourhood. They were told to pick up refuse, to sweep and mop, and whitewash. In effect, a massive cleaning effort was carried out under the watchful gaze of the occupying military force. Here I reproduce two versions of this story.

Estela, a woman in her thirties when I spoke to her in 1992, worked as a caretaker and was active in community projects. She recounted her memories of the *allanamientos* some fifteen years earlier spontaneously, as part of a larger discussion on the history of the neighbourhood.[31]

Estela's Story

At 4:30 a.m. Estela's husband had already left for work. He noticed the trucks when he left, but he never imagined that they were headed to José Ingenieros. They surrounded the neighbourhood, enclosing it in a human chain of young men in khaki.

When Estela heard the military at the door, she was terrified. She went to the window and yelled down to her neighbour. The woman told her not to panic, and to open the door to them. Estela refused until her neighbour arrived. She discovered then that they were searching all the apartments. They looked through everything: inside the toilet, all the shelves, the furniture, everything. They asked her if she lived alone and, at her answer, asked where her mother and husband were. Estela explained that her husband had gone to work very early and that her mother sometimes slept over at her sister's house. They found a book next to her mother's bed. A soldier asked her whose it was.'Can you imagine what it was?!' Estela asked me, still horrified in retrospect. It was *La razón de mi vida*, Eva Perón's autobiography – risky given the suspiciousness with which Peronism was regarded by the military regime. 'A good book,' the soldier commented. Estela told him her mother always read it. While they inspected everything, Estela stepped outside onto the terrace and made signs to her neighbours. They were all afraid to speak.

They found many guns in those searches. One apartment in complex 17 was full of them. They also took foreigners away. Estela's husband is Paraguayan and when they searched the apartment, they asked for his papers. She told them that he carried them with him. Estela's husband had to cross the military line when he came home from work. They accompanied him home to verify his address.

In the afternoon they made all the men go downstairs and clean the passageways. They also made them paint the trees with lime. When the soldiers left, people yelled out to them to come back the next day. There were a lot of people who thought they were necessary [*les hacía falta*]. Estela was not among them.

Raúl and Susana's Story

Raúl and Susana, a married couple, both local political activists, told me another version of the story.[32] The couple is older, wealthier, and more sympathetic to the military than Estela. Asked about the history of the neighbourhood, Raúl replied:

> Over the years this neighbourhood has been purifying itself [*se fue depurando*] because, with the fall of General Perón, or rather, with the fall of Isabel Perón, the military came in. So once the military came and surrounded the three [Susana corrects him, four] complexes with trucks, with jeeps ... They surrounded everything, permitting neither entrance nor exit ... They made an office upstairs here and everyone had to go there with their papers first. And after that army patrols went house to house ... They knocked very politely [*con mucha educación*].*Very politely*. They called at each apartment. They came with rules of conduct [*reglementación*], and they asked if we had arms. If you did, you'd better give them up, because if they searched the apartment after and found the gun, well, then it was more complicated for the resident. So, very politely, we told them we had no arms and they searched our apartment ...
> *Susana*: We invited them in.
> *Raúl*: We invited them in to look in our drawers. They had us open the closet ourselves.
> *Susana*: They didn't touch anything. Very polite. Everything – they searched the whole apartment to see if there were pamphlets from some

political party – everything we had should be handed over to them, and we should tell them first.

Raúl: Or show them. It was also to catch many ... ah ... In that period there were many ... ah ... There was some terrorism. So it was the way to locate it. Because that way they went along purifying the neighbourhood a little. Also, later, the poorer people [*la gente humilde*] preferred to have a plot of land. They sold their apartments, and they bought a prefab and they went farther away. Those were the people who used to live in shanty towns.

As is clear from these accounts, the *allanamientos* are depicted in different ways by different people. Some describe them as terrifying, others stress the well-mannered and correct comportment of the military men, but almost all end the story with the same twist: some neighbour would lean over a balcony or window sill and call out to the departing troops, 'Come back again soon!'

This tale is told so often because it makes a good story, but also because it is an evocative anecdote. It is at once compelling and perplexing. It shows some of what it felt like to live in José Ingenieros and as a poor person in those years. This sort of massive military presence marks one important way that the dictatorship experience of many poor people differs from that of the Argentine middle class. For the military, the mere fact of poverty was politically suspect. Where those members of the middle class who were unaffected by direct repression may have sought refuge in their homes (as opposed to the inherent dangers of public places, especially the street), the residents of José Ingenieros became the targets of military action merely by virtue of living in such a neighbourhood. An obvious objective of actions of this scale was the public display of the brute force available to the military rulers. Likewise the idea that the operation was a census underlines the surveillance and information-gathering power at the service of the state.

Cleanliness and Danger

These first-hand accounts of the *proceso* in José Ingenieros highlight some of the ways in which experiences of dictatorship were complex and sometimes contradictory for many people. The story of the *allanamientos* is especially rich. It foregrounds a theme which cries out for an anthropological reading: the connection between ideological and physical cleanliness. This connection is not merely symbolic; the military was trying to impose its kind of order on José Ingenieros in both senses. It is precisely this discourse of physical and social cleanliness that seems persuasive to some residents. Estela was not convinced by this rhetoric and practice, but Raúl and Susana seem to have been. Raúl saw the *allanamiento* as one of a series of processes which have purified, cleaned, and improved the neighbourhood. This purification was a question of getting rid of terrorists, but also of the excessively poor. One irony here is that later in the same interview Raúl described his own childhood experiences of dire poverty (see appendix).

A tension or contradiction between the apparent order of dictatorship on the one hand and its repressive violence on the other is a common thread in local narratives about the era. As I have noted, most residents are aware of human rights abuses that they now know to have characterized the dictatorship years (in fact, most raise the issue on their own); some are even conscious of the systematic strategy to undermine the powerful labour movement. Nevertheless, many also hold more positive opinions about the *proceso*: there was more order, there were no drugs, one could walk the streets without fear of petty thieves, and so on.

In most cases these opinions seem to be held simultaneously, but separately. One couple, Don Fernando, a construction worker in his fifties, and his wife Doña Mabi, who was about the same age, told me about that period. They were speaking of the *allanamientos*, and of the military in general.

> *Fernando*: The only thing is that they bothered you [*molestaban*], that they came in and out [of the apartment].
> *Mabi*: And they searched us.
> *Fernando*: They searched. One time they took me out of my house because I had a green work shirt on, like this. They asked me: Where was it from? Where did I get it?
> *Mabi*: And they turned everything upside down, the mattresses, everything. Looking for arms, I guess.
> *Fernando*: [This was in] the time of Videla. Because Videla ... was really criminal ... Between Videla and Massera, this one [meaning Menem, the president at the time of the interview] seems like a goody-goody [*buenito*][33] ... But I was content, you know?
> *Mabi*: You don't know the things that happened.

Fernando: Before, there were delinquents. In the time of ... [he means the dictatorship but avoids naming it][34] there was none of this. It was a quiet life.

The couple goes on to ask if I am not afraid to be walking around the neighbourhood alone at night. This last comment serves to underline the extent to which the couple evaluate the dictatorship less in absolute terms than in relation to their experience before and after it. As we have seen, violence in itself was neither new nor unusual in the neighbourhood.

For the military, the *allanamientos* were an expression of their raw power. This power was made manifest not just by the scale and violence of the military action, but also by its ability to humiliate. Residents had no choice except to permit this eruption into their most intimate spaces. The military invaded the only social space that people had left, disrupting it, 'turning everything upside down,' as Doña Mabi put it. Meanwhile, non-familial social interaction had been virtually prohibited except in certain clearly prescribed contexts. How much more humiliating the *allanamientos* must have seemed in light of the neighbourhood's proud and militant history. Squatters who had boldly defied the military, seizing the neighbourhood and actively making it their own, were now subject to the most blatant forms of pacification.

But what was this ritual of cleaning about? It looks like an effort to put things in order, contrasting sharply with the turmoil we can imagine the troops left *inside* people's apartments. The cleaning must also have been intended to humiliate; the men were forced to engage in what would have been seen as the debasing – and womanly – chore of cleaning while soldiers, and everyone else, looked on.[35] It was a harsh rebuke, emasculating, one that underlined the neighbourhood's inability to maintain itself.

Of course the criticism here cannot be considered innocent. From the time of the squatter occupation, the inhabitants of José Ingenieros had organized. They had been very successful at getting together and getting things done. They had transformed the complexes from a construction site to a neighbourhood in both material and social senses. As we have seen, the *proceso* regime was actively engaged in dismantling community organizations. Who might have organized neighbours to clean common spaces after stair delegates had been targeted for repression?

The *allanamientos* also constituted a form of social control that both expressed and marked (that is, identified) the neighbourhood as dangerous and unclean in the social and the physical senses. All this is evocative of Mary Douglas's famous argument about pollution as matter out of place. In *Purity and Danger* (1984), Douglas points out that 'dirt is disorder.' And that 'eliminating it is not a negative movement, but a positive effort to organize the environment' (1984:2). For Douglas, 'ideas about separating, purifying, demarcating and punishing transgressions have as their main function to impose system on an inherently untidy experience. It is only by exaggerating the difference between within and without, about [sic] and below, male and female, with and against, that a semblance of order is created' (1984:4). Douglas's analysis tends to abstraction in that she addresses rules about purity more than particular instances of their application. Nevertheless, she calls attention to the importance of these rules and rituals in buttressing authority by reinforcing specific kinds of social order. She also points to the importance of gender as a central organizing principle of social order.

One important point here, then, is that the military regime was intent on conveying its vision of order as the order. Other forms were not permitted; they were anarchic by definition. As the history of José Ingenieros shows, the *proceso* reorganized as a way of destroying previous forms of cooperation.

These messages were not lost on residents of José Ingenieros who would have been continually exposed to them – in subtle and not-so-subtle forms – in the state-controlled media. More persuasive by far, however, would have been the material social practices – abduction, imprisonment, torture, assassination – which made dissension an act of physical bravery. If it were just fear, a sensible reaction under the circumstances, we might expect silence in response. It is the story's surprising end, the 'Come back again soon!'[36] which makes the events harder to read. This suggests hegemony, that the state through a combination of force and persuasion convinced at least some residents of José Ingenieros '*que les hacía falta*,' as Estela said some of her neighbours put it, that they were necessary.

Given this experience, the local preoccupation with garbage I continually encountered takes on new and more profound significance. The history of José Ingenieros begins to explain the defensive assertion, 'this is not a shanty town!' There were times when it seemed that everyone in the neighbourhood was obsessed by questions of cleanliness and garbage. I found this particularly in the memory workshop (chapter 6). Every time I tried to get people to talk about the history of the neighbourhood, it seemed, they spoke about garbage instead. It took some time until I began to see that they were, in fact, talking about the history of the neighbourhood as they saw it.

Conclusions

I have argued that the *proceso* was a transformative period for people in José Ingenieros and throughout Argentina. Here I have described some of the processes which changed livelihoods and lives. Many politicians and commentators in Argentina have argued for putting this gruesome past behind them: that it is better to move on and look ahead. But things not spoken are not necessarily forgotten, and social practices and networks which have been so traumatically destroyed are difficult to rebuild. It seems to me, then, that any real attempt at reconstruction, at 'reweaving the social fabric,' as Argentines are fond of putting it, needs to start with a considered look at the wherefores, the whys, and hows of its tearing.

An important disjunction that appears in the memories of the *proceso* for residents of José Ingenieros is between what they knew at the time and what they later discovered about what had been happening. While the military was in power, people's readings of the situation was very much shaped by their personal experience and word-of-mouth communication. The repressive apparatus of the state made a concerted effort to limit precisely this kind of communication, by closing down or supervising the locations where social life took place. Creating a climate of fear and distrust, the repressive forces sometimes even penetrated families so that the most intimate interactions – between spouses, between parents and children – were curtailed or distorted. It is important to underline that political repression did not just silence discussion of politics, it could shut down communication altogether. For many, then, it was difficult to 'socialize' their knowledge: to bring it out, discuss it, examine it, build on it. To the extent that these processes occurred with respect to people's knowledge about and understanding of the *proceso*, much of it occurred after the fact.

The examples in this chapter demonstrate the extent to which stories about the past were also commentaries on the present, and the reverse. Although the return of democracy was a crucial transformation in many ways, by the time I was conducting fieldwork in the early 1990s, people lived with a different kind of insecurity. The next chapter, therefore, not only describes the economic legacy of the *proceso*, but also outlines the successes and failures of the new democracy for working-class people, and which constitute the context through which the *proceso* period has been retrospectively interpreted and evaluated.

Chapter 5

After Reorganization, 1982–1992

The initial phase of the new democratic period was very much about the *proceso*. Euphoria was manifest in the mass rallies preceding the elections: between one-and-a-half and three million ecstatic citizens attended the last two rallies in the capital (CISEA 1984:428). Some commentators have characterized the years after the *proceso* primarily in terms of the political consolidation of democracy. By the time I arrived in José Ingenieros in 1991, it was taken for granted (most of the time) that Argentina had, and would continue to have, a formal democracy. The condition of the economy represented a much more pressing concern. William Smith, an expert on the Argentine political economy, calls this problem the 'second transition' (1989:270).

Discussions of transitions to democracy are plentiful in the wake of Latin America's dictatorial regimes of the 1970s and 1980s. The emphasis on process implicit in the idea of transition is helpful, but the concept is also tricky for a pair of reasons. First, there tends to be a kind of progressive assumption lurking below the surface; nation-states will move, perhaps by fits and starts, but in a definite positive direction, towards democracy. Second, the objective becomes a receding target, an end for which citizens are often asked to be patient, accepting compromises in the interim.[1] This chapter briefly sketches some of the most important movements and processes shaping Argentines' lives from the end of the dictatorship through my stay in José Ingenieros in 1992. This characterization runs somewhat counter to a simple notion of 'transition to democracy.' On the political front, the Argentine case is a clear illustration that democratization is not a linear, unidirectional process. With respect to the economy, I emphasize the continuities in economic policies, as well as the deepening economic hardship for working-class Argentines in this period. As I have already argued, residents of José Ingenieros understood the *proceso* in light of the experiences and understandings of the intervening years.[2] Therefore the processes I outline here constitute an essential context to the ones I describe in the chapters to follow.

The End of the *Proceso*

When the *proceso* began to unravel it was for reasons of its own making. The country's ongoing economic ills discredited the regime's grandiose initial claims. It failed to deliver on its promise to provide social and economic order: a functioning economy and institutions that would allow people to feel relatively secure. Also, tensions within the military began to mount. Seeking a way to rally support, the regime led by General Leopoldo Galtieri opted for a war with Britain over the Malvinas, as the Falkland Islands were known in Argentina.[3] The attack launched on 2 April 1982 took South Georgia, South Sandwich, and the Falkland Islands, territories in the South Atlantic. The first stage of the invasion only required subduing a symbolic British force and occupying the islands with their eighteen hundred English-speaking inhabitants on the Falklands. The British reclaimed the Island of South Georgia on 25 April. By 14 June the Argentines had surrendered. Galtieri was replaced by General Reynaldo Bignone, who was to transfer power to civilians as quickly as possible.

In retrospect, one wonders what might have possessed the ruling junta to wage war on a European power. However, Malvinas was a nationalist cause around which the country, including the fragmented military, could rally. Everyone had grown up the with phrase '*Las Malvinas son argentinas*' (the Malvinas are Argentine). They never expected Great Britain to put up a fight.[4] At the time, the ploy worked remarkably well. Throughout Argentine society there was general and enthusiastic support. Even among the regime's most ardent critics, there were heated debates. As throughout the country, people in José Ingenieros rallied behind the cause amidst a media blitz: sweaters were knit, money raised, wedding bands donated, care packages assembled. Only after the fact, with defeat and especially the return of the ex-combatants, did people begin to realize that it had been a tragic failure.

Once it was clear the *proceso*'s days were numbered, human rights came to the fore. The formerly small weekly marches of the Madres de Plaza de Mayo exploded, becoming a forum for the public expression

of solidarity with victims and criticism of the regime. It is hardly incidental that the presidential candidate of the Radical Party (Union Civica Radical – UCR) Raúl Alfonsín, was on the board of APDH, one of
the country's leading human rights organizations.[5]

If Alfonsín centred his campaign on the return of the rule of law in
Argentina, it was not just in terms of the judicial system. His campaign
focused on the possibilities democracy offered for citizens' rights to be
heard and for their concerns to be addressed. He called for a return of
the social welfare functions of the state. In his inaugural speech, he
proclaimed: 'We have learned in the light of the tragic experience of
recent years that democracy is much more than a simple form of legitimate power, because with democracy one does not just vote, also one
eats, one is educated, one is healed' (Verbitsky 1985:53). Many felt that
Alfonsín's popularity was an expression of anti-Peronism, but his criticism was more subtle. He argued that his own campaign expressed a
different opposition: not Radicals or Peronists, but 'democracy or
chaos' (CISEA 1984:430). Alfonsín's campaign thus powerfully inverted the signs of the military regime's equation, with a different
understanding of order.

On 30 October 1983 Alfonsín won the presidential election for his
Radical Party, beating out the Peronist candidate Italo Luder. Even in
historically Peronist Gran Buenos Aires, Alfonsín won 51 per cent of
the vote (CISEA 1984:436). This was the first open and free election –
the first from which Peronism had not been excluded – which Peronism had lost since its appearance on the scene in 1945.

Human Rights Policies during the Alfonsín Presidency

Raúl Alfonsín was sworn in as president on International Human
Rights Day, 10 December 1983. Two of the earliest and most important
attempts by the fledgling democratic state to cope with the immediate
past were the CONADEP, the Argentine National Commission on the
Disappearance of Persons, and the Juicio a los ex-comandantes, the
trial of the nine men who made up the three juntas that ruled the country in succession during the *proceso*. CONADEP's harrowing final
report was presented to the president in September 1984, and was subsequently published as *Nunca Más* (never again). It sold more than
350,000 copies in Argentina.

The trial of the ex-commanders received even more public attention
as it unfolded in the second half of 1985. Carefully orchestrated as a

public ritual (Kaufman 1991), the trial was oral and public, in marked contrast to the usual written judicial procedures of the Argentine legal system. For five months, Argentines heard witnesses lay out the facts in 709 cases selected because they showed the scope, pattern, and character of the human rights violations committed during the *proceso*. Norberto Liwski was among the witnesses. In the end, two of the accused received life sentences, one seventeen years, one eight years, and one three years and nine months in prison. The court found that there was insufficient evidence against those who ruled between 1979 and 1982.[6]

Observers agree that the *juicio* presented an authoritative account. This account, of course, was socially produced under specific conditions. The trial can be analysed for the kind of evidence which it did and did not permit (Acuña et al. 1995; Kaufman 1991; Marcus 1994; Osiel 1986 and 1997; Taylor 1994). Although the prosecution set out to prove a pattern of violence, people could only testify about their own experience; the social character of the events described tended to fall away. Witnesses were presented as individuals, not as members of the social and political groups that are central to understanding what was at stake. Nevertheless, for many Argentines the trial made it impossible to remain unaware of the fact that wide-scale, systematic, and unimaginably cruel human rights violations had taken place under their noses. It also showed that the democratic state was willing and able to exact a price for what the military did when it left the barracks. The political importance of the trial is undeniable, especially given that it set a precedent worldwide. This was the first time a state had prosecuted its own military for such crimes.

Although the *juicio* was a remarkable precedent, the Alfonsín government took steps to try to limit prosecutions, most importantly in the *punto final* (final stop) legislation, putting a stop date on the bringing of new cases, and due obedience law which limited responsibility to high-ranking officials. Despite such concessions, the first significant military resistance occurred on 14 April 1987 shortly after *punto final* was enacted. The *carapintada* – as they became known for their camouflage face paint – uprisings called for a 'political solution' to the problem of the trials; by this they meant an amnesty. The group of dissidents, mostly junior officers, wanted the replacement of the military hierarchy, an end to the 'negative campaign carried out by the media' (quoted in Acuña and Smulovitz 1995:62), and protection for the rebels.

When the president called for public support of democracy, a multitude amassed in the Plaza de Mayo. Participants from José Ingenieros recall the ebullience of the crowd as they spent days in the Plaza intent on keeping the armed forces at bay. The standoff ended on Easter Sunday, 19 April. Alfonsín announced the resolution of the crisis from the balcony of the Casa Rosada, the presidential palace. He sent the crowds home proclaiming: *'la casa está en orden'* (the house is in order).

The *carapintadas* would be responsible for three more rebellions.[7] Although they argued that their actions constituted a critique of the hierarchy, not a threat to democracy, their activity evoked memories of the recent past. The size and language of the public response to the first three of these uprisings[8] suggest that this was a common reading. A chief demand of the *carapintadas* was the 'revindication' of the military for their actions in 'the war against subversion.' They may not have intended to take power, but they did hope to alter the direction of the national debate on the recent past.

The *carapintada* rebellions begged the question many had been asking themselves for some time: what was the function of the military in contemporary Argentina? With the fall of Soviet communism and the emergence of Mercosur, a common market in the Southern Cone, the traditional antipathies had lost their conviction. Even if there might be external enemies, after the debacle of the Malvinas war people could not help but wonder if the armed forces was capable of anything except domestic repression and undermining democracy. La Tablada seemed to offer an answer to these questions.

La Tablada: Echoes of the Past

The open green field of the Regiment of La Tablada faced José Ingenieros. When a political group called Movimiento Todos por la Patria (MTP) took it over early one summer morning, 23 January 1989, residents of José Ingenieros had a front row seat. MTP, which had ties with the former guerrilla organization ERP (Ejercito Revolucionario del Pueblo) as well as other groups, was originally pluralist, populist and revolutionary, but, 'had become a vanguardist, verticalist sect intent on achieving recognition' (Schneider 1987:9).

Military sharp-shooters stood on the roofs of José Ingenieros. In the apartment where I would later live, a kitchen window shattered; a stray bullet was later discovered in the soup pot on the stove. Doña Mabi recalled her reaction to the armed confrontation: 'Bullets came this way. Since the barracks is over there, I didn't really think about it at first. [I thought] maybe it was target practice. I didn't notice it at first, but when the bed shook (I had stayed asleep for a while) ... Then my bed shook! Later I realized the kids weren't here, and since children are curious ... One had been nearby; she had seen it.'

MTP took over the regiment, claiming the *carapintadas* were about to launch a revolt there. The repression was swift and fierce – more swift and fierce than that used to put down the military rebellions that had preceded it. In three days, much of them televised, thirteen commissioned and non-commissioned officers and four draftees were dead. Twenty-eight of the MTP group were dead, two more were missing and five unidentified, twenty were under arrest. Officials say twenty more escaped.[9] Sixty-two people were reported injured (Schnieder 1987:10; Acuñas and Smulovitz 1995:75). Witnesses in José Ingenieros said the military assault was merciless and ceaseless, allowing little chance for surrender. They described the horrifying sight and smell of charred bodies lining the fence. The entire story remains confused.

As one commentator notes, it is not clear who infiltrated whom, but the confrontation at 'La Tablada fit [both the MTP and the military] like a glove. Military intelligence may well have infiltrated the MTP, or at least fed the leadership information to encourage the attack, as circumstantial evidence indicates. And the MTP may well have been correct that a military uprising was imminent. In either case, the leftists who led the attack needed the military coup-mongers as much as the Armed Forces needed left-wing subversives' (Schneider 1989:9).

Perhaps even more disturbing than the assault was its aftermath. The original story began to unravel as many of the earliest reports – that an advance truck rammed the gates killing a guard and that the attackers had modern Soviet and Chinese arms, for example – proved false. Relatives of those who died or were captured insisted that there was evidence of the use of excessive force; the chief of Buenos Aires provincial police agreed, saying a specialized SWAT team of fifty could have put down the attack with tear gas (Schneider 1989:12).

Occurring when the prestige of the armed forces was very low, the uprising could not have had a more positive effect on their image if it had been planned. The swift and decisive action by the armed forces undermined *carapintada* assertions that the hierarchy was ill-prepared to do its duty. The success in putting down a supposed internal threat revived the notion of the armed forces that had dominated during the *proceso*. Once again it was possible to talk and think about an armed forces whose principal role was to maintain internal security: to put down domestic conflict and to gather domestic intelligence. Two days later, President Alfonsín announced the formation of the Consejo Nacional de Seguridad (CONASE – the National Security Council) to work on counter-subversion.[10] Schneider notes that a witch hunt ensued: not only were MTP offices across the country raided, but also communist activists were rounded up. Because human rights, union, and liberation theology advocates had been involved in MTP, the whole left fell under suspicion (1989:12). Of course, most participants in the group were in no way involved in the murky scheme to occupy the Regiment.

This repression evoked the *proceso*. People in José Ingenieros told me they destroyed books and leaflets which they feared might be viewed as subversive. A human rights organizer reported that support for an educational project dried up in the wake of the incident. The reaction to La Tablada shows how close to the surface memories of the *proceso* remained. La Tablada underlines the degree to which discourses and, even more important, practices of the *proceso* era were still available and relevant. This moment marks a turn of the tide, particularly with respect to the military and human rights; it demonstrated the extent to which those demons, despite many valiant efforts, had not been effectively exorcized.

Retrenchment under Menem

By the time Alfonsín gave up his presidency early to president-elect Carlos Saúl Menem because of the economic crisis, prosecutions of the military were virtually halted, but Menem intended to go further.[11] Shortly after assuming the presidency, Menem started talking about a presidential pardon (*indulto*) for those still in jail. Public opinion was firmly against the *indulto*.[12] Nonetheless, 277 people received presidential pardons on 8 October 1989. These *indultos* freed military men convicted of human rights violations, misconduct in the Malvinas war, and participation in uprisings. They also freed civilians jailed for guerrilla activities. Excluded from this first round of pardons were only the very highest ranking military criminals, who were pardoned in due course, on 29 December 1990. Menem said that he signed the pardons in the name of 'peace and reconciliation.'

There can be little question that the Menem years saw a change in the tone of public debate around political and civil rights. Various cases of police violence and the use of excessive force received press coverage in the early 1990s. (One of these is discussed in chapter 7.) Another cause for alarm was the rising incidence of attacks against the press, often in the form of lawsuits, but including threats and violence.[13] President Menem himself often criticized the press for 'abuses of the freedom of the press' (*Clarín* 1991c:19). He displayed other antidemocratic tendencies – in his use of presidential decrees to circumvent the legislature for example, and in some of his comments.

One episode that drew particular outrage occurred amid growing protest against ever-deeper cuts to education funding. The president spoke on Argentina's national holiday, 9 July 1992, in the northern province of Tucumán. He warned students and parents against participating in marches and protests organized by the teachers' union and parents' associations. He cautioned that these marches 'might have a subversive type connotation' and added that this could lead to 'a new contingent of Madres de Plaza de Mayo' (*Clarín* 1992:9). The comment condensed several ideas. First, it used the tainted notion of subversion that was thoroughly embedded in the dictatorial discourse and in the repression it had produced. Second, it suggested that the Madres who so many saw as heroines were the parents of 'subversives' in this sense. Third, it implied that critical teachers and parents might themselves be 'subversives.' Finally, it suggested that, as in the past, such dissent might result in violence and disappearance. The implicit threat was met with outrage from unions, opposition parties, and human rights organizations which responded by organizing two more marches in front of the Congress.

In the decade following the *proceso*, politicians explicitly tackled the political legacy of the dictatorship. The process was neither simple nor linear. Rather, the initial assault on the military view was later softened and qualified, at times even reversed. As I noted in the introduction to this book, it was precisely this sense that the human rights view was giving way that brought me to the present project.

A conversation I had with a friend in José Ingenieros demonstrates the ambivalence which continued to surround the version of events produced in places like *Nunca Más* and the juicio. One night a group of people from the community centre El Hornero rented the video *La Noche de los Lapices* (The Night of the Pencils). This commercial film portrays a notorious incident in which a group of high school students was kidnapped, tortured, and held prisoner for months. Only one teenager, Pablo, survived. According to the film, the students had been organizing a demonstration against the price of the student bus fare. The film is chilling. When we were walking home afterward, one of our group wondered aloud, 'but the story was kind of partial, wasn't it? Maybe there was more to what the kids were doing but [the film makers] didn't show it because [the film] was from Pablo's point of view. He spent four years in prison, so didn't really know what was going on.' Implicit in this comment were questions about the accuracy of the account, the innocence of victims, and the legitimacy of their repression.

The Economic Legacy of Reorganization

Like its social and political legacy – social atomization and fear – the economic legacy bequeathed to the new democratic regime was grim: stagnation, inflation, falling wages, increasing stratification. Some figures are telling: at the end of the *proceso*, the purchasing power of wage-earners was lower than it had been in the 1960s (Smith 1989:270). At 209 per cent, the Argentine inflation rate was the highest in the world at the time. The national debt was US $43 billion; servicing it took half of export earnings.[14]

The focus on the interrelation of political, social, and economic processes of reorganization is particularly important for thinking about what the *proceso* meant for working people in general, and residents of José Ingenieros in particular. What Torrado (1992) calls the *aperturista* or open economic model was radically different from anything seen in Argentina before. The military regime reversed the previous strategies of import substitution. Industrialization was no longer the centrepiece of the development agenda. This economic policy had everything to do with social and political policy.

> [For the armed forces] to achieve the anxiously awaited institutional and political disciplining of the working class, beyond vitiating its corporate institutions and political representation, the most efficient strategy would consist of a drastic modification of the functional economic conditions which had historically sustained the development of this class, that is, the drastic modification of the industrializing model. (Torrado 1992:63)

This fact gave the economic liberals like Finance Minister José Martínez de Hoz an opening. Since the *proceso*'s architects tended to equate developmentalism with Peronism and the big state, one of their aims was to dismantle the state. This fit neatly with the economic liberals' call to open the economy to free market forces.[15] As a result, economic policy shifted towards free-market prices, favouring the most competitive industries. This in turn led to the concentration of capital, opening the economy to foreign capital and imports, and containing inflation through a drastic reduction in real wages (Torrado 1992:63).

As a way of curtailing the power of the industrial working class, the policies were remarkably effective. The years of Videla's presidency (1976–81) represented the longest period of union inactivity in Argentina since 1943 (Delich in Cavarozzi 1992:65). Industry's share of the gross domestic product (GDP) fell by 20 per cent between 1975 and 1982; but more importantly, the number of workers engaged in industry fell by 35 per cent. Real incomes of wage-earners shrank by an estimated 30 to 50 per cent between 1976 and 1982 (Torre and Riz 1993:341).

Also telling is the increase in the number of self-employed, precarious wage-earners, and marginal workers. Between 1970 and 1980 the number of working-class people who were self-employed increased by 43.7 per cent (Torrado 1992:236). In other periods such an increase did not necessarily signify hardship for workers, but during *aperturismo*, it reflected an increase in hidden wage-earners and marginal workers.[16] Working conditions also became more precarious for these workers, who became even more vulnerable to the whims of employers. Days and hours of work grew longer and wages fell considerably, both in absolute terms and with respect to wage-earners (Torrado 1992:247–8).

At the same time, there was 'a new and drastic decline' in social spending, a reduction of about two-thirds compared to the levels of the preceding developmentalist model. Public services were reserved for the poorest members of society. In hospitals, for example, user fees were introduced except for those who could prove they were sufficiently poor. Also, with changing employment patterns, far fewer people had access to union health plans. Health and education levels declined during this period. The housing deficit remained about the same, probably because of decreased migration to the cities (Torrado 1992:441–4). Torrado sums up:

> One can conclude that it is during this period that the phenomenon of 'critical poverty' – at least at statistically measurable levels – spreads in Argentina, that is, the existence of ample social sectors with basic needs unmet or insufficient income to guarantee their basic satisfaction. In

effect, the available evidence suggests that during *aperturismo* a significant absolute pauperization occurs in the working class, at the same time
as relative pauperization of the middle class ... In sum, the interventions
of the state in relation to well-being during the *aperturista* strategy trans-
lates transparently the declared objectives of social discipline. (1992:443)

Proceso era economic policies constituted a crucial element of the reorganization the regime sought. Economic, political, and social policies
combined with organized repression in its more and less naked forms
to rend the social fabric and to isolate people. Corradi puts this well:

on the one hand, state terror confined citizens to looking after themselves
... Meanwhile, the people's strategies to cope with inflation turned them
into speculators and moonlighters. The carrot was no less demoralizing
than the stick ... Everything conspired, from the police state to wild market forces, to turn a person into a maximizing consumer rather than into a
cooperating citizen, eroding feelings of social obligation. (1985:125)

Economic Transition?

As noted, Alfonsín had promised that the return to democracy would
mean a new, more humane economy. His initial attempts reflected this
commitment. He first tried Keynesian measures of social spending to
restart the stagnant economy. The new government introduced job creation and social welfare projects like the National Literacy Plan and the
PAN (Plan de Alimentación Nacional) which delivered food to families
in need. José Ingenieros was a beneficiary of all these programs. The
initial organization of Hornero was a byproduct of the expansion of the
beneficent state under the Radicals.

Very soon, however, Alfonsín's economic strategy proved untenable,
as hyperinflation set in. By the third quarter of 1984, the annual inflation rate was 1,080 per cent (Torre and Riz 1991:348). After only eight
months, Alfonsín returned to some of the neoliberal measures of his
predecessors, a move his critics were quick to point out. He tried twice
to implement major economic plans directed at stopping inflation, but
despite considerable popular and international support, each failed
when inflation again escaped control. By July 1989, eleven months into
the second plan, retail prices had risen 3,610 and wholesale 5,061 per
cent (Acuña 1994:37).

Not surprisingly, the populist Peronist candidate Carlos Menem won the elections held on 15 May 1989 with the majority of the electoral college and 47 per cent of the popular vote. The economic crisis was so profound by the time of the election, and the wait between the election and the inauguration so long, that Alfonsín had to leave office six months early so that the incoming president could take action. Nonetheless, the transition was an important moment in Argentine history. His was the first democratically elected government which had voluntarily handed power to its opposition.

Menem's 'Popular Market Economy'

As a candidate, Menem had emphasized his connection to the Peronist masses, especially those of the interior. On assuming power he quickly moved behind a neoliberal model, however. Throughout his presidency Menem favoured privatizations, opening the economy, and a foreign policy which sought close relations with the United States. Argentine literary and cultural critic Beatriz Sarlo describes Menem's mode as 'a new *mestizaje* in which market liberalism blends with the charismatic political style that President Menem learned in the Peronist movement' (1994:34). Typical of this *mestizaje*, Menem gave his economic policy the remarkable name, 'the popular market economy' (*Página/12* 1991a:6).

Domingo Cavallo, minister of the economy from the beginning of 1991, played a key role.[17] The team was politically effective: Menem wielded the charisma and Peronist credentials, Cavallo the Ivy League MBA and the air of technocratic efficiency (Sarlo 1994:34). Cavallo's Convertibility Plan effectively pegged the exchange rate for a new Argentine peso to the US dollar (replacing Alfonsín's austral which in turn had replaced the peso) and suspended indexation clauses in contracts. The immediate consequence was a decline in interest and inflation rates, and some initial industrial reactivation. The neoliberal policies also concentrated on the debt, especially privatizing state enterprises and using the proceeds to reduce it. In addition, the economy was deregulated and the taxation system reorganized. This was a sea change for Peronism. As Cavallo put it, 'Menem is changing everything that Perón did after the Second World War' (Acuña 1994:47). Nonetheless, and despite a growing cloud of corruption hovering around the Menemist inner circle, many Peronists continued to vote for Menem, and implicitly for Cavallo. The support was great enough to bring the president a victory in midterm elections and then re-election – once the constitution had been revised specifically to permit it.

The Social Costs of Economic Adjustment

Despite the praises sung to the Menemist economic strategy in Washington and the banks, it had serious flaws. Even the economic plan's authors admitted that the cost of restructuring was the *ajuste* – the 'adjustment' but also 'tightening' (of belts). The message that everyone must suffer short-term pain for long-term gain was persuasive to some. While it is true that people from many occupations and classes faced economic hard times, some groups were harder hit than others. Bringing hyperinflation under control was crucial for poor people, but the strategy Cavallo employed created some noticeable and alarming effects in José Ingenieros. With the peso pegged to the dollar, inflation was much lower than it had been, but despite official denials, prices continued upward.[18] Wages were stagnant. The peso/dollar bought ever fewer domestic products and ever more imports. The consequence was a further decline in domestic production. People employed in the putting-out system saw their rates fall, and then orders dry up. The piece workers I knew in José Ingenieros were priced out of the market by imports – most importantly, Asian imports for the seamstresses.[19] Marisa and her family, for example, were working at a feverish pace trying to make ends meet in May 1991. Two years later they had no work at all.

The much-lauded restructuring also shrank the state and its economic redistribution functions, and thus its ability to soften the blow for the poor. Together these effects continued the overall trends that began during the *proceso*: rising unemployment, continuing de-industrialization, and a widening gap between rich and poor with ever more people on the poor side of the divide.

So notable is the change in the social structure and the distribution of wealth in Argentina in recent years that it has produced a literature on 'the new poor' (cf. Powers 1995a, 1995b, 2001; Minujin et al. 1992). This literature points not only to increasing numbers of poor people but also to the increasing heterogeneity of poverty in the country. Authors now distinguish between 'structural poverty' and 'pauperization.' The structural poor (the 'old poor' in a sense) are those whose basic needs are unmet in at least one of the following senses: crowded or unsuitable housing (i.e., earth floors); poor sanitation; a child aged six to twelve who is not in school; or the head of household has insufficient earnings capacity given education and family size. The 'new poor' are thought to be those whose poverty is manifested in their income levels alone. This implies that they once had incomes enabling them to acquire these basic needs. Analysts acknowledge that the distinctions are not perfect, but they are useful.[20]

Although the economic crisis had roots that predate the *proceso*, rates of poverty had been increasing notably since then. In 1974, 5.8 per cent of homes in the *conurbano* had incomes below the poverty line (Murmis and Feldman 1992:57).[21] The number of households below the poverty line hit 38 per cent in October of 1989; a few months earlier inflation had peaked at 196.6 per cent for the month of July (CEPAL in Powers 1995b:36, n 30). When I was conducting fieldwork in José Ingenieros, the poverty figure descended from 25 per cent in October 1990 to 14 per cent in October 1992 (CEPA in Powers 1995:97).[22] By this measure, poverty had decreased in the short term because inflation was brought under control, but it remained well above historical levels.

In one sense, residents of José Ingenieros were fortunate to have relatively high-quality housing, making them less likely to be classified among the structural poor. Many benefited from inflation when it came to paying off the debt on their homes to the Banco Hipotecario. As already noted, 89 per cent of apartments in José Ingenieros were owned by their inhabitants. All the same, the kinds of jobs people in José Ingenieros tended to hold were precisely those that saw deep cuts, both in the quantity of employment opportunities and in earning levels.

Job loss is one effect of rationalization and privatization. As one example, in November 1990 the federal government more than halved its workforce from 671,000 to 284,000 by laying off 103,000 workers and transferring more than 284,000 teachers and health workers to the provinces (World Bank 1994:18). A visible effect of the layoffs in José Ingenieros was the emergence of ever-greater numbers of mini convenience stores, known as *quioscos* throughout the neighbourhood. In José Ingenieros they were usually run out of ground-floor apartments. The owners of the *quiosco* nearest my apartment cleverly offered a telephone message service, since few residents had phones. Many people had taken the severance packages – often as much as a year's salary – that accompanied firings and invested them in small businesses.

These enterprises were not limited to José Ingenieros. A 1991 newspaper editorial in the largest circulation paper, *Clarín*, remarked on the proliferation of *quioscos* and street and ambulant vendors in Buenos Aires, estimating that they numbered some seventeen thousand. It attributed this phenomenon to shrinking salaried employment and it noted that while providing work, this was work without legal protections, reliable wages, or employment benefits (*Clarín* 1991f:16). Another problem was that possibilities were few. What worked for the first few entrepreneurs became a much more precarious enterprise as it was emulated by ever more people. Argentines joked that as this trend continued ambulant vendors and *quiosqueros* will find themselves with no one to sell to except each other.[23]

The Persuasiveness of the Economic Plan

The conundrum for many analysts is the remarkable complacency of most Argentines in the face of a harsh attack on their economic well-being. In this respect, I was struck by a conversation that I had with a group of people in José Ingenieros. We were talking in 1991, a time when there was heated discussion of the Menem government's plan to privatize many nationally owned companies. Luís was a postal worker afraid that his days as a public employee were numbered because he expected the postal service to be sold and its workforce 'rationalized' – that is, he anticipated many layoffs. What was striking was not so much this man's resignation to his fate as his sense that he deserved it.

He said that he was a gnocchi, and that the only solution for people like him was to fire them all and start again. A gnocchi is a particularly Argentine concept. It means someone who, because of political patronage, holds a public job but does not work at all. Argentines use the term because of a modern tradition that holds that if you eat gnocchi (an Italian potato dumpling) on the 28th of the month, and leave money under your plate, you will be lucky with finances in the coming month. Gnocchi is the food of choice because by the end of the month its ingredients, potatoes and flour, are often about all people can afford. By analogy, people who get paid for no work are called gnocchis because they also show up on the 28th of every month, pay day.

When I asked Luís what he meant when he called himself a gnocchi he admitted that he often arrived at work as much as an hour late, and that he did not work as hard as he might. What struck me was that by using the term he identified himself as a freeloader, as someone who does not work and does not deserve to be employed. Also remarkable was the notion that the only solution to his lack of productivity was a pink slip. Arriving at work earlier, or working harder, were not alternatives. He agreed with the government's assertion that he, and people like him, did not deserve a wage.

Luís cannot be dismissed as atypical. Menem and his neoliberal economic plans continued to enjoy widespread support among the Peronist faithful as late as the 1995 elections, despite massive layoffs and the continued erosion of workers' rights. For example, in 1990 Menem imposed right-to-strike limitations on the politically charged Peronist anniversary, 17 October. Many people clearly believed that there was no other way, that the working class would have to cede its hard-won privileges for the good of the nation.

Menem's popularity has to be attributed at least in part to his government's ability to keep inflation under control. It is difficult to exaggerate the intensity of the fear of hyperinflation, a fear fanned by Menem himself. Beatriz Sarlo describes the 'cultural imprints of hyperinflation' in Argentina:

> The population's state of mind can be characterized as the obsession, constantly repeated in public and private discourse, that anything is better than a new surge of hyperinflation ...
>
> The cultural imprints of hyperinflation can today be seen with clarity. In the first place, the idea was imposed that all other economic or social demands must be postponed in the face of the principal objective of achieving stable prices. Everyone – including the sectors most harmed by the new economic policy – agreed that economic stabilization was the central value to be defended above all others ... Thus the discourse of Menem and Cavallo on the virtues of the free play of market forces and the negative effects of state intervention was taken as descriptive of the reality that had to be accepted. The market began to be seen not as an institution reflecting changeable social relations, but as a natural phenomenon whose objective limits had to be accepted.
>
> In the second place, the discourse of the president and the economy minister, together with the rapid drastic measures favoured by Cavallo, tended to convince the population that it was impossible to respect all the institutional formalities if stabilization was to be rapidly achieved. (1994:34)

In other words, further democratization would have to wait.

The fear of hyperinflation is not as irrational as Sarlo suggests, however. Everyone suffered the anxiety of seeing their pay cheques dwindle before they could get them to the bank. As we have seen, the progressive impoverishment of most Argentines has a longer history, but the dramatic effects of hyperinflation in particular can be seen in the shocking fact cited above, that almost two out of every five residents of the *conurbano* lived below the poverty line when inflation was at its peak.[24] Stabilization did matter tremendously in the everyday lives of people in José Ingenieros. It was especially beneficial to the poor, who were particularly hard hit by inflation and could not benefit from currency speculation (Powers 1995a:98–9). In addition, relative stability also made things easier for those who had some money. People could buy the relatively cheaper imports on lay-away. One friend, who had found a well-paying job with a lot of overtime at the Coca-Cola factory,[25] bought a TV and stereo in 1991, both in monthly instalments. The ability to buy almost anything on time was a popular aspect of the economic plan.

The naturalization of the economic scheme of things was buttressed by both local and international political contexts. Locally, few voices, and none from within the main opposition, the Radical Party, articulated any credible alternative to the notion of *ajuste* and privatization advocated by those in power. Likewise, Argentines came up empty when they looked abroad for alternatives. Although Sarlo writes in broad generalizations, evidence from work with poor people in the capital substantiates this view (Powers 1995a:118–19; 1995b), as do the comments of residents of José Ingenieros.

On the other hand, Menem's popularity was not total. Electoral and other political support often seemed to be less a matter of conviction (although it was still often that in the Peronist bastion of José Ingenieros) than a calculated decision that he was the safest option. If one is stuck with a neoliberal, one might as well go with one who seems to know what he is doing, people reasoned.

Conclusions

People in José Ingenieros began this period full of hope. Inevitably, the transition was a more uncertain process than anticipated. Remarkable and disturbing moments, like the juicio a los ex-commandantes, the *carapintada* uprisings, and La Tablada, evoked and played on the past in complex ways. Of most immediate concern to the people I spoke with in José Ingenieros were their continuing economic woes. In this sense, the transition never came. Having waited for a decade for Alfonsín's *con la democracia se come* (one eats with democracy) people were beginning to lose hope that conditions might improve. As becomes clearer in the chapters that follow, the sense of perpetual economic crisis was part of a larger climate of insecurity which characterized José Ingenieros in the early 1990s.

MEMORIES

Chapter 6

The History Workshop: An Exercise in Popular Memory

Local historical knowledge in José Ingenieros is fragmented for the same reasons that social networks were disarticulated by recent events and processes. For many reasons, not least political, people in José Ingenieros seem to have rarely discussed the past among themselves. This fact poses a theoretical and methodological problem: how might one proceed to look at popular memory – that is a shared 'common sense history' (Popular Memory Group 1992) in José Ingenieros? For members of a *taller de memoria* (history/memory workshop), one solution was to paint a mural. The mural, like the workshop that produced it, calls our attention to the difficult relationship between community and place in José Ingenieros. Much of the literature on memory sees working on the past as a way of getting at and thinking about collective identity (Boyarin 1994; Friedman 1992a, 1992b). Here too, the *taller de memoria del barrio* was seen as a location where community had to be remembered, and thus, somehow reconstituted and positively valued.

Through the mural (see colour plate 1), workshop participants rendered a version of the past for themselves and their neighbours. It depicts the neighbourhood's apartment blocks at four different moments represented by four buildings in a row. The first shows the time of the *toma*, when some buildings were not even finished, and when many neighbours lacked access to water, electricity, and gas. The second depicts a later moment with infrastructure installed. Third is the present, with bars on the windows signifying fear and insecurity in the face of crime. Finally we see a future when the gardens are green and people feel safe. In the foreground is a series of silhouettes of people working and painting to better the community. In the sky is a rainbow (being painted and as yet unfinished) and the title 'This is our neighbourhood, this is our history.' The meaning of the whole mural is neither transparent nor expected. This depiction of the period from 1973 to 1992 renders preoccupations and tensions that are central to life in the neighbourhood, however. The contrast between the images in the mural and 'official histories,' both dominant and oppositional, is striking and important.

This chapter describes the history workshops which I instigated and helped organize as sites of the social production of memory. With the history workshop the past-present relation comes to the fore. As I have argued, the past is recalled in specific relationship to the present. This is truer still in groups like the history/memory workshop, where an important justification for the work of the *taller* comes from a conviction that it helps people understand their present dilemmas more clearly.

I describe the *talleres* in some detail here because their processes are telling. Three types of questions are important with respect to the *taller*. First, why and how did neighbours work on the history of their community through the history workshop? Second, what difference does it make to do this remembering together? How is the workshop dynamic in particular, different from individual accounts? And third, what knowledge about the past in José Ingenieros was produced or brought to the surface through the history workshop?

The History Workshop

The history workshop is connected to the movement in social history that focuses on 'history from below.' Workshops are seen as strategies for uncovering subaltern histories and silenced voices. The term itself is used as a gloss for the collective thinking – through of history, generally by participants of the events or members of the communities in question. Such workshops have employed various methodologies with a variety of groups across the globe.[1]

The most obvious Argentine precedents are the *talleres* run as part of the National Reading Plan under the Alfonsín government (Alvarez 1989).[2] Describing the decision to employ specifically history workshops, Hebe Clemente, one of its organizers, writes: 'As these [experiences] emerged, we began to understand that it was here, in the history workshop, that the essential national significance of the Plan resided. In turn, we began to understand their particularly emotional, and especially Argentine load, because we believe that a workshop with these peculiarities whispers to us of the things we lack' (Alvarez 1989:8). Except for a project on railway workers (Accorinti 1990), these history workshops usually focused on small towns, and worked mostly with local intellectuals such as town librarians, school teachers, and people from the mayor's office. That a project of this sort should have been sponsored by the state is striking. In going outside Buenos Aires and the other big cities, it attempted to amplify the field of Argentine history. Part of the social democratic agenda of the post-*proceso* presidency, this plan can be read as trying to construct a hegemonic narrative that casts a wider net, incorporating communities and regions that have usually fallen outside ideas of the Argentine nation. Yet there could have been more variety in the class backgrounds of participants.

When the plan was discontinued with the election of President Menem, a few organizer-facilitators went on to work in a more precarious way in some older neighbourhoods of the capital. Some Argentine labour historians who work in close collaboration with unions have also employed something akin to the history workshop technique (Cangiano 1996, Pozzi 1988).

History Workshops in José Ingenieros

I helped organize two distinct *talleres*. The first workshop came out of El Hornero community centre and lasted from September 1991 through May 1992 (with mid-December through March off for the Argentine summer). A second, more successful, workshop was located in the neighbourhood pre-school, meeting more intensively from August through December 1992. Although core groups of relatively consistent participants formed in each workshop, memberships shifted over time. I was almost always present.

The first *taller* arose almost by accident. As explained in chapter 2, the Hornero community centre had been my entry into the neighbourhood. One of the first things I asked people there was about key dates so that I could look for some reference to the neighbourhood's history in the Congressional Library's newspaper archive. I was told about the *toma*, which was described as taking place in winter (it was cold) 1973, or perhaps 1972. What I found was evidence of a citywide phenomenon and front-page photographs of tanks surrounding what looked like José Ingenieros. After some reflection on the implications for my work of 'correcting' possibly 'faulty' memories, I surrendered to curiosity and indignantly asked my friends at El Hornero why they had kept the tanks from me. I showed them my notes, but I had been unable to take photocopies of the pictures. Their surprising immediate reaction was to organize an outing to the congressional library to have a look. A group of six adults and four children met one Saturday afternoon at the library. We looked through various bound volumes of periodicals, finding and discussing articles on the *toma*. It turned out that the photograph of the tanks was of a similar neighbourhood and had been mislabelled.

The formation of a history workshop seemed like the logical next step. Likely participants from the centre, and others who someone thought might be interested, were invited to meet one Saturday afternoon. Attendance fluctuated from two to a dozen people; most were friends with each other.[3] Participants were longtime residents of José Ingenieros, including both *adjudicados* and *intrusos*, ranging in age from twenty-one to about fifty years.[4] More women than men were in the group for the reasons already discussed. In occupation and income, participants were typical of residents of the neighbourhood; there were housewives, piece workers, domestic workers, a factory worker, and two of the younger participants were students as well.

A conspicuous divide in both *talleres* was generational. Younger participants who had grown up in the neighbourhood were generally trying to reconstruct a history that they vaguely remembered but had yet to understand. They sensed that their parents had mixed feelings about the past, but often did not even know what events generated these feelings. Older people, on the other hand, tended to focus on their personal experience because the *taller* was an environment that accorded this experience significance.

Why a History Workshop?

Given the difficulties of the past for residents of José Ingenieros, people's willingness to participate in the workshop requires explanation. When we started the *taller*, I saw it as formalizing an existing relationship, recognizing the active role of residents in my project, and giving their participation a degree of autonomy. Most participants were already trying to answer my questions and introducing me to people they thought had something interesting to say. Once we sat down to think about the possibilities that a history workshop offered, it became clear that few were interested in working on the neighbourhood's history for itself. Rather, the *taller* was seen as a way to address other more pressing concerns. Several months into the first *taller*, four of us went to talk about it on a local FM radio station. After discussion, participants decided that representatives of the group should present the workshop in the following terms. This list comes from the notes that representatives took with them to the interview.

– We are a group of neighbours who meet Saturday afternoons to drink *mate* and talk about the history of the neighbourhood.
– The *taller* is a space for those of us in the neighbourhood who believe that *our* history matters too.
– The *taller* allows us to talk about our experiences, the ways in which we have lived different moments. We have become aware that although we are neighbours we haven't all lived the same history in the same way. There are four *complejos* within the neighbourhood. There are *intrusos* and *adjudicados*. So, we have different visions of different moments.
– We depict what happened to help us understand the present and make plans for the future.
– We believe it is important that what we are learning not stay only with us; that's why we should go on the radio, for example.

People felt the need to articulate, or perhaps recreate, community identity; they looked to the past as a source of inspiration and example. Some felt themselves to be excluded from History with a capital H, and wanted to write themselves back in.

As we have seen, a principal objective of years of repression had been the fragmentation of all kinds of social networks, and in this neighbourhood it had been largely successful. The discernible result of this recent past was a population that had turned inward. Many who used to participate in community organization were no longer interested. The abrupt and prolonged break in collective activities meant that not only activists and leaders but also certain practical organizational knowledge had been lost. Thus a principal preoccupation of the *talleristas* was to recreate or recover a sense of community similar to that which some remembered from the early days of the neighbourhood. People hoped a history workshop might awaken neighbours' concerns for the neighbourhood. If we could 'resuscitate memory' (*recuperar la memoria*) as they put it, perhaps earlier moments might serve as models for present organization. This was to be a history for the future. As our flyers declaimed, '*Un barrio sin memoria es un barrio sin futuro'* (A neighbourhood without memory is a neighbourhood without a future).

This view of history was common sense for participants; in fact, it is the main reason people considered the *taller*, and my work for that matter, worth the bother. In explaining this to me, many people quoted a popular song written by a Peronist: '*Si la historia la escriben los que ganan / Quiere decir que hay otra historia / La verdadera historia.*' (If history is written by the winners/That means there is another history/The real history).

Thus, like Raymond Williams, they believed in the counter-hegemonic possibilities of history. As Williams writes, 'it is significant that much of the most accessible and influential work of the counter-hegemony is historical: the recovery of discarded areas, or the re-dress of selective and reductive interpretations. But this, in turn, has little effect unless the lines to the present, in the actual process of the selective tradition are clearly and selectively traced' (1977:116).

Argentines are more likely than many North Americans to recognize the malleability of the past. Rewriting the past, as in official school curricula and history texts, had been normal in the switch back and forth between Peronist and non-Peronist, military and civilian, and more and less nationalist governments over the previous fifty years (Shumway 1991). On one hand, this made Argentines in general more conscious of the manipulation of the past; on the other, it made them more sceptical.

This relation to the past helps explain the remarkable reverberations of the Francisco Scilingo case that broke in Argentina in 1995. Although everyone knew that prisoners of the navy had been thrown drugged but alive into the Rio de la Plata during the *proceso* (this, after all, had long been rumoured and, after that, documented in the Juicio and *Nunca Más*), it mattered tremendously to have a confessed 'dirty warrior' admit the fact. The impact of Scilingo's confession can be attributed to the crack in the wall of denial the military had so blithely constructed, but I am not sure that this alone is sufficient explanation. The responses suggests that some people continued to believe that *Nunca Más* and the Juicio were politically skewed accounts until they heard the same facts related by someone directly involved in the actions.

Beyond the demobilization engendered by the dictatorship experience, other factors also made community organization difficult, likewise the much more modest efforts of the *taller*. The shared insecurity caused by the precariousness of the squatters' position in the early years facilitated sharing and cooperation between neighbours. Relative stability at the time of the *taller*, on the other hand, allowed people to take their housing for granted. But as we have seen, stability does not mean economic well-being, and economic conditions in Argentina at the time meant that many neighbours lacked the time and energy for activities unrelated to their most immediate needs. Time was at a premium: many were trying to scrounge odd jobs, or, when possible, work extra hours or hold a second job. One *tallerista* abandoned the workshop when he started working a second, three-quarter-time factory job, for example.

The first *taller* eventually fizzled out, its only public activity aside from flyers and radio spots advertising it having been the radio interview in which we described the workshop. These *talleristas* helped to plan the first meetings of the second workshop, however, occasionally participating in its activities as well.

The community centre based *taller* did not get as far as it might for several reasons. Understandably, people were daunted by the prospect of broaching such a large and complex topic as the history of the neighbourhood. Participants did not feel themselves authorized to act as historians, especially given the lack of written documentation. We had some group discussions and agreed to do interviews, but subjects were hard to convince and demanded more persistence and energy than *talleristas* could afford. Despite the emergence of the idea of a radio program from early on, people's thinking seemed to focus on producing some kind of written product. Members began to feel that nothing was being accomplished and consequently were frustrated. An important part of the problem here was the notion of academic authority, and especially writing.[5] Contrasting this experience with the second *taller* suggests that it is much more difficult to disrupt dominant narratives using some forms of representation.

Taller de Memoria

The second *taller*, was a collaboration between myself and the principal of the neighbourhood pre-school. Alejandra is a talented, energetic, and committed educator, of the generation of politically engaged Argentines who were key targets of the *proceso* years. In the early 1990s she was one of the few outsiders who had developed a good working relationship with neighbours and who could call meetings that people actually attended. Committed to working with the community, she had developed relationships with many mothers of the children in her Jardín de Infantes (pre-school). In previous years the pre-school had sponsored activities as varied as a choir and a workshop on sexuality attempting to reach out to community members. Although Alejandra agreed with my own view of the special significance of history, she was also taking advantage of my presence to strengthen the pre-school's ties to the community.

In this *taller de la memoria* the participants were mothers and grand-mothers of pupils (who could attend because their charges were in school at the time), Alejandra, some staff (including teaching and cus-todial staff), myself, and various others. The pre-school teachers were from outside the neighbourhood, and more likely to be middle class. The rest of the participants (except for me) were working-class people living in José Ingenieros, most since the time of the *toma*. For reasons already discussed and having to do with the gendered division of labour in Argentina, most participants, both caregivers and staff, were women. The lessons learned from the first *taller*, combined with the principal's experience in participative techniques like theatrical games, made this workshop much more successful. The pre-school *taller* occa-sionally had as many as thirty participants and sometimes as few as three; it met twenty-four times over five months, produced a large colourful neighbourhood mural, and continued to be active after I left in December 1992.

An intriguing difference between the two workshops is suggested by their names. The pre-school workshop was called *taller de* la memo-ria *del barrio* in contrast to the first, which was known as the *taller de la* historia *del barrio*. The significance that participants read in the differ-ence was not entirely clear to me, but they were quite insistent about it.[6] Williams's discussion of tradition is suggestive here (1977:115ff). By using the idea of tradition in place of history he underlines the signifi-cance of the past in a more daily sense. Traditions are not just about historical events, however we might understand them, but about how things have been in the broadest possible sense.

Likewise the shift from history to memory as the subject of the *taller* seems to bring it closer to the experience of participants. It is less intim-idating and more accessible; everyone has memories. But these memo-ries, as the group of British historians who call themselves the Popular Memory Group argues, are also less well analysed by those who hold them. Subaltern history, they suggest is 'held to the level of private remembrance. It is not only unrecorded, but actually silenced. It is not offered the occasion to speak' (1982:210). The place of memories in José Ingenieros, especially those that do not fit neatly into accepted accounts, supports their claim.

The Activities of the *Taller de Memoria*

We used as many techniques as we could think of to keep the workshop dynamic. Alejandra's familiarity with theatrical games allowed her to use them as warm-up exercises in many sessions. This also helped to keep us away from writing. Although most participants were literate and some highly so, writing is not social enough for the *taller*, as I had learned. When writing was required, the group deferred to Alejandra and myself (despite my obviously imperfect Spanish). Whatever success we had in the *taller de memoria* was tied to our ability to get out from under the weight of writing.

The pre-school *taller* began by charting the history of the *barrio* on a time line. As for most *taller* activities, the agenda for this meeting was planned in advance by Alejandra and myself. One or two others often joined us in these sessions. More than thirty participants attended this first meeting, a group that would prove to be unusually large.[7] We randomly divided the group in half. I facilitated one group, and Alejandra the other (see figure 6.1 for my yellow group and figure 6.2 for Alejandra's orange group).[8] I drew a line representing the history of the neighbourhood on a large piece of paper. One end was marked '*toma*' and the other 'today.' I then asked people to throw out dates or important events to mark on the line. Someone started by mentioning the date of the *toma* (remembered by most as May–June 1973, but by one person as 1972); various others recounted their versions of the story of the squatter occupation. I wrote down what I heard, while others (usually teachers) told me to note things that I did not catch at first. Of the eighteen people in my half of the group, about ten were talking at any one time. When things seemed to get too chaotic or repetitive, I asked if anyone could think of something that happened further along. The first few times I got comments on 1973 and 1974 but no further. I marked the line in two-year intervals, to encourage filling it in. Finally, when a teacher suggested we progress year by year and as time was running out, we advanced a little.

Several events joined the *toma* on the time line, although many of these were not as fully described as they are here for the purposes of

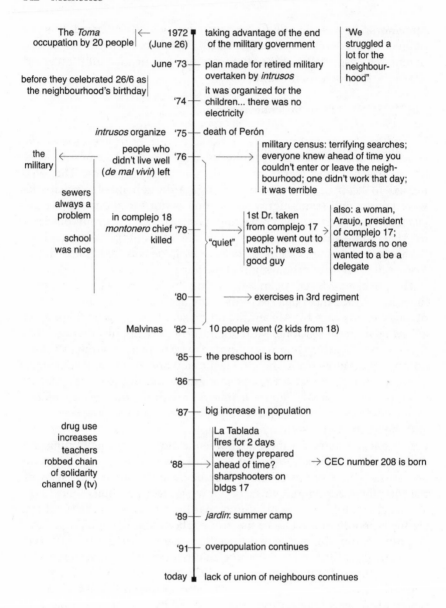

The *Toma* occupation by 20 people |← 1972 (June 26) ■ taking advantage of the end of the military government "We struggled a lot for the neighbourhood"

before they celebrated 26/6 as the neighbourhood's birthday | June '73 — plan made for retired military overtaken by *intrusos*

'74 — it was organized for the children... there was no electricity

intrusos organize '75 — death of Perón

the military |← people who didn't live well (*de mal vivir*) left '76 — ──────→ military census: terrifying searches; everyone knew ahead of time you couldn't enter or leave the neighbourhood; one didn't work that day; it was terrible

sewers always a problem

school was nice | in complejo 18 *montonero* chief killed '78 — ──────→ "quiet" | 1st Dr. taken from complejo 17 people went out to watch; he was a good guy → also: a woman, Araujo, president of complejo 17; afterwards no one wanted to a be a delegate

'80 — ──────→ exercises in 3rd regiment

Malvinas '82 — 10 people went (2 kids from 18)

'85 — the preschool is born

'86 —

'87 — big increase in population

drug use increases teachers robbed chain of solidarity channel 9 (tv) | '88 — → La Tablada fires for 2 days were they prepared ahead of time? sharpshooters on bldgs 17 → CEC number 208 is born

'89 — *jardin*: summer camp

'91 — overpopulation continues

today ■ lack of union of neighbours continues

Figure 6.1 *Taller de Memoria* Time Line, Yellow Group

intelligibility. The coup in March 1976 was noted when a teacher said something like: 'And '76? What happened in '76? It was the coup, wasn't it?' As in other conversations in the neighbourhood, I was struck by how little importance the date of the coup had for many residents. Even people directly affected by the repression had been vague about its date. This was one place where it was clearest that the academic's fixation on dates and changing political regimes is foreign to, and may even obscure, local understandings.

A fuller discussion came out with respect to 1978. I asked how things had been then. 'Quiet' (*tranquilo*) was one of the responses. Another participant disagreed: 'What do you mean quiet?!' and she recounted how, the day of her civil wedding ceremony, a doctor had been kidnapped from his apartment in broad daylight. As she was leaving her home to go to the civil registry, she heard shots and saw activity in the street; by the time they returned, the doctor was gone. (This is the abduction of Dr Jorge described in chapter 4.)

Without a shared public history recounting such events, personal history organizes them. Claudia remembered exactly the time, and probably also details of what happened to the doctor because of the way it touched a momentous occasion in her own life. When I asked for dates, people often estimated them by thinking back to how many children they had at the time, how old a child was, or what the weather was like. Many people keep time in this way, anchoring 'momentous events' in the 'quotidian.' (In this instance, however, Claudia's wedding was the more momentous to her, anchoring her memory of the altercation in the street as a backdrop.) Personal events and national ones are recalled in relation to each other.

This story about Dr Jorge evoked memories of the group of committed physicians who had worked in the neighbourhood, often until one or two in the morning, helping everyone who needed them. Recounting this disappearance, probably the single most widely known kidnapping in José Ingenieros, reminded people of others: the abductions of the other doctors, the president of one *complejo*, and a young woman believed to have been a Montonera. Although the doctors survived, most people believed that they were dead, since they never returned to José Ingenieros. Some who had known the doctors personally knew they had survived. Since these things were rarely discussed, however, this information was not communicated.

People also remembered the Malvinas War in 1981 and fund-raising activities that gained much community support. Another event that generated lively discussion was the 1989 incident at La Tablada. That year was remembered as a low point for the neighbourhood. This annotation was exceptional, describing a mood rather than an event. Crime had been frequent within the neighbourhood and feelings of insecurity intensified when local thieves broke the long tradition of finding victims elsewhere. This mood, although generalized, was given focus for the *talleristas* by the reaction to the mugging of several school teachers. Teachers in Argentina are immediately identifiable because of the white lab coats they wear, so it was clear they had been targeted. The incidents threatened to undermine local schools as teachers became increasingly afraid of going to work. Alejandra had organized a *cadena de solidaridad* (chain of solidarity) in which students, parents, and teachers symbolized their solidarity by collecting hundreds of pieces of paper with hand prints accompanied by expressions of hope for the community. A group of parents went to talk to the assailants to ask them not to attack school personnel. The attacks stopped. No one mentioned that 1989 was also the peak of hyperinflation, nor that it was the year of the *saqueos* (looting).

Other events recorded as important parts of the community's history were the foundations of the pre-school and the CEC, and the tradition of celebrating the neighbourhood's birthday in one *complejo*. This last event was seen as an idea that might be emulated, perhaps even at the instigation of the *taller*.

I know less about what happened in the other group (see figure 6.2 for a visual record).[9]

A little over an hour after the meeting was finally under way it was time to close. Each group quickly recounted what they had learned and recorded on their time line. There was much enthusiasm. Everyone seemed to want to continue and said they would attend another meeting bringing more participants. Although disappointing, it was not surprising that this enthusiasm waned over the intervening two weeks; the next meeting was smaller.

The notable omissions in the time lines are important. First, there was a resounding silence on politics. The only mention was of the Montonero leader who was disappeared, while the doctors were implicitly praised for not playing politics. Yet José Ingenieros has always been an extremely politicized place. As we have seen, the *toma* was an intensely political moment and in the pre-*proceso* years as well, representatives of different political groups had struggled for power within the neighbourhood. In the years that followed, José Ingenieros

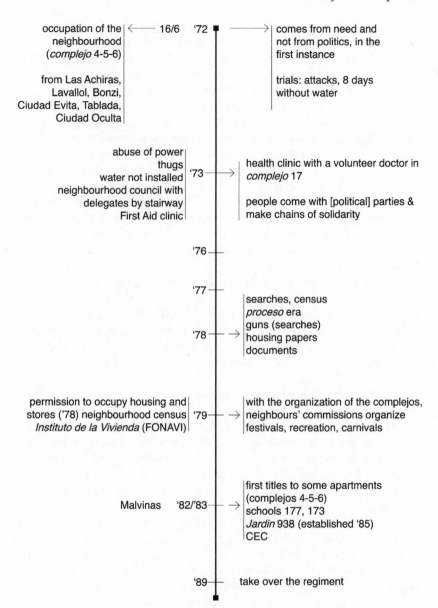

occupation of the ⟵—— 16/6   '72 ■ ——————⟶ comes from need and
neighbourhood   not from politics, in the
(*complejo* 4-5-6)   first instance

from Las Achiras,   trials: attacks, 8 days
Lavallol, Bonzi,   without water
Ciudad Evita, Tablada,
Ciudad Oculta

abuse of power
thugs   health clinic with a volunteer doctor in
water not installed   '73 ——⟶   *complejo* 17
neighbourhood council with
delegates by stairway   people come with [political] parties &
First Aid clinic   make chains of solidarity

'76

'77

searches, census
proceso era
guns (searches)
'78 ——⟶ housing papers
documents

permission to occupy housing and   with the organization of the complejos,
stores ('78) neighbourhood census   '79 —⟶ neighbours' commissions organize
Instituto de la Vivienda (FONAVI)   festivals, recreation, carnivals

first titles to some apartments
(complejos 4-5-6)
Malvinas   '82/'83 —⟶ schools 177, 173
Jardin 938 (established '85)
CEC

'89   take over the regiment

Figure 6.2 *Taller de Memoria* Time Line, Orange Group

continued to be overwhelmingly Peronist, but party hegemony meant that conflict had shifted to competition within the party.

The silence here may indicate that neighbours saw the political history as dangerous. During the *proceso*, discussion would have been taboo at least in the company of those whose allegiance was unknown. A social worker who had worked in José Ingenieros from 1977 to 1981 (but especially during 1977 and 1978) noted that, in talking about the *toma*, neighbours spoke about how dangerous and violent things had been but not about the political stakes. She had spoken to neighbours when these events were in the very recent past. Proudly recounting their accomplishments, they conveyed a sense that it had been like the wild west, the social worker recalled. Almost fifteen years later, such accounts were much more muted. She understood their silence on politics as a response to her status as a representative of the state during the *proceso*, but the *taller* experience suggests such a reaction may have been generalized.

Although they do appear in figure 6.1 because they were mentioned briefly, there was also very little discussion of the *proceso*-era *allanamientos*. This omission is especially surprising because this story had been a leitmotif of my interviews. In both these cases, the younger or newer residents of the neighbourhood may not have known details; others may have not wanted to mention them in public.

Dramatizations in the History Workshop

By its nature, the first meeting of the *taller* had focused on particular events. In the next encounter, therefore, we hoped to shift the focus from specific events to the quotidian. We asked participants to re-enact daily life in the neighbourhood at a specific moment. The resulting dramatizations of *la vida cotidiana* were amusing, vivid collective efforts.

We separated into two groups to construct skits representing different periods. One took the *toma* as its theme and the other the founding of the pre-school in 1983. I was in the first group. As the neighbourhood's origin story, the *toma* was an obvious choice. We began by talking about what people remembered about the occupation of the apartments nineteen years earlier. The main ideas for this sketch came from Claudia and Dora, *intrusas* living in different *complejos*. Dora, the grandmother of a pre-schooler, and in her forties at the time of the *taller*, described entering a ground-floor apartment by crawling in the

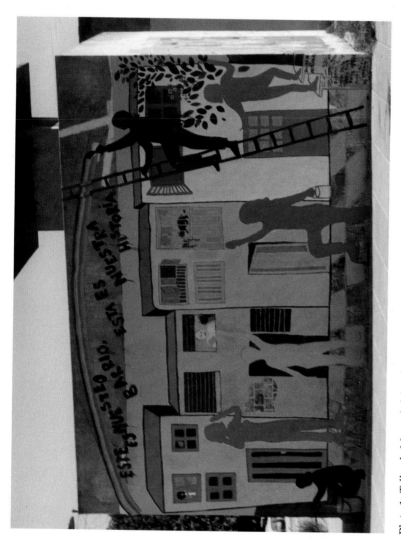

Plate 1. *Taller de Memoria* Mural

Plate 2. The Restored *Taller de Memoria* Mural. The mural was restored in 2000 under the Buenos Aires Neighbourhoods program. Note the omission of the title (top) and signatures (bottom right).

kitchen window. As we attempted to enact this scene, Alejandra asked her to try to remember details: what she had been carrying, how she had felt. Claudia interjected, 'But in fact, the *toma* started in the old houses, with the decision to try to take an apartment.' So we back-tracked, deciding to start with a scene where Dora, sitting down to eat with her husband, informed him that his brother had been by to tell them that people were taking apartments. When her husband, por-trayed by another of the *jardín* mothers, said that the idea was crazy and that he would lose his job, she decided she would go. 'If they put you in jail, I'm not going to look for you!' he said, and off she went. Had she been afraid, Alejandra asked. Dora replied that she was not; she had looked forward to having an apartment.

Claudia's memories were the basis of the second scene. She remem-bered a day when she was about twelve and living in a shanty town. Her father had come home from work to her mother's tale of people taking apartments. Why didn't they take one? He asked if she were crazy, insisted that he had worked hard on their little house, and that the family was fine where it was. 'I know,' he had said, 'you want to be a widow!' All the while, Claudia's mother was folding a blanket and a shirt, placing it under her reluctant husband's arm, and walking him to the bus stop. The pointed depictions of the hesitation of the men were funny, particularly because Claudia's father is known as a man who thinks of himself as a revolutionary. The mostly female group pro-vided a receptive audience for this sort of critique.

The next scene placed the two adventurers in the neighbourhood itself. With the encouragement of other *intrusos*, Dora climbed in the window of a first-floor apartment where she had to stay until a lock-smith could come and open the front door for her. Other *talleristas* played squatters, egging Dora on as she clambered through the win-dow, or telling Claudia's father where empty apartments could be found. Still others looked for apartments of their own. At the end of the sketch, plans were made to pool resources and to cook a communal meal, since few had brought food or had prepared to stay. This closing scene gave the sketch an optimistic ending, and a moral.

The process of elaborating the sketch revealed the degree to which people universalized their personal experience. They had little aware-ness of the important variations between *complejos* and even portions of *complejos*. No doubt this was, again, because these experiences had remained at the level of personal anecdote. In recounting and re-enact-ing the *toma*, there was some pride, excitement, and wonder at how daring people had been. Participants had explicitly, perhaps defensively, maintained their right to occupy empty housing that their families needed.

The other dramatization was about a group of women who organized to clean out an abandoned building and convince the provincial government to establish a pre-school there. They depicted the women's meetings with government officials. Estela, the star of the drama, had actually been central in this effort; she impersonated one after another (identical) condescending bureaucrat: 'Good afternoon ladies. How can I help you? You're from José Ingenieros? Oh. [with disdain] No I'm sorry Mr. X cannot see you today. Leave him the information and I am sure he will get back to you. Thank you.' In the end, of course, the neighbours persevered, and the pre-school was born.

With humour – people laughed aloud in recognition – the group depicted the arrogance and condescension with which civil servants almost invariably communicate, in no uncertain terms, just how contemptible and insignificant they consider the neighbourhood.[10] They also showed that neighbours, especially women, could overcome the daunting array of government officials and red tape that stood between them and services for the community.

Miniature dramas were a revealing way to recall and recount the past. Alejandra's coaching to summon old feelings and gestures shows how this form has potential for a fuller evocation of past events because it is not exclusively verbal.[11] Body memory is potent, and perhaps less mediated. In addition, in acting, people express sentiments that they might not otherwise articulate. The first sketch poked gentle fun at Claudia's father, Dora's husband, and perhaps the men in general, for their initial reticence. The laughs of recognition during the second sketch, responding to the nuances of intonation and gesture as much as to the words spoken, were indicators of a painful reality in José Ingenieros, one that most people would not readily otherwise acknowledge.

Other Activities of the *Taller*

We also engaged in more conventional activities in the *taller*. We occasionally discussed a specific topic or invited someone to talk to the workshop. One visiting speaker was Norberto Liwski, the doctor whose testimony we saw in chapter 4. He told participants about his experiences in NHD 17 from the summer of 1973 to the day of the coup. He was able to describe the health centre and the mothers' organization that had arisen in the *complejo* where he worked and later lived. He explained that, given the precarious conditions in which neighbours lived in those early days, there had been health problems, especially infant diarrhea. As he spoke, he seemed to awaken memories in some. Claudia remembered the clinic and a day care centre. Malena, who had been even younger than Claudia, remembered having been envious as she watched other children playing in the centre from her apartment window. Liwski also recounted the experience of activists from the commission in *complejo* 17. After he left, everyone agreed the exchange was very emotional. Olga, a grandmother who lived in NHD 19, remarked on how little she had known about what had happened in NHD 17. The intensity of the session seemed to confirm my sense of how seldom this history of community organization and of repression gets discussed.

The *Taller de Memoria* Mural

The previous *taller* in the community centre had demonstrated the need for markers of progress. People had felt frustrated by the lack of tangible advance, even when we had rich discussions. From quite early in the process it was evident that the new *taller* needed a clear goal. Although many favoured a written document since this fits into dominant (and participants') ideas of what history should look like, Alejandra and I pushed for another medium which would be both more accessible to other neighbours and more open. Participants considered a radio program, a photo exhibit, a video, a festival, a mural, and a neighbourhood clean-up day.

The group decided that our first project should be a mural painted on some large public wall in the neighbourhood. It is worth noting that Argentina has no mural tradition, unlike Mexico or Chile.[12] As is evident, none of us were professional artists, although we did have a draftsman in our group. For technical expertise we turned to a former pre-school teacher who was also a painter, but the whole project was a collective endeavour. She steadfastly resisted the *talleristas* attempts to defer to her.

Once we agreed the mural was to be the vehicle, we had to think of the history of José Ingenieros in terms of images as opposed to verbal storytelling. Of course the mural has its limitations as an expressive form, but some of these were also advantages: the mural is very public, requiring little commitment from its audience. Also, we did not have to understand the whole history of the neighbourhood, we only had to have a few things to say. The fact-finding part of the project could continue as we worked on representation. The sense that we needed to have everything figured out had been a stumbling block in the earlier *taller*. Remarkably people felt they did not know their history enough to represent it.

The mural's location was the subject of debate. Many blank walls were possible, but several factors were at play. The first decision was whether the mural should face inward, toward other residents, or outward, toward passers-by and adjoining communities. Because José Ingenieros is at the intersection of two major arteries, a lot of traffic passes by. Claudia argued for an outward-facing mural because she was concerned about the image of José Ingenieros. Her children's friends from other neighbourhoods were not allowed to visit her apartment. A long-standing tension persists between residents of *los complejos* and the more 'respectable' *chalets* of Ciudad Evita adjoining the neighbourhood to the south. She felt the need to show outsiders that José Ingenieros was not a bad place. Several others argued that we had things to say that neighbours themselves needed to hear. Eventually it was decided that the first mural should be prominently placed within the neighbourhood, with the understanding that an outward-facing mural might soon follow.

Next was a decision about which of the four complexes was to get the mural. Everyone knew a place in their sector that would be ideal, and each lobbied for her own. We settled on the central complex. A likely spot faced onto one of the few internal streets and also the pedestrian mall frequented by people from all four *complejos*.

Finally, issues of ownership and territoriality had to be considered. The people who lived behind the wall had to give permission, but we did not expect problems here. More worrisome was the issue of *pintadas*. The painting of political slogans in red white and black is an important part of Argentine political culture. In the neighbourhood the various *unidades básicas* had acquired traditional use rights for key walls. One participant had, some years earlier, been physically threatened by a rival group when she and her allies tried to paint over a *pintada* on someone else's wall with a human rights slogan. The wall we eventually chose had neither problem. We could find no currently active political group that claimed responsibility for the old *pintadas* on the side of a small building housing electrical equipment. This location faced the administration office of NHD 18, whose staff promised to keep an eye on it.

Preparing the wall involved many hours of scraping years of *pintadas* off the eighteen-by-twelve-foot wall (it felt like a form of political archeology) and washing it with bleach. We decided to forgo the extra step of painting a white base coat, fearing that a totally prepared surface might prove too tempting to resist. For the same reason people felt we should start painting as soon as the wall was ready. The entire process took a month.[13]

The mural design was generated in workshop meetings. Many also met Saturday afternoons for the dusty work of scraping down and bleaching the wall. Some of those from the first *taller* participated in these sessions, partly because the meeting time was convenient, but also because of the concreteness of the enterprise. Ideas were generated by participants working in groups of three or four. The final composition was a synthesis of these ideas. Although we agreed on a design before going out to paint, it was discussed and altered as we went along.

Although the mural genre might be expected to free its authors from chronology, the possibility was there, and people took it. The mural contains an explicitly linear narrative which one reads from left to right and past to present. The periodization it expresses, however, is somewhat unexpected. The first building, on the left, not surprisingly, represents the *toma*; the next building shows the neighbourhood once it is well established; third is the mural painters' present, and finally the future. Notable here is the omission of the dictatorship as a period. As with the time line when neighbours had to be prompted to talk about the *proceso* years, there is a silence in the mural. Bars on the windows of the third building are intended to reflect a climate of fear of crime in the present. The second building is not easily dated. Shutters and door are closed, however, and paint is peeling off the building that represents a time sometime between 1973 and the present.[14] As noted earlier, this history does not fit neatly with official ones. All the periods except the first are quite fuzzy, and the breaks represented by the coup and the return to democracy are missing altogether.

The mural illustrates one of the most important things the *taller* taught me. What I kept feeling was an obsession with the quality of physical space – sewage, trash, garbage – appeared again here. It was a way of thinking about order – a complicated idea given the history of dictatorship – and community. When people told me 'this is not a shanty town,' it was because they feared this physical deterioration might mislead me. And this deterioration was tied to poverty, but also to the dissolution of community organizations.

These themes, and the tension between them, help explain what is probably the most conspicuous design feature: the juxtaposition of the buildings and the silhouettes. The contrast is partly an artifact of the process; two groups' designs were selected and combined.[15] The buildings express a concern with the physical space of the neighbourhood, and especially its present sad state. Only through working on the mural did participants become conscious that the neighbourhood was not, in fact, in worse shape than it was at the time of the *toma*. Rather, the neighbourhood in general had seen a rise and fall over time. Various *complejos*, and even sectors of *complejos*, had distinct cycles.

The silhouettes address more overtly social themes, especially cooperative community-oriented labour. While the buildings, at least for the painters, express a marked chronology, the silhouettes are more slippery. They were originally seen as both a description of the past and hopes for the future. Created by tracing our bodies onto paper and then painting them onto the wall, the silhouettes inadvertently became a visual pun – referring to the narrative of the mural and to the mural painting itself – which was strongly felt as we worked. This slipperiness was partly intentional; the silhouettes were meant to represent continuity, forming a bridge between the constructive community activity in the past and in the present. The woman getting water from a spigot, who explicitly belongs to the *toma*, is clearly on the same plane as the painters or muralists.

One effect of the mural not to be underplayed is that it is cheerful and lively in the grey concrete context. The fact of our persistent, collective, and community-oriented effort in a central location within the neighbourhood would convey its own message about the possibility of neighbours working together. Traffic on the mall was light when we worked, since we usually painted Wednesday afternoons, when the street was quiet, and during the Saturday afternoon siesta. For those who did see us, though, we presented an unusual sight. Children in particular hovered around and were often handed paint brushes so they could help.

On the Saturday evening when we finished, we threw a party; about thirty people ate *chorizos* (the tastier Argentine equivalent of the hot dog), drank wine, and danced on the pavement in front of the mural

Figure 6.3 Painting the *Taller de Memoria* Mural. The mural's silhouettes create a visual pun, referring to the neighbourhood's history and the activity of the artists themselves.

until about 10 o'clock at night. Many eyed us indulgently, but some joined the festive carryings on.

Popular Memory: Dimensions of Political Practice

The work of the *taller de memoria*, through its activities and especially its mural, calls attention to the complex relation between space, place, history, identity, and politics. Geographers have begun to call their fellow social scientists to task for our underdeveloped understandings of space and place. Doreen Massey, for example, criticizes the notion of place 'as bounded, as in various ways a site of an authenticity, as singular, fixed and unproblematic.' She suggests instead that place should be 'thought of in the context of space-time and as formed out of social interaction at all scales, then one view of place is a particular articulation of those relations, a particular moment in those networks of social relations and understandings' (1994:5). The very history of José Ingenieros militates against the assumptions she criticizes. The construction of José Ingenieros as a space and place is so recent and so obvious a process, and such a difficult one, that it could hardly be overlooked. A key struggle in José Ingenieros was precisely to develop community in the sense that proposes shared solutions to common problems.

On the other hand, neighbours and *talleristas'* ways of describing José Ingenieros (through talk, dramatizations, and the mural) suggest that these essentialized ways of thinking about place are not necessarily academics' constructions. Residents of this neighbourhood often fell into a similar trap. They did so in part, I suspect, because they were struggling to form a shared identity and a sense of community that would underwrite collective action.

Despite all the coordinators' best efforts, participants still represented the history of the neighbourhood by depicting the physical space it inhabits. The portion of the design that includes the buildings was produced by a group working with pencil and paper. For some neighbours, José Ingenieros *is* its grey concrete *monoblocs* (colour, too, was added later). Like the perpetual return to the material conditions of the neighbourhood (garbage and decay), the focus on the buildings equates the community with the space. The crisis of the space *is* the crisis of the community. Thus social problems – lack of community organization, alienation, and crime – are read as physical ones, that is, the decay of the neighbourhood. As we have seen, this issue of garbage is far from trivial. It is tied to problems of community services and community organization, to dominant discourses on social order, and to how José Ingenieros is seen by outsiders.

The two elements of the mural represented in the two superimposed designs – the preoccupation with physical space on one hand, and with community on the other – were recurrent themes in the *taller* itself. They are related to contemporary problems in the neighbourhood, and to distinct visions of the nature and causes of these concerns. By superimposing the figures on the buildings, the workshop participants tried to call attention to the social dimension of these problems. The figures, and also the mural's caption, make an argument about the role community activity might play in improving the space, and remaking the place.

The Popular Memory Group defines popular memory 'first as an *object of study*, but, second, as a *dimension of political practice*' (1982:205). Throughout the *talleres* we were continually reminded of this connection. Like writers on popular memory, participants in the *talleres* explicitly tied history to identity and politics. Further, work on popular memory was seen as a tool for reaffirming or forging collective identities. Activists care about such projects because they believe that fortified collective identities can then be turned into collective endeavours and political action.

The tension expressed in the mural's design became apparent, especially when the significance of our activities was called into question, explicitly in discussion, or implicitly by poor attendance. At issue was whether the *taller* mattered. Was the *taller* just indulgent intellectualizing, as some argued? Some saw the workshop and its talk of the past as abstract, perhaps interesting but also a luxury in the face of the serious problems the neighbourhood confronted. These critics viewed talking and doing as opposed, and even mutually exclusive, activities. We had this debate repeatedly. In the first workshop some participants questioned the concreteness of the project and argued that our work should be more practical. This was frustrating because these discussions usually seemed to sideline what seemed to others the practical and concrete work of the *taller*.

In this context, although not always, the arguments about irrelevance were used by people who had another agenda. Two were running for the administration of a *complejo* and wanted to push the *taller* in a direction that served their campaign needs. They wanted us to do a survey of the neighbourhood asking people about their priorities. As we will see in chapter 8, one effect of the small number of functional community groups is that any remotely persistent one is targeted by people who fear competition or, as here, who are looking for a location from which to launch projects of their own.

I do not mean to belittle the legitimate questions that some had about making the history workshop a priority, however. The relative importance of the history workshop was again called into question when a serious problem with contamination of the water in the neighbourhood emerged. People from el Hornero were absorbed with this issue, leaving them little time for *taller de la memoria* meetings. Alejandra and I found that we agreed with their decision to give priority to the water problem. We discovered, however, that our cooperation through the *taller* facilitated the flow of information and helped coordinate the activities of the pre-school and the community centre with respect to the water crisis. The workshop became a location where concerns could be informally discussed and information exchanged.

Another animated debate about the utility of the workshop arose as we considered possible projects. Neighbours concerned about the lack of green spaces for children to play suggested refurbishing one of the unkempt gardens. Some people said that a playground was something the neighbourhood really needed, and that our energy should be directed at the needs of the children. Others said that although the idea of a playground was good, this was a *taller de memoria*; we should build on what we had learned by staying closer to our theme. Here the presence of outsiders emerged as a concern; by this they meant me, Alejandra, and teachers. Could we say that this was a neighbourhood workshop when at times fewer neighbours than non-neighbours participated? The man who expressed this concern most forcefully also wanted to get away from history-oriented activities 'and really do something concrete.' A relative newcomer to José Ingenieros, activities about the community's history and identity may not have touched him, although he was, contradictorily, one of the *taller's* most persistent and industrious participants. Other members pointed out that, although the neighbourhood had been in need of fixing up for a long time, groups had not successfully organized around this issue; people were, in fact, meeting in the memory workshop. It was worth taking some time to consolidate a base using something that seemed to be working.

The *taller* temporarily petered out after the completion of the mural. This event, unfortunately, coincided with the departure of my co-organizer (a promotion moved her to another part of the province), the end of the school year, and the fact that I too would soon be leaving. We made a photo display about the mural-painting process seen at the pre-school and in an administration office near the mural.

When I was involved in it, the *taller* seemed always on the verge of extinction. Just when it was about to take off in a flurry of activity, something would happen to set the whole thing back several steps (a meeting with poor attendance, a discussion that seemed counterproductive). Nonetheless, people did meet to reflect on their history in the *talleres*. The reasons they did, and the ways that they did, point to the place of history and memory in social life. Authors such as Passerini (1987) and Portelli (1991) have shown something of the complexity of popular memories, but the *taller* experience begins to point to their roles. Popular memory is a location where people can begin to produce histories in which they figure – literally, in the case of this mural. These *talleres de memoria* show how slow and complicated this process can be. The double image of the mural stands as a metaphor for how difficult it is for people to put themselves fully into the picture. It is also a compelling illustration of the past-present relation.

In the end, what matters is the significance that neighbours assigned to the workshop. For them, history-telling was an important part of history-making. At least some saw the *taller de memoria* as an experience that could help to recreate social ties by helping to forge a common, positively-valued identity in the face of the social atomization produced both by Argentina's repressive past and by the economic liberalism of its present.

Before we leave the story of the *talleres*, consider a final image (reproduced in this chapter). In February 1994 I received a letter from friends in the neighbourhood bringing me up to date on their activities. This new mural was painted on the side of el Hornero just before Christmas. This wall is on the edge of the neighbourhood, facing outward. In the face of dominant discourses marginalizing the community, the struggle to paint an optimistic image of the future continues.

Chapter 7

Narrative Truths

In the *talleres* people collectively thought through and worked out a local history. The workshop was an explicit attempt to remember collectively. How, why, and with what success this was done casts some light on the social production of memory in José Ingenieros. The choices members of the *talleres* made are telling: to put an optimistic spin on local history, and to leave the *proceso* as a recognizable period out of the mural altogether. Such choices merit further consideration. In this chapter, we turn our attention to the significance of these kinds of choices, some of them very public, some less so.

The stories here point to an important distinction that Donald Spence describes between 'historical' and 'narrative' truth (1982). In the first part of this book we were largely preoccupied with what happened in Argentina and José Ingenieros between roughly 1972 and 1992. This only explains part of the significance of the past for residents of José Ingenieros, however. It tells us little about what people make of this past. Spence points out that narrative truth privileges the logic of storytelling, of *making* sense, over that of fact.[1] Where narrative truth comes into conflict with historical truth, the active intelligences of storytellers are made manifest.

This chapter opens with the consideration of a compelling 'mistake' in the narrative of an activist couple. The fact of the mistake foregrounds the way storytellers construct their tales. It calls particular attention to the ways they read the past and the present through each other. Understanding what, why, and how Susana and Raúl told me what they did requires multiple contextualizations. Their account must be read against national and local history and against their own recent political realignment. It has to be seen as a story about both the past and the present.

Susana and Raúl cannot be made to speak for all their neighbours, however. Lest we be tempted to read their account as representative of a particular class or local perspective, the chapter goes on to consider an incident in which other residents of José Ingenieros express a quite different perspective. In this second encounter, three original residents of José Ingenieros met with hostility when trying to tell a story that ran counter to official versions of the recent past in Argentina. The unhappy experience of Anahí, Marisa, and Rosa calls particular attention to the role of audiences, and thus the fact of storytelling as a social encounter. It also suggests why and how people might choose to remain silent. It calls attention to the difficulties posed by unpopular narratives about the past. Too often silence is mistaken for forgetting. I want to underline here the ways in which silences are produced (Trouilliot 1996) by the difficulties that the past poses for people in the present. The chapter thus returns to the *talleres* to consider some silences, evasions, and elisions manifest there.

Raúl and Susana's Narrative

Questions about the form and function of historical narratives reasserted themselves for me one morning in early summer 1992. I was interviewing Susana and Raúl, a middle-aged couple we have already met, who had moved to the neighbourhood in the *toma*. Just after I started living in José Ingenieros, Miguel, a young Hornero activist, had taken me to meet Susana and Raúl, parents of a friend of his. He told me that both had long histories of Peronist militancy and that they would have interesting tales to tell. The couple asked about my project and offered to talk to me. A formal interview was finally arranged almost a year later. By then my Spanish was much improved, and although we had hardly met in the interim, they would have heard more about me through their son and his friend.

We had agreed that I would go to their apartment one Monday morning at ten because mornings were better for Susana, who worked late. At first, when I knocked on the door, there was no answer. I had almost given up when a voice told me to wait. I waited. Raúl opened the door, saying, 'Oh, it's you! Wait a minute.' And closed it again. A bit later, when he invited me in, it was clear I had woken everyone up. Nonetheless Raúl generously asked me to sit down, opening the shutters, and told me they had returned from the country at four that same morning. Their apartment was one of the most carefully finished that I had seen in José Ingenieros, a fact they noted when I complimented them on it. The floors were tiled, furniture was comfortable and in good condition, and a small addition added light to the living room of their large ground-floor apartment in *complejo* 18. Clearly they were among the wealthier families in the neighbourhood. Until shortly before the interview both held relatively well-paying jobs. Raúl's was a product of his political activism and connections.

Susana arrived a few moments later, explaining that they had been visiting her natal home in Buenos Aires province, outside the city. She had decided not to go into work – possible, she said, because it was something she never did – so we had plenty of time. When I expressed interest in her trip Susana proudly showed me the video they had taken of her sister's house in the country, complete with gardens, orchard, and farm animals. The tape began with part of a speech by Aldo Rico, the *carapintada* colonel-turned-politician who was creating a stir at the time. Although we did not rewind to see more, we watched intently as Susana pointed out her favourite parts of the speech.

After the video and with *mate* making the rounds, we chatted a bit more. The couple then agreed I should turn on the tape recorder so I could capture all the details as they told me about the history of the neighbourhood. Throughout, two well-behaved grandchildren wandered around, intermittently shushed by an adult in deference to the tape. Occasionally either Susana or Raúl left with one of the children or to refresh the *mate*. This was a particularly rich interview because both Susana and Raúl are engaging and loquacious speakers with a strong sense of what they wanted to say. We discussed life in the neighbourhood over the years, politics, Peronism, and their recent conversion, after years of faithful activity on behalf of the Peronist party, to Aldo Rico and his new party, Movement for Dignity and Independence (MODIN).

We had spoken informally for a while and the recorded interview lasted almost an hour and a half, so I had been in their apartment more than two hours when I turned off my tape recorder and made signs as if to leave. It was here that Susana and Raúl began to speak more freely of Rico and their reasons for leaving the Peronist party. Rico was a real Peronist, *'Peronista de Perón'* and *'Peronista de '47,'* they said, 'not like Menem.' I asked if that meant the first and second (1945–55), but not the third government of Perón (1973–4). They assented, replying that Perón with Evita was one thing, Perón with Isabel quite another. They told how they had worked hard for the return of Perón during the eighteen years of his exile. The work had been illegal; they had been forced to work underground. If someone had a picture of Perón, they might be arrested. They went on to explain that this had been the time of General Videla and the junta. There were many kidnappings, they told me, they even took grandchildren. Las Madres de Plaza de Mayo are still looking for their grandchildren, they said. Many times they would kidnap a child and sell it for adoption. It was terrible. They killed many people. For example, people had been held prisoner in the nearby Puente 12. I asked about the date; they hesitated a moment, and then said that all this had occurred before the return of Perón in 1973.

I also asked what this period had been like in José Ingenieros but was told that the neighbourhood did not yet exist. The government they were describing was responsible for building the apartment blocks in which we were speaking. The government that removed Isabel Perón was different, they went on, 'otra cosa.' During that government the average worker still lived pretty well, 'se vivía bastante bien,' things were fine, and there were lots of public works projects. The main problem had been that the military government had dramatically increased the national debt from $40 to $90 million, using large public works projects to justify such high expenditures. In fact, things were cheap; it was the time of *plata dulce* (easy money).

As I listened, I was amazed. Susana and Raúl had found a solution to the problem that had plagued many of the accounts I had heard. People often remembered the last dictatorship as relatively benign, but in subsequent years they had been unable to avoid the knowledge that an official policy of abduction, torture, and murder had prevailed throughout. Susana and Raúl seemed to have resolved this contradiction by misremembering when the notorious human rights abuses had occurred. They described specific well-known actors and places from the 1976 to 1983 period, but associated these with a previous, more aggressively anti-Peronist period of military rule. What can we make of this story, then? What were they trying to tell me?

Mistakes and Meanings

Historians Daniel James and Alessandro Portelli have both fruitfully examined significant errors in oral accounts.[2] James shows how and why, despite photographic evidence to the contrary, the working-class Peronists he interviewed insisted that they were in downtown Buenos Aires on 17 October 1945, demanding Juan Perón's release from detention. They thus write themselves into what is arguably the most important event in Peronist history (1987, see also Torre 1995). Portelli documents a similar mistake in his article on the political significance accorded to the death of a twenty-one-year-old steel worker in Terni, Italy (1991). When people systematically misremember Luigi Trustilli's death as having occurred during a massive 1953 strike rather than a less momentous 1949 anti-NATO rally, they express a different kind of truth: 'they allow us to recognize the interests of the tellers, and the dreams and desires beneath them' (Portelli 1991:2). These analyses point to the ways in which the quirks of memory supply a key to the interpretation and significance that rememberers attach to the stories they recall and retell. One can begin to make sense of Susana and Raúl's mistake in similar terms. We have to shift our focus to what they are saying in the larger sense, that is, to the underlying narrative truth that this specific version of events expresses.

In thinking about what Susana and Raúl were saying to me, on one hand, and about why the chronological shift made it easier to say, on the other, a host of political, social, and personal histories come into play. First, we must keep Susana and Raúl's audience in mind. Not only were they speaking to *la canadiense,* but they also knew that I worked with, even lived with, people from El Hornero, a decidedly non-Peronist community centre.[3] The couple were well known in the neighbourhood and would have been wondering what I had been told about them, especially in light of their turn to Rico. Despite our discussions about confidentiality, they might well have suspected, perhaps even hoped, that I would report back to people I knew in the neighbourhood (they had suggested I use their real names).

In speaking to this audience, then, they were trying to make several points. First, they wanted to express their concern about human rights violations in Argentina's recent past. They would have assumed that, as an interested foreigner, I would have known and disapproved of such violations. They may have wanted to make their knowledge and their real concern for the victims of such abuses clear. Particularly interesting here is the reference to Puente 12 because it is a clandestine detention centre close to the neighbourhood in which some neighbours were held. They thus show their knowledge of a local site of repression.

Perhaps most important, though, the story serves to draw some distinctions that are central to Susana and Raúl. These are distinctions between different periods of military rule and between different arms of the state's repressive apparatus. It is not incidental that their comments on the human rights violations should have followed from their explanation of their defection from the Peronist party to Aldo Rico's new party, MODIN.

At the time of the interview, towards the end of 1992, Rico had become a political phenomenon. He had done surprisingly well in some regions in the recent national elections. The new party, MODIN, often considered fringe, startled everyone by coming third in the Buenos Aires gubernatorial race.[4] In the Peronist party bastion of La Matanza, Rico attained 55,887 votes compared with Eduardo Duhalde, the Peronist/Menemist candidate's 197,500. Rico also came ahead of the Radical Party candidate. His nationalist message presented one of the strongest critiques of the economic program.[5]

After Raúl had lost his relatively lucrative job to the forces of rationalization in the Peronist-run municipal office, the couple had thrown their lot in with MODIN. Previously they had run a Peronist *unidad básica* (neighbourhood-level political office) working as *punteros políticos* for the party – a job that involved channelling patronage from the government and party apparatus to supporters, and political support from the neighbourhood to the party. They broke their lifelong ties to the Peronist party by helping open a local office of MODIN in José Ingenieros.[6]

To understand the relationship between Susana and Raúl's mistaken recollection of the past and their recent change of allegiance, one has to consider the depth and emotional charge of their Peronism. For people like Raúl and Susana, Peronist allegiances are not just about what the party stands for, either in the present or historically, but also what it represents, and how it has mattered in their lives. For many residents in communities like José Ingenieros, this identification is so powerful that it constitutes a central element of local culture, shaping practices, experiences, interpretations, and politics in ways that are central to local life. (For a discussion of the historical construction of Peronist identities, see the appendix, which highlights how the history of Peronism has helped shape the identities and dispositions of residents of José Ingenieros.)

A deeply Peronist political identity informs Susana and Raúl's reading and interpretation of the political scene. As we saw in chapter 4, Rico had been catapulted to national renown when he led a military rebellion against then President Alfonsín's democratically elected government during Easter Week 1987. Although he did not begin his political career as a Peronist, Rico's style and rhetoric had become increasingly populist, and at the time of the interview he had recently started quoting Perón.

Susana and Raúl supported a military man whom they liken to Juan Perón at his best (Perón with Evita, as they put it). Their move to Rico was part of their critique of the current government. In a taped portion of the interview, Susana described Menem's regime circa 1992, asserting, 'this isn't the doctrine of General Perón. This is a government shared with other political forces. It's a liberal government. It isn't a Peronist Government. That is, they haven't taken General Perón's doctrine into account. That is exactly why we, at this moment, feel cheated and we have decided to work for another military man who will re-emerge.' Yet Rico's military past, while harkening back to the great leader, also creates certain problems. The military had fallen into considerable disrepute because of its years in power during the *proceso*. The most important causes of its loss of prestige have been the human rights record and the debacle in the Malvinas Islands.

An obvious effect of the displacement of the sordid military history of human rights violations onto a previous period is that it helps get Rico off the hook. There is no doubt that he was on active duty during the 1976 to 1983 period, and if one acknowledges that this is the same period when clandestine abductions, torture, and murder of Argentine citizens was normal throughout the military, one has to wonder where he might have been and what he might have been doing.[7]

When talking about Rico, Susana and Raúl are at pains to point out that he was one of the few officers who led his men with courage and concern for their safety during the Malvinas War. They note that he had relatively few casualties (six of forty men) and that he 'led from in front.' They thus draw on a long Argentine nationalist tradition that distinguishes between 'good' and 'bad' militaries, branches of the military, and military men.

They also point out what they consider to be an important distinction between the military and the police. At an earlier moment in the interview, and as we saw in their description of the *allanamientos* (chapter 4) they describe the polite manner and correct comportment with which the military searched their apartment. By contrast, they had a much less favourable impression of the police. This is tied to an experience in which their son was arrested for selling merchandise in the street. They were only able to get him out of jail by pulling strings and activating their Peronist party networks. In marking the difference, Susana and Raúl point out that Buenos Aires provincial police are only required to have a grade three level of education, and are less respectful and less well disciplined than the military.

Finally, by seeing the pre-1973 military government as the most repressive, Susana and Raúl can define themselves as members of the targeted group. Peronism, and all evocations of Peronism, were banned for the eighteen years of Perón's exile from 1955 until 1973. By tying their committed, even heroic, work towards the leader's return to the same period as the country's most ferocious repression of dissidents, their bravery is underlined.

The more recent dictatorship was more complicated for Peronists. Although much of Peronist thought and practice was also suspect during the *proceso*, the military did not see the 'Peronist' and the 'subversive' as so completely synonymous as they had once been. Naval chief and member of the first junta, Admiral Massera, had marked sympathies to a certain kind of Peronism, for example, and fancied himself a potential successor to the great leader. Meanwhile, in José Ingenieros, there seems to have been some cooperation between the death squads and right-wing Peronists when it came to identifying their historic foes on the left both within and outside the movement.

All and all, then, this 'mistake' is quite a neat trick in that it solves a number of problems for Susana and Raúl. What is remarkable here is the transparency with which the past is reimagined to better fit the needs of the present. No doubt this radical revision becomes easier in a context where there has been very little discussion of the events in question. Were people to speak more freely about the past, someone might have pointed out Susana and Raúl's error to them. The general silence on this past helps make such a revision possible. As local political activists, Susana and Raúl are probably more concerned than most with presenting a coherent and convincing story. Furthermore, they would probably have been self-conscious about their move to Rico. They might have thought that my friends and I would have disapproved. They might have seen the interview as a chance to set the record straight.

Contradictory Memories

Although Raúl and Susana's is the most radical (and creative) separation, it points to a dilemma apparent in many accounts of the *proceso* era. Doña Inés, for example, heatedly and aggressively denied that anyone from the neighbourhood had disappeared. In constructing time lines in the *taller de memoria* there was some disagreement about the character of this period. One woman's suggestion that it was a quiet period is countered by others' memories of violence. The second time line, in particular, conveys both positive and negative characteristics of the *proceso*. On one hand, *talleristas* recalled *allanamientos*, on the other, festivals and carnival celebrations.

As I have noted, people often separated what they saw as good aspects of the last dictatorship from bad ones simply by talking about them at different points in our interviews. One of the clearest examples of this process can be seen in the excerpt from the interview with Don Fernando and Doña Mabi in chapter 4. This separation is probably partially due to the fact that the full knowledge of human rights abuses emerged only after the transition to democracy. But I often had the impression that people simply did not know how to understand the connection between aspects of the *proceso* which they see as positive and negative.

Making the connection might require radically rethinking ones' understandings of the recent past, a rethinking that could prove emotionally difficult.[8] Many people do not think about or perhaps even see the ways in which the disorganization of the present moment is also a product of the destruction of forms of social organization under the pressures of dictatorship, for example. This is not to say that such an analysis is available only to academics, however, as we shall see shortly. Without a clear sense of the relation between repression and superficial order, people's memories are divided, requiring remarkable acts of creative remembering – what I have been calling mistakes – to resolve the contradiction.

Raúl and Susana's account also calls attention to the specificity of the stories people tell. They are marked not only by personal experiences and understandings, but also by the social and political position of the tellers. In this case by a Peronist identity, by a negative experience with the police, by an inherent respect for at least some military men, and by disillusionment with the Peronism of Carlos Menem and a subsequent political conversion.

I want to emphasize here that I do not think that people are lying when they make these kinds of errors. Rather, the story Susana and Raúl are trying to tell and the message – here about Rico – they are trying to communicate makes more sense when told this way. We might ask what the revisions and amendments protect. Rico? Raúl and Susana? Or their narrative truth? What can they do with their Peronism,

the Peronism Raúl so compellingly describes by recourse to his childhood memories of gifts of shoes and toys (see appendix), when it
seems to have deserted them? Not only had the Peronist system's
patronage failed them when Raúl lost his job, but also the supposedly
Peronist president has abandoned what Susana describes as the politics of General Perón. They clearly see in Rico the possibility of a second coming. Also clearly, the second coming they hope for is of Perón
in his more nationalist and militarist guise.

Audiences

Stories about the past need to be thought about not only, perhaps not
even chiefly, as texts, but as social events. They are socially produced
under specific conditions and for particular purposes, sometimes
more, sometimes less consciously. Context, intent, and audience are
essential factors shaping narratives in crucial ways. Many stories I
heard were specifically told to and for me. The *taller*, in contrast, saw
people telling their story to a wider audience, one that included their
neighbours in the *taller*. For the mural, it was wider still. Even so, the
audience's exact constitution was a point of contention, as we saw in
the debate over the placement of the mural. Not only location, but also
the content of the mural was shaped by a sense of its audience. Given
the decision to address local people rather than outsiders, some saw
the mural as a call to action, exhorting neighbours to participate. The
desire to convey an optimistic message is apparent in both the *taller*
mural and the later Hornero one directed outward. In the *taller*, however, the audiences were still basically sympathetic and supportive. A
hostile audience is something else altogether.

A Hostile Audience

One day in March 1992 three women from José Ingenieros were taken
by surprise when confronted by a hostile audience. Anahí, Marisa, and
Rosa were invited to speak to a group of students in a course designed
to train social activists (*Capacitación de Operadores Sociales*). The reader
has already met the shy but self-possessed Anahí, who was young but
active at the time of the *toma*. The articulate Marisa had been a small
child at that time. Rosa, the third woman, no longer lived in José Ingenieros, having left during the *proceso*. Over *mate* a few days later, Anahí
and Marisa told me the story that follows.

Rosa, Anahí, and Marisa were invited to speak to a group of students in a course designed to train social operators, or social interveners. Organized by the National Youth Secretariat, the course was designed for young people from the northern province of Formosa. The invitation had come from a man who knew them and the history of José Ingenieros well. He had suggested that they speak about community organizing, the history of the neighbourhood, especially the dictatorship and its relation to community organizing. Having received few details about the nature of the event or what was expected of them, the three women had briefly discussed a strategy, but by their own account, were ill-prepared for the encounter. The speakers had travelled across the width of metropolitan Buenos Aires to arrive at a classroom full of people and three chairs at the front, facing the rest; they found this intimidating, they told me. They had no time to get their bearings so decided just to tell the story chronologically.

All three had been *intrusas*. Rosa was the eldest so spoke first, describing the neighbourhood's early days. Anahí spoke next, and finally Marisa, who was only a teenager at the end of the *proceso*. They roughly sketched the history of the neighbourhood: the invasion of the public housing development before it was completed or occupied; the struggle to complete construction, establish infrastructure, and be awarded title to the apartments; the violent repression that had begun the night of the March 1976 coup and had included disappearances and *allanamientos*; the present-day problems of physical decay and crime and local attempts to address some of these through the community centre. In telling me about it, Marisa and Anahí described how they sensed from the reaction in the room that their account was not going over very well; there was considerable resistance as they described the *toma* and the *proceso* era repression. In reaction, Marisa said, they laid the facts out more starkly.

When they finished their presentation, there was silence. Then questions began. The first was about the *toma*: was it not an assault on law and private property? Rosa suggested that the *toma*, good or bad, should be seen in its historical context. Someone asked what the speakers' connections were to subversive organizations. Rosa replied that many people had come to the *barrio* to help in the early days. One knew these people by their first names. When things got rough they stopped coming around. No one knew where they were; local people were left to face the consequences (*dar la cara*). She thus articulated what must have been old resentments towards the generally young, mostly middle-class activists who had worked in poor neighbourhoods in the early 1970s. The outsiders could leave when the mere fact of being in José Ingenieros became dangerous. Another audience member said that the only part he 'salvaged' (*rescató*) from the presentation was the discussion of community organizing; what did all this history have to do with anything? The three women tried to point out that the two aspects, the history and the organizing, were inseparable.

Upon reflection, Marisa thought only three or four people had been overtly hostile, although the overall tone of the questions and comments had seemed confrontational. One questioner turned out to be a police officer working with the US Drug Enforcement Agency. On the other side, a young woman had gotten up to affirm that she thought that what the guest speakers were saying was important because (paraphrasing), 'anything that happens to human beings is of interest to all of us. These may be things people do not want to hear but they are part of history and we have to hear them.' A young man whose father worked in a penitentiary was apparently much affected by the women's account; he followed them around the rest of the day, asking questions about what things had been like in the neighbourhood in the old days. Sometimes his friends said that they had been better off with the *milicos* (slang for military), he told them, but he had disagreed because the military 'did lots of things.' He thought that people just did not want to know about it. Note here that even the supportive people in the audience spoke in vague generalities.

After the session, the talk's organizers had apologized to their speakers. Searching for explanations, they theorized that the negative reaction of the audience might be traced to the fact that all participants were from the northern province of Formosa. Not only were people more conservative there, they suggested, but also the main sources of employment were connected to security forces: police, military and *gendarmería* (border police). Also, since the course was designed and organized by the state, those who attended were probably selected '*a dedo,*' that is, for their political connections to those in power – they were Menemistas.

We might also attribute some of this reaction to youthful resistance to tales of bygone eras, and the lessons to be drawn from them. Furthermore, these students would probably have been enmeshed in a social work approach to social problems, one aimed at defining problems so as to permit containing and fixing them. The reference to the past, then, became a complicating encumbrance. The history that Rosa, Anahí, and Marisa recounted was also a story where neither the state nor its subjects were obedient to the students' probable understandings of their appropriate roles. In and after the *toma*, residents of José Ingenieros had been successful in disorderly ways; the state had thwarted, rather than aided in the construction of a functional community.

Anahí was deeply upset by the reaction of the students. It was one thing for someone who had not experienced this history first-hand to have to put up with this sort of thing, she told Marisa and me, but quite another to have suffered, lived with fear for years, and kept working, only to find you have to put up with the same criticisms from young people. She was also upset that she had been put the position of having to deal with such an audience. It is not surprising, then, that neither Rosa nor Anahí, both of whom had close relatives who fell victim to repressive violence, mentioned their personal experiences. Exposing them to such an unsympathetic audience would have been painful.

This presentation took place in 1992, after democracy and democratic thinking was supposed to have been firmly replanted in Argentine soil for almost ten years, after the juicio a los ex-comandantes, *Nunca Más*, and a whole host of other public reckonings. This is part of why these events were disturbing; they reminded the three women how marginal their understanding of recent history might be, and how easily it might be undermined. That Rosa, Anahí, and Marisa should have been so ill-prepared for a hostile reaction, suggests, I think, the great care with which people decide when and where to speak about this controversial past. All three know people like Doña Inés who do not agree with their version of events, yet they do not often have their version challenged.

Silences

Anahí, Rosa, and Marisa's experience with the future *operadores sociales* points to some ways in which the past can be difficult. The fact of political, emotional, and narrative difficulty is often overlooked in discussions of oppositional histories. These difficulties can lead to silences – silences which are often read as forgetting.

Of the many historians who call attention to narratives about the past, Luisa Passerini's work is particularly helpful because her treatment of working-class memories of Mussolini's Italy suggests some parallels to the Argentine case. In *Fascism and Popular Memory* (1987) she addresses a vexing problem: how do you understand the history of a working class, or a working-class culture, under a fascist regime? She eschews the kind of romanticization that imagines 'a consistent anti-fascism and unwavering participation by the whole class (not just a limited nucleus) in clandestine opposition,' arguing that such an image 'makes it impossible to understand to what extent a class undergoes and survives the experience of defeat' (1987:5).

Of course, the Italian case differs in myriad and important ways from that of Argentina, not least, as Susana and Raúl's account suggests, because the history of Peronism places Argentine working-class people in a much more ambiguous relation to the leadership of military men. Yet Passerini's openness to a more nuanced and less heroic tale also acknowledges the real difficulties people face in trying to carry on their lives under less than favourable conditions.[9] This attention to the ways individuals make sense of their pasts allows us to go beyond assumptions about worker resistance or acquiescence to the problem of how people make do.

One manifestation of the difficulty of this past for the people Passerini interviewed was a marked silence in many accounts as informants skipped from the 1919–21 period to the 1943–45 period (1987:68). Clearly the silences Passerini encountered were meaningful: they call attention to the particular narrative structures of people's stories.[10] She describes reading through and around the things people did and did not say to construct her understanding of life in Turin under fascism. For residents of José Ingenieros as well, the past, especially the past of the *proceso*, is difficult. Few of their stories are heroic.

People fall silent when faced with unspeakable stories, when words are too dangerous or desert them altogether for political or psychological reasons. Words may be dangerous in another sense, of course, when one does not know how to say what one wants to say and have it come out right. Attend, for example, to the problem Raúl has describing the military era *allanamientos* in the neighbourhood, and the terrorist threat: 'It was also to catch many ... ah ... at that time there were many ... that is ... There was a little terrorism. So this was a way of locating where it was. Because ... this ... This way the neighbourhood was purified a little ...' We have seen another example of this awkwardness in the silence of Don Fernando, who rather than naming the *proceso*, skipped the word altogether (chapter 4).

Of course, silences can point to things forgotten. Juana had been a social worker for the provincial Instituto de la Vivienda, the branch of the federal government that had managed the neighbourhood. From about 1978 to 1983, along with regularizing the tenancy of apartments, Juana's job included trying to organize residents of José Ingenieros to look after and improve the neighbourhood. Describing the period to me, Juana expressed frustration at what she read as residents' laziness and lack of initiative; she had found it nearly impossible to get them to form an administrative commission. Residents knew, however, that their neighbours had been subjected to harsh repression for having engaged in such activities. By 1992 Juana seemed to have forgotten the larger context that helped explain the reluctance of residents to participate. Just as for Susana and Raúl, accurately remembering would have posed problems for Juana. Remembering that she was working for the militarized state raises troubling questions. Might she and her colleagues have unwittingly put people at risk? The stories recounted in chapter 4 suggest just this.

On another occasion, Julieta, another social worker who had been part of Juana's team in José Ingenieros, mused: 'Later, with experience, one has one's own evaluation of things, no? Mariana [another member of the team] and I have done it; we're friends and stay in touch. We have made our own reading of our performance there.' In remembering, Julieta's tone was muted and her comments few.

Many people were more actively silent in the context of the present work. There were those I could not ask, who would not meet me, or who, if I met them, would not talk about whole periods of neighbourhood history. For example, one man who had spent years in clandestine and then legal detention agreed to meet me if we spoke only about the neighbourhood in the time leading up to, but definitely not including, the *proceso*. Some of these silences would have been based on an entirely legitimate privacy, others on a fear for what the future might hold, and how their words might come back to haunt them. There were also questions I would not ask. For example, I heard stories from victims about violence, but did not explicitly ask for them.

When the Past Does Not Fit

The difficulty of the past is important in a second sense. Working-class people are often struggling against the grain of dominant versions of events from which they are often excluded (Steedman 1986, 1995). The political transition of 1972–3 is one clear example. When I described how I saw the *toma* as part of the dramatic events of the transition, people could see how their history was in fact part of national history, but such a reading took prompting; it is not one suggested by dominant accounts.

Likewise, in thinking about the *proceso*, various more or less official

versions circulate; none fits comfortably with how people in José Ingenieros understand the period. The public discourses about the *proceso*
left little room to contemplate the role and place of the majority of
Argentines. Most people were only observers whose approval or dis-
approval was assumed but not explored (Parelli 1994).

Writings on popular memory (Popular Memory Group 1982, Swedenburg 1991) use Gramsci's notion of common sense[11] to describe the practical knowledge that subalterns have about their past and present. These
authors emphasize how difficult it is for popular sectors to articulate a
history that runs counter to the official stories that exclude them. I would
argue, nonetheless, that these authors are not attentive enough to how
these histories and experiences may diverge from those more official
ones. The history of residents of José Ingenieros departs in important
ways from official versions, and even from oppositional histories like
those of the human rights groups. These are differences in experience
(the squatter occupation, the *allanamientos*) and memory, but also in
interpretation. As we saw in chapter 4, Norberto Liwski confronted this
lack of fit in the blank responses of human rights activists when he
described the multiple kidnappings after the mass for Cirila Benítez.

When certain kinds of knowledge and information are dangerous or
difficult, they become all the more isolated. Being unrecorded and
silenced, they are seldom worked out, and they can begin to seem
unreliable in the face of dominant versions expressed repeatedly and
authoritatively. Those who would express another point of view find
themselves speaking out of chorus. In the *talleres*, we saw how participants felt unsure about their own history. Their decision to focus on
memory rather than history is related to their sense of history as coherent and authoritative, I think, and speaks to the insecurity they felt
about their knowledge of the past.

When the Past Is Organized Differently

Another of the ways in which popular memories can be dissonant with
official accounts is in how they are organized. Sensitivity to the ways
informants describe the past means paying attention to how they order
events. There is often a poor fit between the categories that organize
official versions and those that people use in their own histories. I was
often struck by how relatively irrelevant dates and even political
benchmarks were to many informants. Confusions about the dates of
specific and important moments (the *toma*, for example) were very

common, likewise changing governments. This was particularly evident in the time lines. Where events were dated, the dates were often vague or even incorrect.

This suggests that some shifts in political regimes may not have been as obvious or important to the people I spoke with as one might think. The significant exception here was the return of Perón. Often people were able to recall whether they had been in the neighbourhood by the time of the events in Ezeiza, although again this was often in the context of personal experience. One man remembered someone having managed to set up a TV in the street amid the chaos of the *toma* so that people could see what was happening. Others were part of the massive columns that had marched there to receive the leader. In a third instance, as Inés recalled (chapter 3), *intrusos* used Perón's return as a deadline after which they would no longer cede apartments to any *adjudicados* who could prove they had been assigned them. Overall, though, the periodizations which political analysts and historians use are not widely employed by residents of José Ingenieros. The hard lines that many commentators draw between the rule of Isabel Perón and that of General Videla, for example, are not so important in the chronologies of most of the people with whom I spoke.

Women, in particular, often sorted out dates through a kind of family time. Doña Elena could date her arrival in José Ingenieros as an *adjudicada* precisely: she had been pregnant when she arrived, her son had been born two months later in April. By counting backwards from her son's birthday, she could tell me that they arrived in February 1973. In other interviews as well, events were dated by which children were present, and their sizes at the time (one child was just old enough to wander away, another was being held). As we saw in the discussion of the *taller de memoria*, Claudia remembered the exact date of a kidnapping during the *proceso* because it occurred on the day of her civil wedding ceremony. I do not mean to exoticize here. I know I catalogue my life in similar ways.

Narrative Choices in the *Talleres de Memoria*

All this is not meant to imply that an oppositional history lurks under the surface here, perhaps organized differently, waiting to express itself. As many of the more political members of the *taller* were well aware, local historical knowledge was no more organized than anything else about the neighbourhood. The next chapter explores the community organization part of this equation. Given the above discussion, though, I want to reconsider some failures, or at least limitations, of the *talleres*, and thus problems surrounding memory work.

First, recall that the *talleres* were not autochthonous. They were actively organized and to some degree sustained by outsiders, most importantly Alejandra and myself. As with other more important forms of collective effort in José Ingenieros, maintaining the *talleres* was always a struggle, although, as I hope is clear from the description of them, the energy and enthusiasm of participants was often genuine. In this sense, the mural was an attractive choice for a form of representation. As we noted at the time, it required almost no commitment from its audience – in contrast to a theatre production, for example, which would have required that an audience show up at certain times and places. In addition, the commitment it demanded from *talleristas* was clearly defined and circumscribed. This may also have been a drawback. Although people talked about additional murals in locations that had lost out to the one we finally selected, painting a mural was a neatly self-contained activity. The idea of an outbreak of mural painting was attractive, but did not come to pass.

The design of the mural was also imprecise. Just as Anahí's reaction to the difficult audience suggests that people avoid coming into conflict over historical narratives that are out of tune, so the mural itself is peculiarly neutral on some central issues. The decision to be positive and upbeat – with the colours, the title, the silhouettes – may have also been an evasion of more difficult and contentious issues. *Talleristas* could avoid discussions like the ones I have tried to engage in here, about the connection between the neighbourhood's contemporary problems and its history. I do think some of these ideas are implicit in the juxtaposition of the two designs, for example, but as I have argued above, part of the problem for people in José Ingenieros is that such arguments and connections are not developed and discussed.

Conclusions

In trying to capture, or to recapture, subaltern histories, analysts sometimes exaggerate their unity and coherence. Gavin Smith (1997) uses the evocative metaphor of a stream cutting its way through limestone, sometimes bubbling up into the domain of official history – in confrontations with the state, for example – sometimes continuing, away from view, in subterranean streams. Smith's aim is clearly to complicate our tendency to romanticize or simplify the histories, memories, and silences of subalterns, an aim that I wholeheartedly support. But the metaphor seems to imply a degree of coherence that is not present among the people with whom I spoke. This lack of coherence has to do both with the difficulties I have described above, and with the radically diverse perspectives of residents of José Ingenieros. Even from the few stories recounted here, it is clear that Susana and Raúl, and Rosa, Marisa, and Anahí have very different experiences, memories, and interpretations of life in José Ingenieros during the *proceso*. This contrast could seem too neat, however. I do not want to suggest that there is a group of forgetters and another of rememberers. For one thing, to remember some things is to forget others.

Susana and Raúl, Don Fernando and Doña Mabi, Marisa, Anahí, and Rosa, and the *talleristas* all express decidedly working-class visions of events. Their experiences and understandings are tied to their class position, but not reducible to it. In the literature, but even more in conversation, one encounters fantasies about working-class memory – as false consciousness or as a direct line to the truth – which are evidently too neat. As we have seen, even members of substantially the same social categories have distinct ways of understanding, making sense of, and talking (or not talking) about the past. This is a messy business.

The Popular Memory Group advocates attention to the processes of the 'social production of memory.' Beyond official public representations, they argue, 'a knowledge of the past and present is also produced in the course of everyday life. There is a common sense of the past which, though it may lack consistency and explanatory force, nonetheless contains elements of good sense. Such knowledge may circulate, usually without amplification, in everyday talk and in personal comparisons and narratives' (Popular Memory Group 1982:210). By pointing to common or good sense, they invoke Gramsci's notion of hegemony (1971), reminding us that such sense is made in contexts of domination.

For José Ingenieros, what is so striking is the way in which the kind of knowledge that the Popular Memory Group describes was precisely not allowed to circulate. The repressive apparatus of the state and the culture of fear that it generated were remarkably effective in preventing people from speaking to their neighbours about their common experience. Often people did not know the extent to which their personal experiences of repression were not unique. The fact that I have been unable to come up with even an estimate of how many residents might have been disappeared is only one example of how effective this silencing has been. Most people I interviewed had witnessed or knew of one or two disappearances but they did not seem to be the same ones.

Argentines often lament the 'forgetfulness' of their fellows. The example of José Ingenieros shows how we need a much more subtle and complex interpretation of the silences, omissions, and even errors that lead them to such a conclusion. These silences are sometimes the result of forgetting, but forgetting is in turn socially produced. The social production of particular accounts, including ones where things have been forgotten, is the difficult part of the process to capture – one which anthropologists and their fieldwork methods may be better positioned than most to follow.

Chapter 8

Of Memory, Trash, and Politics

The past is alive in José Ingenieros, even when it is neither discussed nor acknowledged. The shared experiences of the last three decades live on not only in the more obvious senses of what people have learned and what they know, but also in friendships and enmities, in confidence and mistrust. Gavin Smith (1991) has argued that community dialogue for the rebellious Peruvian peasants he worked with is often expressed in the language of contention: that the passion of disagreements often suggests the depth of people's connection, of their sense that something very important is at stake. For the analyst as well, these struggles can be particularly telling. Two contentious projects from the time of my fieldwork in José Ingenieros suggestively raised the spectre of the past for neighbours. One was the Asociación Vecinal Pro-Policía, a group based in *complejo* 4-5-6 that worked to bring a police presence into the neighbourhood. The other was an Italian-funded community health project, known locally as *el proyecto de salud*, which aimed to improve public health in José Ingenieros. Both groups raise, yet again, themes that engage the history of the neighbourhood: law and order, health and sanitation, and community organizing and political patronage. These two projects and the concerns they express are not just connected thematically; they emerge out of José Ingenieros in a much more daily sense as well. The characters in the drama have histories in the neighbourhood, as do the antagonisms that engender or at least fuel the struggles around these projects. They engage community politics.

In this chapter I describe these two projects and the conflicts they occasioned. I also discuss how these examples demonstrate the importance of the past-present relation, shaping how people see, understand,

and act. If, as I have argued, the *proceso* was largely about creative destruction, disorganizing certain kinds of people at both sectoral and local levels to better carry out a new political-economic agenda, then we are left with the question of how and to what extent this works in particular circumstances. Throughout this book I have called attention to popular memory because it is a useful way of thinking about how such processes are materially manifest within the lives of individuals and groups of individuals. It starts to pry open the black box of the much-discussed 'disarticulation of social ties.' For me, as for many of those who agreed to collaborate with me, this is the point. It is precisely because history weighs so heavily in contemporary efforts to organize people, to improve the neighbourhood, and to make community, that it is salient.

Crime and Punishment

La Asociación Vecinal Pro-Policía, spearheaded by the energetic, articulate, and nearly unstoppable Doña Inés, arose from concerns about crime in the neighbourhood. As participants in the *taller de memoria* noted on the time line, the incidence of local crime rose sharply in the late 1980s.[1] Previously, I was told, kids may have been on the wrong side of the law, but they had gone outside José Ingenieros to commit their crimes. The neighbourhood's tough reputation may have even helped protect residents in those days; local thieves went elsewhere to hold people up, but outsiders seldom dared trespass. Residents were particularly alarmed when young people they knew personally, who they had seen grow up, turned on members of their own community. People describe the eery sensation of having been mugged, only to see their belongings for sale or being used by their neighbours.

As we have seen, Doña Mabi and Don Fernando recalled the *proceso* in the context of their current preoccupation with crime.

Fernando: Before there had been delinquents,[2] in the time of [the *proceso*] ... there had been none of that. It was a quiet life.
Mabi: [interrupting her husband] My daughter says, 'there was always [crime], *mamá*, it's just that now they are more advanced.' That's what she says. But ... now we are afraid to go out. You can't go around at night.

Doña Mabi admitted that her fear was not entirely rational, but she felt hemmed in by the sense that she could not walk her neighbourhood at night. Like most of her neighbours, she had no car and even if she could afford them, taxis refused to service the neighbourhood.

For Don Fernando the crime problem was particularly associated with drugs. My information on drug use is anecdotal, but there were clearly serious problems. Many boys sniffed glue. Some parents tried to pressure local merchants not to sell glue, and especially not to minors. People were also injecting drugs, usually crack-cocaine. We often found used syringes in our ground-floor apartment's small garden. People in the community know who uses and who sells. Some complain that the police also know and are on the take. Most find the situation upsetting, but they also find it difficult to demonize drug users they know personally. Many of those with serious drug problems steal to support their habit. Ironically some neighbours who complain most vociferously about local youth crime are seen buying stolen goods from drug users at very low prices. People sometimes even place orders when they want something in a different size or colour, effectively commissioning more thefts.

Policing the Crisis

On one level, the place that discourses of law and order have taken in Argentine society in the last thirty years lends credence to the sort of argument made by Stuart Hall and his colleagues in *Policing the Crisis* (Hall et al. 1978). They make the point that 'moral panics' around crime are social phenomena that imply law and order reactions. Related arguments about Argentina suggest that members of poor or so-called marginal communities are victims of state power in the guise of police forces (Oliveira and Tiscornia 1990, Schocklender 1992, Herbel 1993). The figure of the 'subversive,' the object of demonization and systematic state violence during the dictatorship, has been transformed into the 'delinquent.' This move has occurred in several senses.

Ideologically, dissent and social problems are laid at the door of certain kinds of people; the delinquent became the new epithet, both in political circles and in the press. Lest we interpret the construction of such discourse as disembodied, it is worth noting how they are materially produced. The only crime statistics are generated by police forces and passed on to the news media at the discretion, and in the language of the police. One indication of this is the ubiquitousness of the phrase 'according to police reports' in press coverage of crime and its repression (Oliveira and Tiscornia 1990:16).[3]

The continuity between the subversive and the delinquent also occurred institutionally. The police forces and prisons continued to be staffed by personnel who were present during the dictatorship, and their treatment of prisoners has been similarly brutal. A hunger strike conducted by prisoners in September and October of 1994, for example, protested inhumane conditions in a prison dedicated to eighteen- to twenty-one-year-olds. Investigators found conditions appalling, and also found that over half the prisoners had served more time awaiting trial than the allowable sentences for the crimes of which they were accused (CELS, personal communication).

Simultaneously, if on another front, the U.S.-sponsored project of a Latin American war on drugs legitimized the continued existence of a military that had otherwise seemed to run out of reasons. Menem's eagerness to cooperate with the United States in the war on drugs helped give Argentina favoured status as an especially good Latin American ally. By engaging in cooperative exercises with the Argentine armed forces, the United States, in turn, lent an air of seriousness to a military institution that failed in its only modern engagement against a foreign power in the 1982 Malvinas War.

In a context where fear of hyperinflation seemed to silence dissent on the nature of the political-economic agenda, the idea of a crime wave dislocated the social character of the crisis; crime became a question of individual moral defect. The connection between the economic crisis and crime is likely more direct. The unprecedented outbreak of food riots and looting during the peak of hyperinflation in May and June 1989 and again in 1990 suggests a strong connection between crime and the economic crisis. At the time, the government described these events in terms of delinquency *and* subversion (Midré 1992).

In some senses such a model is too easy, however. As critics of Hall and like-minded theorists have noted, street crime does happen, and people in working-class communities do want protection from it. For example, many residents of José Ingenieros were uncomfortable about staying away from their apartments overnight if it meant leaving them empty and unattended. They were convinced that they would be robbed, or their apartments occupied by a new family. Such fears are not, one should note, unique to José Ingenieros. People in other working-class neighbourhoods had similar concerns. So how, considering the preceding history, do we make sense of the fact that groups in communities like José Ingenieros call for state presence in its most repressive form?

La Asociación Vecinal Pro-Policía

The Asociación Vecinal Pro-Policía arose out of a sense that crime in the neighbourhood, particularly mugging and theft, was out of control. Residents were upset that police did not give them the service accorded wealthier neighbourhoods.

I learned more about the Asociación one cold, damp fall evening early in 1991. Doña Ines came to the community centre of El Hornero for an interview. Four members of the community centre came in to listen and occasionally interject. Rumours had been circulating that the building was being eyed as a potential site for the local police office that the Asociación proposed to establish, so the subject of the association's activities was a contentious one when Inés brought it up. She raised the topic in the second half of the interview.

> The latest thing that I am doing is getting a patrol car for the neighbourhood's security. Two years ago the neighbourhood was under attack. We had a [bad] element ... but if they had gone to rob somewhere else ... (it's still bad, no? Because the other people they rob are people like us) but they robbed here, you know? The old lady's purse, the kid's sneakers, they stripped and beat one old man. There was a group. So we got organized and looked into it, to see what was happening. We went to the police station. They didn't give us the time of day. Police officers were around here: but it's a better bet to stick with the delinquents than some police that we had at that time [chuckling].

Chacho, one of the El Hornero activists, interjects, 'but this is a social problem that happens everywhere.'

> Inés (irritated by the interruption): This is the situation, let me explain: they have put a social label on us. Once a patrol car came; I don't know what happened; they stoned it or something. In this country they lump everyone together. How can I explain it? If there is one delinquent, we all are. If there is one rapist, we all are. If there is one (as there is everywhere), one drunk, we all are. So we are 'the people from the *monoblocs*.'
> Chacho: No, but that happens everywhere. It's not just here. It's a social problem.
> Inés: No, but I am telling you about this specifically. We went from here to La Plata [the provincial capital]. I went to every organization; they told us all kinds of lies. I can't tell you. I say to the chief of police: '*Comisario*, what

can we do so they patrol us a little here?' Sure the patrol cars enter to ask for [free] stuff: pick up some wine here, something else there. Fine. They don't earn anything, but they never come into this neighbourhood [to patrol].

The Asociación's response to the provincial police's insistence that they could not patrol José Ingenieros because of financial constraints was to offer to defray the expenses. Doña Inés and her group charged four pesos per month (US$4 at the time) to each household that wished to participate in the Asociación. This, it was said, was to pay for the gas in the police car. The idea was that police would patrol the neighbourhood, and a local office would be established as a community base for the patrolmen.[4]

The initiative sounds like the community policing projects that are so popular of late in Canada and the United States. However, no similar discussion was going on in Argentina at the time. Despite superficial similarities, there is little resemblance to the very public storefront police offices. When the office was finally established in José Ingenieros, the only window facing the street, in the door itself, was painted over.

As Doña Inés noted, José Ingenieros fell into the group of neighbourhoods seen as too risky for anything but a full-scale police effort. Except for the police officers who lived in José Ingenieros, they were seen in the neighbourhood only en masse, usually in a raid to arrest someone in particular. In this light, the solution that Inés and her allies settled upon was mobilizing political connections and community resources to try to introduce a more regular police presence, addressing the perceived rise in delinquency with repressive force.

Although more than forty households paid the fee, many more did not. The objections to Doña Inés's plan were varied. Some neighbours agreed with her assessment of the situation but were incensed by the implication that they should pay the police to do their job. They saw the contributions not as a way to defray expenses, but as a payoff. As Don Fernando, who first told me of the plan, saw it, upwards of forty families (potentially as many as 850) paying four pesos a month would add up to a healthy sum. Others had more fundamental disagreements. In the wake of the dictatorship, many were inherently suspicious of a police force that had proven to be not only cruel but also corrupt. This was not merely an ideological position, although for some of the more politicized it was that. It was also produced precisely by the experiences described in earlier chapters: the early hostile official response to the *toma*, the guerrilla activities of the early 1970s, and the repression and *allanamientos* of the *proceso*. I do not want to suggest, however, that people's non-cooperation with the Asociación's project necessarily sprang from reasoned critique. Like everyone else trying to organize in the neighbourhood, Doña Inés and her group came up against considerable apathy, indifference, and unwillingness to participate in or contribute to new initiatives – reactions that were themselves the result of previous experiences.

Fear

One way to characterize the differences of opinion on this issue is in terms of fear. The place of fear in this debate points to the visceral quality of knowledge, beliefs, and ideology. On one hand, there was a tangible fear of crime and criminals in José Ingenieros. Media alarm about crime, what one study calls 'the social construction of images of war' (Oliveira and Tiscornia 1990), combined with local experiences and information to make fear of street crime an important issue in the neighbourhood.

This fear is evaluated against a fear of the police. Occasionally local kids are killed in police confrontation. Several young people from the neighbourhood told me about one incident just after it happened in February 1992. Two young men from *complejo* 17 were shot and killed by the police in San Justo, the administrative capital of the Partido de La Matanza. Anita told me that a service was held for them in *complejo* 18 and that many young people were upset and crying.[5] Although one man was a gang member, recently released from prison, everyone agreed the other had been a nice guy, son of an *empanada* seller,[6] with a job and a girlfriend, who just happened to be in the wrong place at the wrong time. People said he had just accompanied his friend to drop something off. According to a local version, one fellow had an old gun, was committing a robbery. He got caught and fired at the police, but the gun did not go off. The police shot him ten times. José's comment: 'they just kept on shooting.'[7]

Tito showed me a clipping from *Crónica*, a popular working-class newspaper. According to Tito, the newspaper photos showed only one victim, because the other had taken three shots to the head and more to the body. He argued that this could only happen if the victim was lying on the ground. Tito, who used drugs and was himself in trouble with the law, said the two men were taking two or three kilos of cocaine to a house in San Justo. According to the article, two suspicious characters were seen about to enter the house and were shot in the street. In Tito's version, they were killed inside, and the paper did not mention the drugs because the police had made off with them. As he recounted the story, Tito was depressed. 'How many kids, people I know, have they killed just this summer?' he asked.[8] We have no way of knowing which account of the incident is correct. It is worth bearing in mind, however, that the press version was probably supplied by the police while Tito is well positioned for access to other versions. He did not deny the delinquency of the activities he and his friends engaged in. Nevertheless, he was upset because the police were corrupt, used excessive force, and in this case killed an innocent man.[9]

Six weeks earlier Tito had been one of three youths picked up when an off-duty police officer had been killed while working security at a neighbourhood butcher shop. Fortunately for Tito, the store owner saw him when he arrived at the police station and asked, 'What are you doing here?' He was released.[10] Nothing terrible happened to Tito while in custody, although Marisa's mother, Carmen, had been speculating ominously. 'You know what they do to them there,' she said.

When I discussed these events with others, they clearly frightened not just people like Tito but also those who might not expect to become targets of police violence. My account of the recent shootings raised the topic of the police one Sunday afternoon at a barbeque with a group of friends. When Roberto (an *adjudicado* we met in chapter three) was less outraged than others by the events, his wife reminded him that there was no capital punishment for robbery (the offence described in the newspaper account). Later he showed that he too had a critique: he complained that the provincial police are poorly educated. When he went to get a document from them, it was always littered with spelling mistakes.[11] Elena, a mother of three and in her forties at the time, said this type of discussion made her extremely dubious about the police. Every time she had to go into the police station for some errand she wondered if she would come out alive. Would she one day get into an argument with someone and end up dead?

The discussion reminded everyone of another anecdote. A man from the *barrio*, an infamous torturer, was renowned for the dubious distinction of having died during sex after a big lunch. Apparently he was with his lover, not his wife, at the time, so the police covered up the fact. Elena, who seemed to take some pleasure from his ignominious end, said her deceased neighbour had been nasty; not only was he a torturer, but he did things like rape women with electric prods. Roberto looked especially horrified. Elena had added the gory detail because he had seemed to have some sympathy for the man's fate.

An Argument

An argument about the Asociación and its goals in the later portion of the interview with Doña Inés delineated the tension between the fear of crime and the fear of the police. Here it is helpful to recall that Chacho was a dark-skinned young man in his twenties while Doña Inés was a middle-aged fair-skinned woman. Both were political, poor, and had lived in the neighbourhood for the past twenty years. Chacho interrupted the flow of Inés's argument in support of the Asociación:

> *Chacho*: Doña, can I ask you something?
> *Inés*: I'm happy to talk.
> *Chacho*: In what ways would a police detail help our neighbourhood?
> *Inés*: Offering security ...
> *Chacho*: Whose security?
> *Inés*: Mine.
> *Chacho*: Yours?
> *Inés*: And that of my neighbours.
> *Chacho*: Not that of the neighbours. First, several things have to change, primarily the police institutions.

The two went on to discuss the corruption of local police, and their alleged connections to the drug trade in particular. It was clear Chacho opposed the Asociación's goals.

Inés ascribed what she saw as Chacho's cavalier attitude to his youth and his sex. He protested that he has a mother and a grandmother to think about. Still, Inés was correct in a sense. Chacho may have been at less risk than she of being mugged, but as a dark-skinned young man, the stereotype of the delinquent, he was far more likely than she to fall victim to police violence.[12]

Their disagreement *was* also ideological. Not long after the discussion had heated up Chacho raised the thirty thousand disappeared as an argument against bringing in the police. In public Inés simply said she did not agree, but later, in private, she emphatically insisted that no one from the neighbourhood had disappeared. Chacho's assertions about the corruption of the system were countered by Inés's, 'The system isn't screwing me. The guy [mugger] is!'

This debate, like the disagreements and antagonisms it represented and perpetuated, was enlivened by the fact that its participants knew each other and had a shared history. The 'delinquents' in question were not media-created spectres; they were real people neighbours knew personally. Marisa, a fourth person in the room, underlined this shared and personal connection with Inés: 'You know our neighbours, the boys who played with me when I was small? The majority have been killed by police, are in jail, or you see the condition they're in.' Here it was boys like Tito she was describing. What both Marisa and Inés knew, but did not mention, was that Marisa's brother was in a residential drug treatment program having narrowly escaped the nightmare of the prison system by the good luck of having encountered a progressive judge.

Finally, this argument was tied to a tussle over resources. The two groups laid competing claims to a neighbourhood building. Inés wanted to put the police station in the space that the Hornero group was using for a community centre. The relatively congenial tone earlier in the discussion deteriorated as Inés's plan to use the building for the *comisaría* entered the conversation.

Inés: I am going to make this simple. I believe in my neighbours. There are many good people here. There are many hard-working people here. The only thing we don't need is more lies. They should let us work and organize the neighbours ... Right now we have the patrol car project organized. Why? Because we wanted to get together with the people from the chalets [Ciudad Evita]. This locale has been offered three times for the *comisaría*. Why? Because it is appropriate for a *comisaría*.

Marisa: Inés, build another place, and stop screwing around with El Hornero and the *comisaría*!

Inés: Fine. That's your idea. Each with his own project. In a moment, I'll tell you ...

Marisa [getting angry]: But it is good to do projects where there is nobody else, not in a place where people are working, where they have lots of plans.

Inés: Listen, when the *comisaría* project was put together not a soul came here ... To get a project going you have to walk two, three or four years.

The sense that resources are limited leads people to advance their own projects at the expense of others, often even in direct competition with them.

The competing designs on the Hornero building also represent different analyses of the nature of the 'crime wave' and thus responses to it. Chacho and Marisa insist on the social nature of the problem and that there is a 'system' with interests opposed to their own:

> *Marisa*: The system benefits from lots of drug-addicted kids. It keeps them busy, so they don't ask for work: because for them there isn't any. Because they are the unemployed. There is no place for them, Inés.
> *Inés*: But one has to realize ...
> *Chacho*: So we need to work so that folks realize. I believe the police are not the solution, and they will never be the solution.
> *Inés*: Look. I believe in the system. Don't lump everyone together.
> *Chacho*: Why not?
> *Inés*: In all the dealings I have had with the police, I'll tell you, I have met two corrupt officers.
> *Chacho*: Two?
> *Inés*: So this is what I want: in my neighbourhood the police have to be respectful.
> *Chacho*: But that's not how it is.

Another key element in the debate is that for Chacho and Marisa criminals were produced by the failure of society and the community, and for Inés by the failure of families. These analyses in turn imply remedies: prevention or repression. Thus Chacho and Marisa felt the Hornero space should be used for activities which build community and keep children busy in constructive ways, while for Inés it should be used for a police station.

In 1992, some time after this argument took place, the Asociación managed to secure a local police detachment, in the *feria* between *nucleos* 4-5-6 and 18 rather than in the Hornero building. We might say that the state presence in José Ingenieros was strengthened, but it was a tenuous victory for the Asociación, it could have gone the other way. In fact, the detachment was no longer there in 1995. The implications of the state's presence or absence are material for the people who will or will not get mugged, as they are for those who will or will not get arrested. However, the outcome was determined in part by how these local conflicts played out.

Finally, the fact and history of people's personal relations is underlined yet again by Doña Inés. As the discussion became increasingly antagonistic, Inés successfully shouted down many attempts by Marisa and Chacho to interrupt the flow of her explanation. In a much more defensive stance, Inés deployed her history of activism and good works in the community to shore up her credentials. She traced the history of her participation from the days of the *toma*. This was part of a rearguard action as she began to lose ground in the argument with Chacho and Marisa. At one point, she turned to Anahí, who is older than the others and was an active teenager at the time, for confirmation of her involvement in equipping a local school.

The struggle around the police provides one compelling example of how the past-present relation matters. One can only understand what is going on in this debate against the backdrop of national and local history. It is important to know that in its early days the neighbourhood was terrain contested by competing armed political factions, that plain-clothes military and police did disappear people, that crime is a problem, that youth have been killed. These larger processes evidently affected and shaped people in particular ways; thus Inés's reading of what the police represent is very different from Marisa's or Chacho's. Further, Inés's position seems to require the negation, at least in part, of the *proceso*. Her insistence that no one from José Ingenieros had disappeared should be read in this light, I think, given the context in which she made it.

Health and Territoriality

Public health issues were a pressing concern in José Ingenieros throughout the time of my fieldwork.[13] Most alarming were problems with sewage, water quality, and garbage – problems that also had particularly strong resonances for the identity of José Ingenieros and those who lived there. When an Italian non-governmental organization, in cooperation with an Argentine partner, offered to fund a small community health initiative in the neighbourhood, then, it entered a particularly charged terrain. One might expect such a project, arriving at a time when public health was a major concern, would be received as a gift. Things were not so simple, however. The health project evoked a variety of reactions from neighbours and significant outsiders, reactions ranging from support and active participation to antipathy and antagonism. Here, as with the Asociación Vecinal Pro-Policía, one needs to look to the past to understand how the project was understood locally.

It is significant that the development project should have focused on public health. Health is one of the few topics considered sufficiently vital in José Ingenieros to generate some interest and enthusiasm (although I address some important limits to community engagement below). Health remains an issue around which people are sometimes willing to work in a relatively nonpartisan way. Children were construed as the particular focus of the preoccupation about public health as shown by the name of a group formed to address health issues at this time: 'Por la salud de nuestros chicos' (for the health of our children). It was thus reminiscent of the unusual successes that Alejandra, the director of the jardín, had in mobilizing the community in the cadena de solidaridad and the taller. Initiatives that focused on children were less likely, it seems, to be construed as political.

The health project had its origin in the same moment as the Asociación Vecinal Pro-Policía, the period of economic emergency of the late 1980s (1987–9). Responding to the social and economic crisis which hyperinflation deepened, the government of Italy promised to assist Argentina in a one-year project. The resulting aid package addressing health and housing took several years to make its way to the ground with the title, 'Assistance, Promotion and Development of Maternal and Infant Populations in a Situation of Social and Economic Emergency.'[14] When it finally arrived, one of its manifestations was a community health project in José Ingenieros.

A main condition of the accord was that the aid be delivered through an Italian non-governmental organization, CISP, partnered with an Argentine non-governmental organization, CODESEDH, and local government agencies.[15] CODESEDH identified communities it felt would benefit from the project, ones which had local organizations permitting community participation. Not surprisingly, it suggested community groups that its members knew and trusted. Norberto Liwski, the doctor whose account we heard in chapter 3, is the director of CODESEDH. It is no accident then, that one of the two locations for the project was El Hornero in José Ingenieros.[16]

In an attempt to avoid the pitfalls of many development projects, this health project included a period of consultation and planning with at least some members of the target communities. The obvious advantage of this strategy was that these members helped to identify local needs. The Italian team imposed certain conditions, the most important of which, apart from the requirement of community and government participation, was that the project be self-contained. This was to be one-shot funding; it could not establish any enterprise requiring ongoing support after the year of the project's life.

The question of community participation turned out to be a difficult one. On one hand, the project needed to have a realistic sense of how most effectively to spend its money; on the other, it needed to be planned quickly and quietly. Quickly because the Italian project organizers were in a hurry to get things done before the money evaporated, and quietly because too broad a consultation process would arouse local expectations that might then be disappointed. One of the most conspicuous scars in community life in José Ingenieros, perhaps in Argentina in general, was precisely this sense of disillusionment. Too often, people felt, promises had been made and broken. The surest way to undermine whatever legitimacy the project and those involved in it might have was to inflate expectations. Initially a few of the most active members of El Hornero travelled on city buses across town for meetings with the CISP field officer, an Italian anthropologist known affectionately as *el tano* (slang for 'the Italian'), and members of CODESEDH at their office.[17] Planning meetings later moved to José Ingenieros and involved more people. Up to this point, participation remained limited to those from El Hornero. Although residents of José Ingenieros, the Hornero members are an unrepresentative group, as indicated by their participation in the community centre. It is unclear how a broader consultation process could have worked in the given time frame, but the lack of one became a point of contention in the public meeting described below.

The plan the project finally launched in José Ingenieros met both funding requirements and local needs. The project would address three types of problem: it would improve the infrastructure of local health clinics in NHDs 17, 18, and 19[18] by furnishing such equipment as infant scales, cots, sample slides, refrigerators (for vaccines) and radiators, also performing some minor renovations; it would address the sewage problem by cleaning and diagnosing the sewage lines, performing strategic repairs, and, if indicated, enlarging or supplementing the sewage lines; and it would fund and organize a course in community health promotion.

Given that the Italian aid package tried to incorporate and respond to community needs and to ensure that no new obligations would be incurred by any level of government, the degree, quality, and character of the resistance it encountered were surprising.

The Sewage Crisis

The sewage problem was a major community concern. Raw sewage would back up through the system, overflowing onto the street and even into people's apartments. Many saw this as a grave health hazard, particularly for small children who could be seen playing in the 'puddles.' The anxiety here intensified early in 1992 as the cholera scare sweeping across South America made its presence felt in the Argentine press.[19]

The reasons for this deterioration remained a topic of debate in the neighbourhood and among government officials. Some arguments focused on technical explanations, others on social ones. First, the infrastructure was never designed for the population it served in the early 1990s for two reasons. The housing development was designed assuming typical nuclear families, but because of the economic crisis, and because affordable housing continued in very short supply, increasing numbers of people lived in the apartments. Extended family arrangements were common, often bringing together three generations in one apartment. There had also been some illicit and unplanned expansion within the neighbourhood for the same reasons. Although the overwhelming majority of squatter occupations date from the *toma*, people continued to occupy and make housing out of the unfinished public buildings in the neighbourhood. Similarly, some ground-floor spaces that were originally open were filled and inhabited.

A second explanation for the sewage problem was that the infrastructure, which may not have been high-quality construction in the first place, was poorly maintained. Government agencies were reluctant to accept full responsibility for a housing project that had been illegally occupied. Each *complejo* had local administrators who were supposed to be responsible for collecting fees and maintaining buildings and infrastructure.[20] As we have seen, this was less than successful for a host of reasons, corruption being the principal of these, as neighbours were quick to point out. In 1991 and 1992 the municipality of La Matanza had done some cleaning of the sewage lines because of the obvious health hazard that their overflow represented. Officials insisted, however, that these problems were not their responsibility.

Finally, some placed blame squarely on residents of the neighbourhood. People were accused of doing anything from not using screens on their drains, to flushing diapers. These accusations reached outrageous extremes with the comment of a municipal official who told me that the sewage problem was caused by women flushing their aborted fetuses down their toilets.[21] The exaggerated violence of this last assertion points to some underlying themes of the debate. Are the problems with infrastructure a product of poor planning or shoddy construction in the public housing project? Or ought they be attributed to a culture of poverty? The former places the blame on the government, or at least on the local administrators of the neighbourhood. The latter deploys stereotypes of ignorant or even barbarous residents reminiscent of the original PEVE philosophy. The image of the fetuses is also striking for the way that it lays the blame on women in particular. It also refutes the idea of the family that underwrites much of the community-oriented activity that does still take place in José Ingenieros.

The crisis intensified when in June and July 1992, amid the cholera scare, local schools closed for several days because water tests registered high levels of biological contamination in water from school taps. School lunch programs were also affected. Considering the seriousness of this threat to the community, the difficulty of organizing an effective response was striking. Clientelist relations were activated with some, but only temporary, success. When the municipality had the main sewage lines cleaned to reduce the likelihood of their overflowing, it was widely understood to be the result of pressure from local Peronist activists. Meetings were organized but groups proved incapable of sustaining them over time.

The Meeting at El Hornero

This was the context in which members of El Hornero held a public meeting in order to present the health project to the community. The meeting was complicated by the fact that it fell on the fourth day that *complejo* 4-5-6 had been without water because the well's pump had burned out from overuse.

The previous weekend people from El Hornero distributed stacks of flyers to the administration offices for distribution to the three neighbourhood *salitas* (clinics), and door-to-door in *complejo* 4-5-6. Those distributing flyers discussed the health project and suggested neighbours attend to learn more about the project and how they could become involved, found the reaction was mixed. The Hornero representatives on the planning committee, Marisa, Magdalena, and Anahí, had asked the project partners to stay away so that the meeting would clearly be a community affair. Representatives of the NGOs would be invited to a later meeting.

Around 7 p.m. one chilly Tuesday evening about twenty-five neighbours crowded into the small Hornero office (because it had a heater). Marisa had the thankless job of chairing the meeting. She began by outlining the health project, but only got about halfway through before things fell apart. Marisa explained that the project would supply some equipment to the three local clinics. A woman from 4-5-6, the one *complejo* without a clinic, interjected, 'But this has nothing to do with us! We need everything and have nothing! And I have no intention of working for the other neighbourhoods.'[22] She went on at some length about how impossible it is if your kids get sick, not that she has small children anymore. At this, a woman from *complejo* 18 responded, 'Well, if that's your attitude, I'll leave. We live in 18, but we came to help and support you because when your sewers clog up, everything comes over toward us.' To which the first woman responded, 'It's not our fault you live in a ditch!' As this went on, things became increasingly hectic with ever more people speaking at once. People were arguing that the clinics were used by people from 4-5-6; listing the ills of the neighbourhood; arguing for and against an administration; arguing for and against paying the expenses owed to these administrations, and more. Marisa let this go on for a while. When debate began to run down, she noted that everyone knew about the problems of the neighbourhood, that the things people were saying were perfectly true but asked that the group try to think of where to go from here. It took her a few tries, but eventually she began to achieve a kind of silent consensus.

Just when we got to this point, an unknown man who turned out to be from the neighbouring *chalets* of Ciudad Evita and to work for the municipal delegate started to say, 'But let's talk about something the people care about. They want to know what you are going to do about the sewers.' At this Marisa started to explain this part of the project, but only got as far as cleaning and repair when she was again interrupted with questions of, 'who is going to do this?' and, 'who is going to pay for it?' One woman (the 'I don't care about anyone not from 4-5-6' person) said that she did not believe the Italians would do it for free. How much would it cost? The discussion continued in this vein for a while.

The man who worked with the municipal delegate started asking questions and making criticisms: Who were the people in the community centre? Why was the flyer for the meeting so badly designed?

How had people been invited to the meeting? Why had it failed? Other questions concerned the workings of the plan with the Italians, and reasons the community at large was not more aware of it. Aside from the value that these criticisms may have had, their effect in the meeting was to discredit El Hornero and to distract attention from the matter at hand.

Some of these questions were legitimate, but it was striking that the people from El Hornero were being treated as *punteros políticos* or social workers – that is, as professional helpers rather than as members of the community. People seemed not to know or understand that El Hornero was a community centre operated by volunteers. One woman from 4-5-6, for example, kept demanding that Marisa find answers to her questions, refusing to believe that she was just another neighbour. She then got up to leave, as did most others because it was 9 p.m. People finally agreed to meet at 10 o'clock the next morning to go to the administration offices in *complejo* 17 and find out exactly what was going on. Only three people appeared the next morning: two from El Hornero and one other. There were no follow-up meetings.

This story illustrates the trials and tribulations facing people trying to organize neighbours in José Ingenieros in the early 1990s. It is possible that the members of El Hornero should have been more politically astute. Nonetheless, some major impediments to organizing are quite clear here. First is the ongoing debate about how 'the neighbourhood' should be understood and defined. Some feel that each *complejo* constitutes its own *barrio*, others choose to draw the map more inclusively. This seems to be largely a question of identity, since people do, in practice, move freely between and among the four *complejos*. Although the Hornero people wanted the project to establish a *salita* in the building they used in 4-5-6, and the *complejo* had once had a *salita* (now occupied by a family), distances are small. No part of 4-5-6 is more than a ten-minute walk from the existing *salitas*.

Second, there is evidence here of deep cynicism about organizing. People were pessimistic about the utility of community organizations; they did not believe that anyone operated merely in the interest of the community. Because El Hornero, which at the time had about ten active adults on its board, was not sponsored by any political party, it was assumed that it was either a secret front, probably for some socialist or communist organization, or that its participants were on the take.[23] I often heard this sort of commentary in other contexts.

Doña Inés put a surprising twist on this logic one afternoon when

Anahí and I went to speak with her in her apartment about the project.[24] She and her husband said that they did not want to hear ideas from local people. If someone came from outside with good ideas, they might listen, but they wanted to meet el tano before making up their minds about him. They also wondered what the Italians sought to gain from all this. They were unconvinced by my attempt to explain the politics of international development aid. Inés's thoughts on this question illustrate the kind of double bind that this sort of cynicism produces. She adamantly opposed any kind of activity that meant collecting money from neighbours; they always get burned, she noted. Boasting of her ability to get things fixed for free through the manipulation of myriad contacts, she spoke about working políticamente (politically) so that things were given to the barrio, in the old Peronist populist tradition. On the other hand, she accused those who did not collect money of working políticamente, this time in a negative sense. For example, Inés insisted that the president of El Hornero was on the take, despite our protestations. It was taken for granted that activists worked for some personal, party and/or otherwise nefarious end. The implication was that the only person capable of working for nothing and with communitarian goals was Inés herself. Although Inés was unusual in her energy, her activism, and her strongly held and loudly expressed views, she articulated the logic that underwrote a more general kind of resignation for many neighbours.

Third, this meeting shows how a local Peronist network attempted to disrupt an organizational attempt it did not control. In the end, this is how Hornero members interpreted the role of the man from Ciudad Evita.[25] Although he insisted he wanted to help, his interventions had a marked disorganizing effect, and he never reappeared to deliver on his promised contributions.

The health project came up against a peculiar kind of competition from local political organizers and civil servants in other ways. The patronage problem may have been particularly acute because the Italian field agent had decided against the advice of community members in selecting the level of government with which to work. Local activists suggested working with provincial officials, but el tano thought the most logical intermediary was that closest to the local, the municipality of La Matanza. Although officials were initially supportive of, or at least not hostile to, the project, it became increasingly clear that it was seen as a threat to the authority and legitimacy of some. It seemed to suggest that all was not well, and that the municipality had fallen down in its duty. As we have seen, José Ingenieros was a nearly impenetrable bastion of Peronist party loyalists. Patronage had always been an essential part of the unwritten terms of that contract. Thus any other source of help or, still worse, community organizing, seems to have been seen as a threat to the status quo.

The part of the plan which involved improving the municipally-staffed community health clinics may have been read as a critique of their quality. In any case, just as the project began to make some small improvements, the municipality was suddenly independently making its own. In one instance a small addition onto the clinic itself, a renovation that had already been planned, approved, and budgeted for in the project, was complicated when municipal officials started their own renovations. Improvements not originating with the Peronist-machine-run municipality were seen as a direct threat to local control. It seemed that precisely because the project had targeted local health issues, the municipality suddenly became active in the same area. This was evident in two other cases as well: that of a semi-private ambulance insurance plan, and in improvements of the sewage system.

On the other hand, part of the municipal government was much more helpful. Those responsible for sewage infrastructure saw the Italian funds as an opportunity to repair some chronic sewage problems in the neighbourhood, and contributed the resources they did have (machinery, labour) to the endeavour. These diverse responses recall our earlier discussion of the state as a collection of people and institutions with various reactions and agendas.

The Community Health Promoters' Course

Of all the aspects of the health project, the training course for community health promoters was the one that best expressed the underlying vision of those involved in the project.[26] Planning discussions at El Hornero concluded that the object of the project was to enable people to act in a useful way within the community about health in the widest sense. The public health promoters were seen as people who would be prepared and enabled to act as activists on issues of public health in the community. Designed for homemakers, adolescents, older people, and only lastly nurses,[27] the course was held in El Hornero on Saturday afternoons after shops were closed. Working groups met during the week. About sixty people signed up; twenty-eight eventually graduated.

Thirteen classes on distinct topics were taught by a variety of instructors between the end of September and 22 December 1992. Classes usually combined lecture and workshop formats. The curriculum was established in planning meetings with representatives of the three organizations.[28] The teachers of each session, however, were identified and invited by CODESDH. Some experts from the municipality of the La Matanza were invited to teach particular classes as a way to include the municipality. Their participation also established contacts which might be useful in the future. When the philosophy and political position of the teachers ran counter to those of the community organizers, however, problems sometimes emerged.[29]

Memories of Community

While police presence is an issue one might expect to scare up conflicts emerging from the neighbourhood's recent experiences of repression, a community health project seems politically neutral. It is striking then that the health project evoked powerful memories as well. Although the connection to the past is not immediately evident, it is as deep as it is subtle. The most dramatic association between the health project and the local past was through the clinic that had operated in NHD 17 in the time between the *toma* and the coup. As the reader may recall, the clinic had been a focus of organizing in the *complejo* in those heady days. Although Liwski reappeared some twenty years later to participate in the health project, the continuities were not just of personnel. The project also represented a return to a philosophy of community organizing and participation.

A connection between the health promoters' course and the experience of community organizing around health in the mid-1970s manifested itself in an early planning meeting. It was significant that those who made the connection did so while avoiding actually naming it. Here, again, a conspicuous silence surrounded the politics of the neighbourhood's early days, but the resonance with the past formed an emotionally charged subtext to the discussion. When el *tano*, acting as devil's advocate, asked why the group believed a course training community health promoters might work, especially given health promoters would probably not be paid for their labour, Rosa described how she had seen it work before. She explained that the idea was for people to be trained to observe, to pay attention when they chatted with their neighbours, notice kids who are sick, and the like. At this

Anahí and Gloria recalled that an earlier experience in the neighbourhood had been very effective.

The group returned to the topic later in the meeting when Anahí
asked *el tano* about his impression of El Hornero. Self-conscious, he
responded in part that the organization was young and still needed to
mature. Magdalena broke the silence that followed noting that it was
difficult to organize. People were very apathetic. Perhaps this was why
the group spent more time and energy trying to make the project happen than on bureaucratic details, she suggested, responding to the
implicit criticism. Anahí added that a few remembered another time,
when *complejo* 17 had a health centre like the one they were hoping to
build. Some discussion about the different characters of the various
clinics in those days followed. The one in 17, Gloria recalled, had been
the most active. She remembered a health worker coming by her home
for follow-up visits. At this, Rosa started to say that it was no accident
that organizing was so difficult in the *barrio;* her voice broke and she
had to stop. Anahí continued with an eloquent testimonial about the
cost of these efforts: 'Just as Rosa is crying now, this organization has
cost us tears.' Many in the room did not know that Rosa had lost her
husband and two sons to the *proceso*. Neither did they know Anahí's
story. When I asked later, *el tano* confirmed that he had had no idea that
people were talking about the neighbourhood's experiences from 1973
to 1976 and about the subsequent repression.

Roberto, an *adjudicado*, and thus a longtime resident, was among
those who did not know about Ahaní and Rosa's personal losses. He
later told me he had decided to take advantage of the charged atmo-
sphere to make another point. His eyes moist, he spoke of working
with the kids in the *barrio* through El Hornero; volunteers had almost
nothing to give but affection, he noted. He proudly noted that one
child he had seen grow up was now working on the centre's newsletter
and had written an article describing its impact on her life. People
were moved by this as well.

For community activists and those involved in the public health
project, these memories were complicated. Nevertheless, some saw a
positive model in the past. They also found some satisfaction in returning to a project that had been so brutally interrupted. A course very
like this one had been in progress in March of 1976 when some organizers and participants had been targeted in the first sweep of the new
order. For others, though, these associations spelled danger and mili-
tated against participation. Twenty years earlier Dr Liwski had been

known by a nickname, so some only realized who he was when they finally met him, once the course was under way.[30] Some believed him to have been killed in the *proceso*. Given all this, it is remarkable how little Liwski's previous connections to the neighbourhood were discussed, even by those who remembered him from before. For example, his name did not come up in the meeting discussed above (which he did not attend).

The connection of the health project and the neighbourhood's past was raised again one evening when a group of us was eating dinner in Marisa's apartment, and discussing the upcoming health promoters' course. Someone recalled that such a course had been offered once before, in 1976 just before the coup. We marvelled that some of the same people who had originally participated in the project, and had been persecuted and abducted in the interim, would finally be able to realize the project. Carmen, a woman in her fifties and a potential participant in the course, interjected that if it were so dangerous, she did not think she wanted to participate.

Nevertheless, many people did participate in the health promoters' course. This required considerable time and effort, and although it was free and some people may have hoped that some kind of employment might eventually result, no obvious economic gains were to be had for the trouble taken. In class discussions, neighbours soon identified social issues as real threats to public health. A project addressing infant diarrhea targeted the neighbourhood's sewage, water, and garbage problems. Working groups planned informational and educational campaigns, a neighbourhood cleanup day, and a program to build larger and sturdier waste receptacles. They also resolved to address the technical aspects of the water contamination and sewage problems. The course concluded with a festive dinner shortly before Christmas where the head of public health for La Matanza received the working groups' proposals. Despite the problems it encountered, and as Norberto Liwski noted in a conversation some years after the fact, the health project successfully raised the awareness of health in the neighbourhood. Furthermore, the concept of health it promoted was broad, including not just the health clinics but also environmental health.

Conclusions: Order and Chaos

What can we take from these two stories? First, one needs to acknowledge the real difficulties facing anyone trying to organize neighbours in José Ingenieros. These impediments may have been as severe for the Asociación Vecinal Pro-Policía as for the health project or those attempting to address the sewage and water crises. These difficulties originate precisely in national and local history. One question hardest to face in José Ingenieros in 1991 and 1992 was why people have been systematically unable to organize around such basic concerns as raw sewage running in the streets where local children play. As Rosa pointed out, however, it should not surprise us that organizing is difficult. Many forces conspired that it be so, from the multiple injuries of the *proceso* – and it bears repeating that these were not only the violent repression of those perceived as political opponents, but also lesser if no less effective forms – to the neoliberal economic policies that leave everyone scrounging for patronage goodies or an extra job.

Not least of these impediments is cynicism. Few people had the authority, respect, or credentials to mobilize their neighbours. Expectations of corruption were so high that scandal no longer excluded elected officials from office. People in José Ingenieros reasoned that all politicians were corrupt, so corruption was inevitable. Part of the responsibility for this view lies with all those who have seen taking as a prerogative of any kind of power (no matter how small), but it is also important to remember that generations of military governments have justified seizing power in these terms. Military governments have repeatedly told Argentines of the unbridled, self-interested corruption of democratically elected officials. I often heard assertions that people in El Hornero were on the take when I knew them not to be. One has to wonder how many other everyday assertions of corruption or hidden agendas were unfounded. In addition to a culture of fear, then, one could argue that the recent history of Argentina has engendered a culture of cynicism. Perhaps a cause, but also a result, of such cynicism is the continued adherence to the patronage game – in this case, a Peronist patronage game. If you cannot trust anyone, go with someone who can give you something you need.

Another factor here is the violence of politics in the few years between the *Revolución Argentina* and the *proceso*. In the conclusion of chapter 3 I argued that the brutality of those days is remembered far more readily than the enthusiasms, but it may also be true that people see them as linked. Beyond describing people in El Hornero as corrupt, some saw the centre as a front for a socialist or communist organization, a characterization I also know to be false. The fact that such labels were dirty words is a product of the fifty-year antagonism between

Peronism and the left. These labels also point to a sense that even the most moderate forms of utopianism are dangerous. This is a danger people in José Ingenieros have learned about first-hand, from the political violence of intergroup battles and from the violent repression of groups on the left by the military regime that followed.[31] As early as 1978, social workers were asking what was wrong with people in José Ingenieros that they could not form an administrative commission. As we have seen, however, people had been shown in no uncertain terms that taking on such a responsibility might be fatal. One way or another, community leaders, the process of learning how to be a community leader, and perhaps even a sense of community, were lost as resources to the neighbourhood.

For people from José Ingenieros, making positive use of their history seems more difficult. In part this is because it requires reading against the grain of dominant versions. Discourses portraying the experiments of the early 1970s as an unmitigated disaster are hegemonic; one even hears it from former activists.[32] As we have seen, though (especially in the context of the *taller de memoria*), some people attempt to mine the past for organizing strategies and positive models of community.

One incident from after my fieldwork suggests that this experience still supplies a resource in times of crisis.[33] When privatization of the utility companies under Menem threatened service to José Ingenieros and other neighbourhoods, residents used a strategy from the old days to resist. The power company has long had trouble collecting from neighbourhoods like José Ingenieros because households were not individually metered. The local administrations were sometimes unable to collect from many residents, and thus paid only portions of their electricity bills. Previously, the political costs of cutting service to entire neighbourhoods were too great, so although relationships were contentious, service usually continued. More recently, however, the newly private power company tried to force payment (probably from the government rather than consumers) by supplying only as much electricity as was paid for; they consequently cut off power at intervals. Without electricity the water pumps were out of commission, so part of the neighbourhood lost water as well. Neighbours argued that the problem arose because the company was too cheap to install individual meters to measure household electricity use. Responding to the power outages in José Ingenieros, neighbours stopped traffic in Camino de Cintura, one of the main arteries bordering the neighbourhood. Residents thus created enough disruption to call attention to their demands, just as they had two decades earlier when they called for Auriliano Araujo's release from police detention. In both cases they were successful. This sort of one-shot mobilization, however, is the easiest to emulate and execute. Clearly it is more difficult to reproduce the kind of sustained organizations of which Araujo was a leader.

In light of their history, it is remarkable that people do continue to organize and act in José Ingenieros. When they do, the leaders are more often women than men. Two reasons for this come to mind. First, feminine forms of organizing through friendship and kinship networks may work better in the present conditions.[34] Male leaders still tend to be tied to the party and the state, an increasingly precarious position given current trends. By virtue of their relative exclusion from traditional institutions of power (see also James 1995), and especially the most important positions in those institutions, women are also less sullied by them (Kaufman 1997).[35] Secondly, most of the issues that still mobilize residents are seen as particularly important for children (and therefore mothers): health, education, and safety. The strong notion of children as innocent, and therefore more deserving of help than adults, is common sense here. In informal discussions among neighbours about what should be done in the neighbourhood, one of the most common proposals was to restore local green spaces and furnish them with swing-sets and teeter-totters. When is organizing not seen as politics, one might ask. When it is about children.

The problems that engage people have another characteristic: they all address questions of social and physical order and chaos. The importance of garbage was impressed upon me everywhere in José Ingenieros. It was the perpetual return to physical order, a preoccupation manifest in the mural itself, that called my attention to its thematic importance. Physical order is read as a marker of social order. Thus the original planners of PEVE saw the *nucleos habitacionales transitorios* and *definitivos* as civilizing devices. Those who organized and executed the *proceso* era *allanamientos* meant it as a lesson in physical as well as social cleansing. In the early 1990s outsiders and neighbours alike read problems of sewage, garbage, and the general deterioration of infrastructure as markers of social chaos that brought the *monoblocs* closer to the social standing of the *villas*.

These connections are not fallacious. There is, in fact, a link between forms of physical disorder and social disorder. Although local activists would not frame it this way, they would probably agree with the underlying logic. The disagreements, though, arise from where to lay the blame. Doña Inés is an articulate spokesperson for those who locate the problem at the level of individuals and families. She sees the disintegration of the *barrio* of which she was once proud as the result of the moral failings of her neighbours. Others hold a view closer to my own, locating the crisis in the loss of forms of community and cooperation.

Clearly the kind of crises I have been describing are not unique to José Ingenieros, or even working-class Argentina. They are part and parcel of the crisis of late capitalism (Harvey 1989). Just as the 'moral panic' around crime shifts people's attention from the underlying causes of crime to their own fear and the moral deficiencies of criminals, so the repeated denunciation of neighbours' selfishness and untidiness seems to place the problem with individuals.

This is not altogether surprising. In working to organize neighbours, one's attention is trained on local problems, local formations and deformations. As community activists, Inés, Marisa, and the others had to deal with the individual manifestations of these problems on a daily basis. What is difficult to see is how the larger processes that promise to organize, make, and remake social life are responsible for the chaotic characteristics of everyday life in José Ingenieros. Again, the *allanamientos* are so very striking in part for the clarity with which they show this contradiction. But the same can be said of economic restructuring. Reorganizing the nation requires destroying communities strong enough to resist it; remaking the economy creates massive joblessness in working-class neighbourhoods. Seeing this is sometimes difficult in part because it seems to say that one has no power to change things.[36]

Though seeing this is difficult, some people do. Some continue to address their energies to the community: as public health promoters, participating in the schools, and community organizations. Rarely did I feel things were as grim as the situation I have just described when I was living in José Ingenieros. I knew people like those in El Hornero who were committed to a vision of community and cooperation. People like Anahí, Marisa, Malena, Gloria, Roberto, Estela, and Chacho acted out their belief in the possibilities; they continued to invest time, energy, and caring in community projects. There is cause for optimism in their refusal to accept disorganization as an inherent characteristic of their neighbourhood, their culture or their class.

Chapter 9

Conclusion: The Weight of History

By telling the story of José Ingenieros, relating how people there recount their history, and by considering the presence of the past in the neighbourhood, I have tried to examine how political-economic processes such as dictatorship and economic restructuring affect people and social life. This story matters because the people in José Ingenieros and working-class Argentines more generally matter – even though they are increasingly considered marginal to their country's plans and prospects. This account also casts light on the nature of political, economic, and cultural processes with much wider effects.

The story of José Ingenieros also shows how culture is a location of power. Culture is not, as state-sponsored and popular conceptions often suggest, the realm only of ethnicity, of ethnic foods and costumes, of music and crafts. This view, expressed in multiculturalism, conveys a vision of culture in a celebratory mode; it sounds like a festival. Culture is also the more and less dreary ways in which people live out and understand their lives and the world around them; it is the taken-for-granted and common sense in Gramsci's sense. Gramsci's work continues to nourish anthropological interpretations because it provides a way of thinking about relationships of domination and subordination, not only in political institutions and structures or in everyday social relations, but in the play between the two.

In this conclusion I revisit some of the main themes that emerged in the course of this study and which help us think about this relationship between culture and power: the state, popular memory, and Raymond Williams's 'structures of feeling.'

The Argentine State

The Argentine state – that is, the state-apparatus and the state-idea – has been a central figure in the story of José Ingenieros. Different state projects have played themselves out on, against, and through residents. Although the neighbourhood witnessed moments when state power seemed chillingly organized and coherent, attending to how these projects are implemented in particular places at particular moments reveals more complexity and contradiction than one might expect if guided by the state's representation of itself. For example, social workers working during the *proceso* sometimes responded half-heartedly to the dictates of their superiors.

Despite the brief time frame, the idea of the state shifted radically in the decades under consideration here. Two images are especially vivid: the authoritarian military regime of the *proceso*, and the elected neoliberal rule of Carlos Menem. The coup of 1976 was a move by the military, not itself coherent or unitary, to occupy the state-apparatus to a remarkable degree. To this end, military men were placed in positions ranging from the presidency of the nation to the administration of José Ingenieros. Statements from the de facto regime are shot through with paternalism, presenting the image of a stern father which belied the physical, political, and economic violence which the government/military was carrying out.

Menem's government had a very different image. The second democratically elected regime since the *proceso*, Menem's neoliberal project portrayed itself as 'shrinking the state.' Studies of such restructuring policies in Latin America point out how neoliberal regimes present themselves as anti-state. For example, in their careful and damning analysis of Chile's 'free-market miracle,' Collins and Lear note that neoliberals believe themselves to be merely technocrats, and their policies to be the only non-ideologically driven ones (1995:45–6). In this view, the Chicago Boys whom Collins and Lear describe remind us of Abrams's observation that, 'in capitalist societies the presentation of the state is uniquely pervasive, opaque and bemusing. Centrally it involves the segregation of economic relationships from political relationships, the obliteration within the field of political relationships of the relevance or propriety of class and the proclamations of the political as an autonomous sphere of social unification' (Abrams 1988:78). Neoliberals' argument that they are doing away with the state is precisely this kind of obfuscation. It only makes sense if one accepts their assertion that the state is manifest mainly in its social-welfare functions – which they are cutting – and not in the policies and practices that regulate (or choose not to regulate) the market. Also writing about the so-called retreat of the state in Chile, Schild notes that this is very much a managed retreat (1998).

It is also helpful, I think, to see how these two ideas of what the state is and should be enter into dialogue with each other. Given the history of bureaucratic authoritarianism in Argentina, and in Latin America in general, one can see how clipping the wings of state institutions might hold a certain appeal. Suspicion of the state engendered by authoritarianism may have something to do with the (at least partial) persuasiveness of neoliberalism in the 1990s – as measured by Menem's re-election, for example.

Much of the Latin Americanist literature refers to the period after the last wave of dictatorships as the 'transition to democracy,' suggesting, if not a hard line between dictatorship and democracy, at least a clear and positive movement in that direction. Arguments that challenge this view risk minimizing the importance of electoral democracy – a position that strikes me as irresponsible given what we know about how much worse things are under dictatorship. However, the case of Argentina shows how the return of formal democratic institutions such as elections are insufficient. Institutions like the police and the civil service are faces of the state which people in José Ingenieros encounter regularly, and which do not seem to have been so dramatically transformed as one would hope. The Argentine case – particularly the erosion of civil liberties under Menem – also reminds us that there is no reason to assume a steady increase in democratization over time. Further, the economic processes which William Smith refers to as the second transition are crucial. Although it seems that formal democratic institutions are secure, they are insufficient. As my discussion of the culture of cynicism suggests, the immiseration and exclusion of growing segments of the Argentine population threatens to undermine not just the legitimacy but also the principles of a democratic culture.

In the context of the current neoliberal hegemony, we may tend to accord the state-apparatus both too little and too much importance. On one hand, the neoliberals would have us believe that the state is disappearing (and good riddance). Yet the state still matters tremendously, despite efforts of reformers to act as if they are only deferring to pressures from Washington or the banks. On the other, critiques of particular political regimes may focus our gaze too narrowly. Watching CNN one day, I was startled to hear, after my years of fixation on things Latin American, a group of African journalists describing the local-level social consequences of structural adjustment policies across their continent. It could as easily, I thought, have been a group of Latin Americans wondering how their countries were to 'develop' when the banks insisted that they cut their spending on education and health care back beyond the barest of bare bones. How were Africans to construct a future when they were creating generations of uneducated and hopeless young people?

When in Argentina, and later when trying to write about what life is like in Argentina, I have often been tempted by the logic of many critics inside the country to see their tragedies as peculiarly and distinctively Argentine. Certainly I have tried to convey the particularities of the Argentine case in this book. This focus on Argentina, and more specifically on José Ingenieros, should not, however, eclipse the ways in which their tragedies are connected to our lives in Canada or the United States, or lives in Africa or anywhere. When thinking about the Argentine death squads, for example, we must recall that their strategies are historically and practically connected to U.S. policies in the region. The similarities between techniques of torture from one country to the next are products not of accident, or parallel invention (to use an old anthropological concept) but of training from United States' advisors at the School of the Americas in Panama. Likewise, structural adjustment policies formulated in institutions such as the International Monetary Fund and the World Bank play out in specific ways in Argentina against the backdrop of shifting alliances and strategies, but they are global policies and practices.

By taking an ethnographic approach, I have tried to illuminate the intimate aspects, experiences, and implications of these global processes. Focusing on the lives of people in José Ingenieros helps to show what such processes mean to and for particular people and communities. The historical frame, and especially the contrast between different historical moments, has helped show how changing relations of power at global or national levels shape people's lives in the places they live and work.

The Past Weighs on the Living

Throughout this book I have tried to show how and why, as Marx put it, the past 'weighs like a nightmare on the brains of the living'

(1963:15). A focus on the past-present relation is a strategy for examining how relations and structures of power actually insinuate themselves into people's lives. Because they are so evidently political, understandings of the past are among the places where we can most clearly trace the interconnections of culture and power.

Jacques LeGoff, one of many authors who have turned their attention to history and memory, writes: 'Overflowing history as both a form of knowledge and a public rite, flowing uphill as the moving reservoir of history, full of archives and documents/monuments, and downhill as the sonorous (and living) echo of historical work, collective memory is one of the great stakes of developed and developing societies, of dominated and dominating classes, all of them struggling for power or for life, for survival and for advancement' (1992:97–8). Shifting his attention to academic interests in other people's histories, he continues: 'It is incumbent upon professional specialists in memory – anthropologists, historians, journalists, sociologists – to make the struggle for the democratization of social memory one of the primary imperatives of their scientific objectivity ... Memory, on which history draws and which it nourishes in return, seeks to save the past in order to serve the present and future. Let us act in such a way that collective memory may serve the liberation and not the enslavement of human beings' (1992:99). LeGoff captures two of the fundamental impulses of work on social memory: to detail the central place and importance of narratives about the past for social groups and institutions; and to see this work on memory as a political project.

LeGoff's stirring call to the barricades of social memory, however, also points to the hazards of this kind of work. In a rush to give voice to the voiceless, we sometimes imply a kind of coherence which may not be present, and which potentially misrepresents and silences the complexity and contradictions inherent in social memories. We tend to think of popular memory as a kind of voice of the people, but which people, which voice? Swedenburg, for instance, shows how the political necessities behind constructing a Palestinian national past elide internal class divisions among Palestinians (1991).

As the *taller de memoria* shows so clearly, to write about the past is to rewrite it. To speak is also to hold silent. The mural tried to remind neighbours of former ways of being that had been eclipsed. But it also inscribed silences, and condensed a set of problems which it did little to resolve. Where was the *proceso*, for example, in the mural which the workshop group painted? What did it mean if the *proceso* was absent?

Although it was productive methodologically, the problems with the mural and the history workshop also point to tensions between what we as researchers hope for and expect, and what comes out of such enterprises. In the final analysis, popular memory may have as much to do with how the popular is shaped by the dominant as the other way around.

I have come to think of earlier writing on popular memory as still too dichotomous. This is not to say that a coherent oppositional history is impossible, but rather to emphasize the problematic political and cultural process of building a popular memory. These dilemmas point to related problems, I think, for the forging of collective identities and the ability to act collectively. The problems posed by the theoretical and practical challenges of popular memory may thus be particularly instructive. Thinking about popular memory helps us interrogate the processes through which certain social and political orders start to seem logical and inevitable. This focus helps us think about how and why people are (or are not) persuaded by Peronism, dictatorship or neoliberalism, for example. To understand their appeal is to begin to comprehend processes of domination and their persuasiveness. The attention to memories and histories demonstrates the importance of cultural processes shaping language, people's senses of self, and even their notions of the natural order of things. When a union activist told me that pity meant something different in the early 1970s, he was trying to convey something of the nature of this sort of historical transformation. He remembered a time when the world looked very different, when people acted in distinctive ways, when it was possible to do things that no longer seem humane.

Structures of Feeling, Resources of Hope

Transformations like the ones the union activist described are clearly not just about political-economic structures. They are also transformations in people's intellectual and emotional orientations to their worlds. As we have seen, people in José Ingenieros in the early 1990s were struggling to address their collective needs and to organize, mostly when situations became immediately intolerable. But the modesty of such efforts is startling given how intense and vital the activism of these same people was only a generation earlier. In the 1970s they needed housing and they took a housing complex and made it their own. The much more modest efforts of the 1990s often disintegrated even before they were fully articulated. In this book, I have examined why and how this came to be. Of course the larger context and climate is crucial, but the processes that produced these differences also took their toll on people's sense of their place in the world and their capacity to act. These are cultural transformations.

Raymond Williams's writing on working-class experience is compelling in part because, as a Marxist literary and cultural critic, he struggled to show how and why both culture and political-economic relations of power mattered. His notion of 'structures of feeling' (1977, see appendix) was partly a critique of the radical separation between the material and the ideological in Marxist thought. Both Williams and Carolyn Steedman (1986) remind us of the place of emotional orientations. More importantly, they take these things seriously. They show the connections between feeling and people's thought and action.

Steedman especially advocates attention to working-class women's stories, 'of lives lived out on the borderlands, lives for which the central interpretative devices of a culture don't quite work' (1986:5). It is precisely because these lives are lived on the borderlands that their stories and understandings do not fit neatly into recognized and recognizable patterns. Lack of fit makes it difficult for working-class women like Steedman's mother to articulate their own stories, but she has emotional orientations to the world that express something of her experience and what it has taught her. Steedman's discussion of the politics of envy (1986:7), produced by being taught to want things you cannot have, is especially rich. She writes: 'We live in time and politics, and exclusion is the promoter of envy, the social and subjective sense of the impossible unfairness of things' (1986:111). Thus, in the context Steedman describes, envy (a feeling) is about a social experience and understanding which has political implications. Of course, the particular structures of feeling produced are socially and historically specific. Steedman suggests that we think about the distinctiveness of working-class women's (and I would include working-class men here too) experiences and understandings from their places on the margins. She reminds us that such experiences and understandings are constructed out of particular personal and social histories and out of material conditions, and they take specific shapes and meanings. One might think of the concepts of the culture of fear (Corradi 1992) and the culture of cynicism in this light. These phrases describe a collection of reactions and orientations which are neither coherent nor explicit, but are born of historical experience and shape how people live in the world.

In Appendix A, I use the notion of structures of feeling to describe the most powerful example of such cultural processes in Argentina: Peronism itself. As I argue there, Peronism is not a party, or a movement; it is a social formation, a whole complex set of relations in which people are deeply implicated. As Raúl's story about receiving toys from the Peróns as a small child suggests (see appendix), these beliefs, sentiments, and convictions are tied both to ideas and to the material conditions of life. The effectiveness of these ideological and material processes explains why the slogans and language of Peronism continued to work in the 1990s. It explains why Peronists turned to Rico more easily than to the Radical Party or why President Menem tried to use the language of Peronism in talking about restructuring by calling it the 'popular market economy.'

Likewise, thinking about the relation between experience, culture, and power begins to suggest some explanations for the persistence of the reflexes and suspicions of the dictatorship era. It may help to explain why, as we saw with the Scilingo case, it took twenty years for military men to begin to talk about what they had done and to question why and how they had done it. Likewise, it may help explain the even more startling fact – that people seemed to be surprised by what Scilingo had to say.

Another pattern Williams and Steedman help us understand is the gendered disposition manifest in the stories of 'valiant ladies' described in chapter 2, and which we have encountered repeatedly in the history of José Ingenieros. As the reader will recall, I take the term from Doña Inés who describes señoras valientes defending their monobloc shortly after the toma, arming themselves with Molotov cocktails and boiling oil. We met them again in the way the (mostly) women of the taller depicted the toma and their efforts to establish a pre-school. The most startling valiant ladies story was undoubtedly the defence of Dr Jorge who, despite local women's efforts, was abducted during the proceso. Anahí's story can be understood in these terms as well, I think. These tales offer clues to how women in José Ingenieros understand their place as active participants who have long been engaged in forging the social world they inhabit. In all the señoras valientes stories, women act as agents, addressing relations of power. They defend their right to a decent life for themselves and their children; they reassert community values; they defend local accomplishments.

The prominence of women in community-oriented activity more recently may suggest that the values, feelings, and ideas – the structure of feeling – that fortified the valiant ladies remain some of the most powerful 'resources of hope' (Williams 1989) in José Ingenieros. To transform this structure of feeling into something more politically salient, such values would need to be effectively mobilized for a new local politics, to inform not just some instances of individual action, but also collective community action.

In the end, what I have tried to tell here is a story of culture and power. I have tried to show how everyday life in communities and neighbourhoods in Argentina and elsewhere are marked, rearranged, and deformed by the larger structural processes that happen at national and international levels. The difference between the past and the present speaks to the weight of history. It speaks to the damage done by repression and neoliberalism. It speaks to the struggles of my friends in José Ingenieros and people like them who are trying to make do and get by in this neoliberal age.

Epilogue

I am writing this epilogue from Buenos Aires in 2001, where I have returned for fieldwork on a new project. The news is full of another *ajuste*. The most recent negotiations with foreign lenders produced loans at credit card rates (between 14 and 16 per cent) (Restivo 2001). A new economic crisis is in full swing. Surprisingly, although Menem[1] was replaced by a centrist coalition (made up mostly of the Radical Party and left Peronists) under President Fernando de la Rúa in 1999, Domingo Cavallo had recently been asked to join this new (and supposedly quite different) government as a 'superminister.' Cavallo's zero deficit plan requires almost universal cuts to state spending to cover any shortfall. The first month of the plan saw an across-the-board 13 per cent cut to almost all state payments (salaries, pensions over $500, and suppliers; interest payments are the exceptions). Percentages are to be recalculated each month according to the new figures. Several general strikes resulted. Coalitions of the unemployed set up demonstrations with roadblocks around the *conurbano*. A *remisero* (car service driver) told us he had picked up a fare on her way back from taking her savings to Uruguay. People congratulate my Argentine husband on having emigrated. Some say they want this new plan to work. Others are convinced Cavallo is lying because he is Cavallo. The media warn of a risk to world markets: 'the tango effect.'

Part of what makes people so depressed about this new *ajuste* is that it is one more setback for a country already experiencing some of the worst economic conditions in living memory. Despite changes in governments and shifts in political orientations, the economic processes I witnessed ten years ago continue. Their cumulative effect is bleak. Statistics for May 2001 show that poverty rates are higher than they were during the 1989–90 bout of hyperinflation. Some four million people, nearly one-third of residents of Gran Buenos Aires, are poor as measured by incomes below the value of the family shopping basket of good and services.[2] For the sector of the *conurbano* known as the second ring and including La Matanza, poverty rates are at an alarming 48.9 per cent. Even more disturbing, the extreme poverty rates, measured by insufficient income to meet caloric needs, constitute a significant part of the recent increase, now totalling 1,247,000 residents of Gran Buenos Aires, more than 10 per cent of the population. More people are underemployed or unemployed. Incomes have fallen and more people are poor.

The spectre of crime and its violent repression also looms larger than it did ten years ago. A new report presented at the Second International Conference on the Construction of Collective Memory, authored by three federal judges and a provincial judge, denounced security forces for systematically torturing detainees in prisons and police stations. They decry the 'generalized, systematic use of torture in all its forms, in investigations and in the treatment of detained people, especially in the Province of Buenos Aires, where there is a situation of state violence that is evidently authoritarian' (Abiad and Torresi 2001). The authors explicitly connect the practices they observed to those of the *proceso*. A related report focusing on the province of Buenos Aires notes a dramatic increase in the populations of police stations: in November 1999, 2,100 prisoners were in police holding cells, in April 2001 the figure had soared to 5,797 (Clarín 2001a). In La Matanza, 'almost every police station houses more than three times its capacity' (Coriolano Report, Resolution 153 in Clarín 2001a). Only forty-five days earlier, new legislation extended police powers, paving the way for further abuses.

Although the facts these recent reports relate are disturbing, their existence, and the context in which they were presented, might be seen as mildly encouraging. That such high-ranking judges are speaking out on these issues, and that they participated in a conference on the construction of collective memory, are both encouraging developments. In a similar vein, the City of Buenos Aires has established a new Memorial Park commemorating the disappeared. The cause of human rights has also been doing better in the courts in recent years. Although a decade ago the recent *indultos* had seemed to end prosecution of military men, there has been a return to the courts for people the press now calls *represores*. Like the more famous incident in which a Spanish court tried to extradite Chilean ex-dictator Augusto Pinochet from Britain, Argentine military men are being sought for trial abroad. Spanish judge Baltazar Garzón requested the detention of forty-eight Argentines for extradition to Spain, including Jorge Rafael Videla, Emilio Massera, Leopoldo Fortunato Galtieri, and Carlos Suárez Mason. Cases are being brought by other foreign courts as well. Although Argentina, like Chile, has refused extradition, these *represores* now find they cannot travel because they are wanted by Interpol. Meanwhile, in Argentina human rights activists have taken advantage of the loopholes in the legislation that halted prosecution in the 1980s. Videla, for example, having been freed by the *indulto*, is again under house arrest (because of poor health) for kidnapping babies of the disappeared; he is also being tried for his participation in Plan Condor, through which the Southern Cone regimes cooperated in the repression of citizens who had fled to neighbouring countries. Massera, already sentenced for kidnapping babies, faces charges for appropriating the property of prisoners of the notorious Naval Mechanics School clandestine detention centre.

La Globalización Insolidaria

The transnational legal proceedings seem to present one its kinder faces, but most people are more concerned with the economic consequences of globalization. In a speech on Argentina's Independence Day, 9 July 2001, Raúl Alfonsín described the country's current woes as partly caused by *la globalización insolidaria*. Although the former president was talking about the large-scale processes which seemed to cut whole sectors of the world's population adrift, the phrase resonated at another level as well. In a conversation a day or two later, a friend, a working-class woman and senior citizen, commented that there was no room for solidarity in today's Argentina. My friend had been cautioning me about how much more dangerous Buenos Aires had become in the last decade. I was warned not to take my daughter to the playground alone because someone might kidnap her. She also told a story about a neighbour who had recently been robbed two weeks in a row on his way home from the bank, the second time in front of his house at midday. Not only had they taken his wallet, money, and credit cards, and driven off in his car, but the thieves had the gall to call the next day offering to sell him back his identification. The discussion of the unfortunate neighbour evoked tales of all sorts of tricks that people used in order to steal from others. People can follow you home from the bank, she explained. You have to be careful because a pregnant woman or an old person or a child can approach you, asking for help only to lure you to his or her associates who will take your money. 'There's no room for solidarity anymore,' she told me, echoing Alfonsín's lament. The 'climate of insecurity,' as it is referred to in the press, is a different kind of fear from that employed by the *proceso*, but it too has its evident antisocial effects.

Developments in José Ingenieros

Meanwhile, José Ingenieros is witness to another globalization effect: a new mall has been built across the street on the land formerly belonging to Regimiento La Tablada. Like other sectors of the state, the army has sold off property to generate income. Instead of a wide green field, the land in front of NHD 17 now holds Auchun, a French-owned hypermarket, some stores, and a food court. Plans for a multiplex cinema are reportedly under way. Easy, a big-box hardware store (similar to Home Depot) faces the *rotonda*, which had already been fixed up and illuminated. Behind the mall, developers are building a '*country*' (Argentines use the English word), a gated community of homes for the middle class. Amid these recent developments, an old rumour resurfaced in José Ingenieros. It was said that the neighbourhood would be razed. Residents were quite worried, and some even went to the provincial capital of La Plata to try to find out if there was any truth in the rumour. They seem to have been satisfied with the assurance that no such plan existed. When I asked why anyone would believe such a thing – razing a neighbourhood of this size is no small undertaking – Anahí told me people believed that the presence of José Ingenieros would be a problem for the developers of the *country* given the neighbourhood's reputation as a haven for delinquents.

Countries, housing developments with special security measures like fencing and private security guards, are a response to the perceived threats posed by the widening gap between rich and poor (Caldeira 1996). In light of the climate of insecurity and of responses to it, people in José Ingenieros believe that their community might be targeted for demolition. When a pair of apartment blocks was demolished in another 'dangerous' neighbourhood, Fuerte Apache in Cuidadela, the rumour became more plausible. Destroyed ostensibly because the deteriorating structures were unsafe, the blocks were also reportedly home to some of the community's most threatening residents.

The development of the Tablada land is indicative of changes in Buenos Aires over the decade since I conducted fieldwork in José Ingenieros. The arrival of large supermarkets, and especially the everything-under-one-roof hypermarkets, and the burgeoning of gated communities (the national newspaper *Clarín* now has a weekly advertising supplement dedicated to *countries*) are both part of larger processes associated with the ongoing socio-economic transformation of Argentina. As elsewhere, malls and hypermarkets are replacing the local shops that characterized most Buenos Aires neighbourhoods until recently. Although the baker, the butcher, and the greengrocer still exist, they now face stiff competition from international concerns. Despite the threat to small local businesses, most residents of José Ingenieros no doubt enjoy the new mall that has popped up on their doorstep; it represents a particular convenience given that one problem for low-income people is that these stores are often accessible only by car.

I was taken aback by the changed landscape of the rotonda La Tablada. Another far more subtle change surprised me as well. The *taller de memoria* mural had been restored recently (see colour plate 2). I asked a friend from the neighbourhood to enquire about who had undertaken the job. She reported that the mural had been restored under a grant from the Provincial Employment Institute, under a program called Buenos Aires Neighbourhoods. Mr Roca, longtime administrator of NHD 18, had submitted a proposal in which restoring this and another mural was part of a larger program that included repairing and maintaining the neighbourhood's public spaces like stairways, gardens, and garbage areas. My friend writes: 'In particular, the mural represents a positive symbol [*un símbolo valorativo*] for the community, and seen from outside it contrasts with that stigma which marks the population: delinquency, violence, drug addiction, etc. Sr Roca commented that the technicians who came from La Plata to evaluate the project admired the work of art which this population has and which is part of the neighbours' patrimony.'

This is all rather unexpected. The beautification project happened in the year 2000, in a country in the throws of a remarkable downsizing of state services. For example, at about the same time, the federal government, having already divested itself of roads, telephones, and trains, was selling off the airports, the postal service, the passport agency, and border controls (so much for the old model of the state). However, 2000 was also the year of a presidential election campaign in a country where people were getting ever more desperate, and increasingly tired of waiting for the drastic reorganization of the economy to achieve its miracle.

Eduardo Duhalde, the governor of Buenos Aires Province and former vice president to Menem, was running for president at a time when his province had an official unemployment rate of around 18 per cent. Plans like Buenos Aires Neighbourhoods were make-work projects trying to take the edge off the state reform agenda. We have seen how this sort of project, helping neighbours clean up, might have been quite persuasive, speaking rather directly to local concerns (although not persuasive enough; Duhalde lost).

Still, the restoration of the mural as part of a larger cleaning up, and its characterization as patrimony, raises some questions of their own. The *repainting* of the mural adds another layer of erasures to those already discussed – erasures involving both the image and the story of its creation. Most striking in the restored mural is the omission of its title: 'This is our neighbourhood. This is our history.' More subtle is the painting out of the names of those who made it. When Roca described the mural to provincial authorities, he associated it with another mural next to it and painted by a youth group in 1988. The authors of the *taller de memoria* mural, as we have seen, were not especially young. They were mainly grandmothers, mothers, and teachers, all associated with the pre-school that was the institutional home of the History Workshop. The idea that the mural was painted by young people somehow downplays it. This idea of the mural as patrimony raises the real unanswered question in all of this: what do people in Jose Ingenieros now think the mural says? The enthusiasm expressed by Roca and the 'technicians from La Plata' may be tied to the mural's attempt to put a positive spin on things. The colours of the original are brighter still in the new version. This optimism was present in the original mural but is played up in Roca's characterization of it. Clearly the original artists wanted to rally people around a positive vision of community, and there is certainly nothing wrong with that. Yet the restoration of the mural raises questions about its political message, reminding us that telling the story is only part of the process.

Meanwhile, other more substantive changes have taken place inside José Ingenieros. NHD 4-5-6 now has running water instead of well water, and NHD 17 is in negotiation with the privatized water company, Aguas Argentinas. A little playground has appeared in *complejo* 17, fruit, my non-Peronist friends tell me, of pre-election efforts by supporters of the current La Matanza Borough president. Other neighbours have started planting trees donated by the government as well. The problem, Anahí tells me, is that they do these things on their own, without the participation of the neighbours. Yet she is not pessimistic either: 'There are always attempts, people trying to do something, people with new projects.' Recently, a new group of young people, all raised in the *barrio*, have taken on the administration of NHD 17. Their predecessors had reportedly appropriated one of the *complejo*'s parking lots, charging 40 or 50 pesos a month for about forty cars, pocketing money themselves rather than using it for the upkeep of the *complejo*. The new administrators are full of ideas and enthusiasm, and, when I spoke to Anahí, had just called a general meeting of the *complejo*'s residents. The neighbourhood's popular democratic tradition refuses to stay buried.

Peronist Identities

Peronism so permeates Argentine culture that anyone who wants to deal with Argentina after 1945 is forced to confront it. In particular, the vast majority of residents of José Ingenieros are Peronists, while the rest bear the stamp of a life spent in their midst. Although an explanation of Peronism as movement, ideology, institution, and party is far too complex to address here, I will try to sketch some crucial elements of what Peronism means for the Peronists I knew in José Ingenieros.

One of Peronism's particular characteristics is the broad spectrum of political positions and social groups that have seen themselves as represented by it. Most Peronists agree, however, that the three main banners of Perón's Peronism were social justice, political sovereignty, and economic independence. Of these, social justice was always the most controversial, although it was also encoded in the party's official name, Partido Justicialista. Both political sovereignty and economic independence were to emerge from the Peronist doctrines known as 'The Third Position' and 'The Organized Community' (Gillespie 1982:17–18).[1] The persistence of these ideas as fundamentals of Peronism is underlined by the extent to which dissident Peronists in the early 1990s concentrated their critiques on President Menem's deviation from them.

The formal structure of Peronism placed Perón at the apex of an organization with three branches (literally *ramas*): political, the party, 'a dispenser of patronage while in office' and responsible for getting Peronist candidates elected (Gillespie 1982:19); feminine, led by Eva Perón; and labour, represented by confederations of Peronist Unions.[2]

Peronism's special qualities as a movement are essential to its role in creating Peronist identities. Gillespie cautions:

Many commentators have been guilty of allowing the problem of how Peronism should be characterized to be dominated exclusively by the controversies over its political and social identity, thus attaching no importance to Peronism's status as a *Movement*. In emphasizing this latter feature, attention is drawn, not only to Peronism's composition, being one of vertically-integrated classes and social-forces, in contrast to the horizontal class base of many parties, but also to the fact that membership was more a question of identification than of affiliation. To be *peronista* did not necessarily imply regular political activity, and formal affiliation procedures, except in the fulfilment of electoral registration requirements, were generally alien to the Movement. Membership in the Movement was generally a question of identification with Perón and with the Argentina of Perón, and, after 1955, not just as a memory of previous golden years but through appreciation of the stark contrast between the past and what ensued: the crises, draconian political and economic measures, and what many saw as a 'surrender to imperialism' of vital areas of economic activity, which characterized the 1955-73 interregnum. (1982:19–20)

To describe an Argentine as Peronist is not merely, perhaps not even chiefly, to describe his or her political or party affiliation. To many working-class Argentines Peronism is a deeply felt identity. It is, or at least has been until now, an identity that transcends the vagaries of daily politics and specific issues.

'El peronismo es un sentimiento'?

Gillespie, who powerfully details the fate of the Peronist guerrilla organization Montoneros, goes further than most in addressing the particular relation of the 'Peronist masses' to Peronism. In general, however, the meaning of Peronism for working-class people in Argentina has received little of the academic attention lavished on Peronism as a whole. Three notable exceptions are Julie Taylor's *Eva Perón: The Myths of a Woman* (1979), Daniel James's *Resistance and Integration* (1988),[3] and Javier Auyero's *Poor People's Politics: Peronist Survival Networks and the Legacy of Evita* (2000). It is hardly coincidental that these authors find themselves deconstructing the popular and academic romanticizations and demonizations of the Peronist working class. As James puts it, 'the working class is present in [writing on modern Argentine history]; political reality and the nature of the dominant

Argentine political and intellectual discourse clearly compel such a presence. Yet this presence has a certain unreality about it. The working class usually appears as a cipher, almost an ideal construct at the service of different ideological paradigms. The essence of these abstractions derives from broader notions concerning the relationship of workers and Peronism' (1988:2). James's book is about the Peronist union movement and its relation to the rank and file between 1946 and 1976, but the argument can be made for the Peronist masses in general. That is, not just the highly organized workers who have been sometimes called the Argentine 'labour aristocracy' because of their relative privilege and collective power, but also other sectors of the working poor and of the lower middle class who have tended to be vehemently Peronist.

Julie Taylor made a similar discovery in her examination of the myths of Eva Perón. Despite the widely held belief that the Argentine working class had sanctified or mythologized Perón's charismatic and powerful second wife, Taylor found little evidence of this. Her working-class informants, she notes, 'summarily dismissed versions of the myth which, according to newspapers, pamphlets, texts and books, they were supposed to have generated. The talk would turn quickly away from the saint and Madonna and return to the concrete benefits Eva had provided. On only one element was there agreement: to do what she had done, Eva had made great personal sacrifices. Yet while they admired this sacrifice, it did not take on the religious aura of martyrdom' (1979:4).

That said, one must also note that one cliché of Argentine political life is the saying *el peronismo es un sentimiento* (Peronism is a feeling). Some Peronists are offended by this phrase because it suggests that their Peronism is an irrational belief. Beto, for example, a longtime Peronist militant resident in José Ingenieros, rejected this characterization when I suggested it:

That's not really how it is. It's living it, and by living it you teach. You don't need to read a book and repeat what a book says, you have to practise it. So, I tell you, it's not a feeling, right? It's a conviction, and coherent, and from the moment [you understand this], you put it into practice ... Because things were good. We had work. Money was worth something ... The system ... the government of Perón gave me what I wanted. That's really something. You look at history from Perón all the way back, it never happened before – [no one] gave the humble people what they wanted, they never participated. That's why I repeat that it's not a feeling. Whoever says that it's a feeling is putting it badly I think, as a Peronist.

As Beto makes clear, Peronists' profound commitment to the movement is an artifact of material social processes by which Peronism brought fundamental change to the lives of working people. Concrete gains in the standard of living and material conditions of working-class Argentines were accompanied by a profound shift in what it meant to be a worker.

Perón's Argentina

Perón's rise to power was associated with the enormous growth of the urban working class. The industrial workforce that in Argentina was 436,000 in 1935 had more than doubled to 1,057,000 by the time Perón was elected in 1946 (James 1988:8). The shift from international to internal migrants was also crucial; rapid industrial expansion had attracted 1.1 million migrants from the interior to Gran Buenos Aires between 1935 and 1947 (Rock 1993:198). Despite this industrialization, real wages declined.[4] New immigrants were left to confront the problems of relocation without the help of the state so that in 1937, for example, 60 per cent of working-class families lived in only one room (James 1988:8). Throughout this period the labour movement was divided and weak.

After the coup in 1943, Perón as secretary of labour addressed some basic needs of the working class. The extent of their support for him was dramatized in the events of 17 October 1945 when thousands of workers marched into downtown Buenos Aires demanding, and achieving, Perón's release from confinement. He then ran for and won the presidency.[5]

In material terms the working class fared well under Perón's two presidencies. In 1945 the Law of Professional Associations introduced a global system of collective bargaining. Unionization grew, from 30.5 per cent of the wage-earning population in 1948 to 42.5 per cent in 1954. By Perón's second presidency (1951–5) the unions were used to incorporate the working class into the state. Although this meant a high degree of state control, its advantages were considerable from the point of view of organized labour: an extensive social welfare system (under the Ministry of Social Welfare, the Foundation Eva Perón, and the unions themselves); labour leaders gained a great deal of power and prestige; and there were undeniable concrete gains for the working class.

Between 1946 and 1949 real wages rose by 53 per cent. Perhaps more telling, national wages increased appreciably as a share of national income.[6] As James notes, 'together these factors managed to give the Argentine working class and its labour movement a weight within the wider national community which was unparalleled in Latin America' (1988:12). Indirect wages and the quality of life for working-class people also improved. Advances included free and obligatory education, health coverage or free medical attention in public hospitals, public housing, extension of the pension plan, family allowance, and indemnification for wrongful dismissal (Torrado 1992:412).[7]

Perón also moved to address the housing crisis. Some half a million new homes were built during Perón's administration, most of them low-cost workers' apartments. The rate of new construction per capita in the early 1950s (8.4 units per 1,000) placed Argentina among the world's highest. Schools, hospitals, clinics, and recreational facilities were also built (Rock 1987:263). One such neighbourhood was Ciudad Evita, the subdivision of single-family bungalows that borders José Ingenieros to the south.[8] The contrast between the quality of worker housing represented by these pretty homes and those of the *monoblocs* would be reason enough for nostalgia.

As important as these facts are in engendering working-class support for Peronism, less tangible and less quantifiable changes may be just as important for people's long-term commitment. James has developed this argument with respect to the rank-and-file members of the Peronist unions. He argues convincingly that Peronism was 'a political movement which represented a crucial shift in working-class politics and behaviour, and which presented its adherents with a distinct political vision' (1988:14). This vision included a critique of the old ways of doing politics in Argentina, especially the corruption of the *década infame*. It incorporated elements of the Argentine nationalist tradition. It also recast citizenship, which is the significant constitutive membership in the nation, so that it implied the inclusion of the working class. One strength of Peronist discourse was its acceptance of working-class people for what they were. In this it contrasted with the left traditions that often conveyed a note of condescension. James argues that Peronism 'took working-class consciousness, habits, life styles and values as it found them and affirmed their sufficiency and value. It glorified the everyday and the ordinary as a sufficient basis for the rapid attainment of a juster society, provided that certain easily achievable and self-evident goals were met' (1988:22). These conditions were that workers continue to support Perón and maintain a strong union movement. The Peronist vision may have been more popular, and more credible, precisely because it was *not* revolutionary. It operated within a sense of limits. As early as 1945, *'Perón cumple'* (roughly, Perón delivers) was a central slogan of Peronist politics.

Another important part of Peronism's attraction for working-class people came from the 'heretical social power' it expressed. Inversions of the traditional Argentine social order are central images in both Peronist and anti-Peronist understandings of the movement. One inversion was Eva Perón's affectionate use of the term *cabecita negra*, referred to in the introduction. The date of 17 October 1945 is another lasting image, when a flood of working-class people penetrated the very heart of Buenos Aires in defence of Perón. The fact that after their long march into the capital many sat with their feet in the formal fountains of the Plaza de Mayo, the symbolic centre of the nation, stands etched in the national memory as a defining moment of Peronism (Torre 1995).

Working-class Identities

The redefinition of what it meant to be working class is a significant part of Peronism's attraction for those who remember what things were like before. The stories of residents of José Ingenieros show the radical shift Peronism implied for their identities. They recount the pride they felt as people like them became socially significant. They saw their experience acknowledged, expressed, and valued.

Separating the economic benefits of Peronism from these less tangible ones is difficult. Raúl struggled to explain to me the place Peronism occupied in his life. In the process he conveyed something of the emotional impact of material goods. He remembered his own childhood:

All the children would go to pick up their toys. They gave them out in the post office. They gave out toys all over. That's something that really stays with you. I was born in 1939 which was really a difficult time, and these were the first toys I ever had. There was no money to buy a child a toy. There were times when we didn't have shoes to wear. We did have shoes to wear to school, but we had to take them off when we got home [so as not to wear them out]. We had to go barefoot. One really remembers those

things. That's why we have always fought for Peronism. Because Peronism always struggled for social justice, which is something that doesn't
exist today.

The high-quality toys, distributed to all children, were not the only
way that children benefited from the Peronist state. There were more
practical gifts as well: higher wages for their parents and a broader
social net; the incorporation of Argentines into the educational system
which reached its all-time high, with primary education achieving near
total coverage (Torrado 1992:412).

Carolyn Steedman, speaking of a 1950s English childhood, argues
the importance of such gifts from the welfare state to a poor child's
sense of social significance and of self. Of her own experience she
writes:

> The 1950s was a time when state intervention in children's lives was
> highly visible, and experienced, by me at least, as entirely beneficent ... I
> think I would be a very different person now if orange juice and milk and
> dinners at school hadn't told me, in a covert way, that I had a right to
> exist, was worth something. My inheritance from those years is the belief
> (maintained with some difficulty) that I do have a right on this earth.
> Being a child when the state was practically engaged in making children
> healthy and literate was a support against my own circumstances, so I
> find it difficult to match an account of the welfare policies of the late
> 1940s, which calls the 'post-War Labour government ... the last and most
> glorious flowering of late Victorian liberal philanthropy,' which I know to
> be historically correct, with the sense of self that those policies imparted.
> If it had been only philanthropy, would it have felt like it did? Psychic
> structures are shaped by these huge historical labels: 'charity,' 'philan-
> thropy,' 'state intervention.' (1986:122)

Such gifts as the toys and shoes Raúl remembers so warmly can
become the very stuff of a child's understanding of himself and his
place in the world.

In Argentina, adults received even more important gifts, including
sewing machines or a house. Such gifts would have dramatically
altered the quality of life for whole families.[9] By giving women sewing
machines, Eva Perón's Foundation gave women greater control over
their own productive labour.[10] The introduction of female suffrage in
1949 was another important way in which women's character as citi-

zens was recognized and transformed. All these material changes in the everyday lives of working people did indeed create new feelings that, as generations of anti-Peronists have learned, one underestimates at one's peril. Even Perón, some have argued, struggled to control them.[11]

When people spoke of Peronism, I was constantly reminded of Raymond Williams's concept of structures of feeling. The lived experience of the Peronist period, especially by contrast to those before and after it, seemed to engender a kind of practical consciousness whose processes were akin to the one Raymond Williams describes. Beto (the militant quoted above) resists the word 'feeling' for its negative implications, but Williams's notion of feeling is neither irrational nor mystical. It is a conviction, as Beto argued, born of concrete, historical experience. Williams writes:

> The term [structures of feeling] is difficult, but 'feeling' is chosen to emphasize a distinction from more formal concepts of 'world-view' or 'ideology.' It is not only that we must go beyond formally held and systematic beliefs, though of course we have always to include them. It is that we are concerned with meanings and values as they are actively lived and felt, and the relations between these and formal or systematic beliefs are in practice variable (including historically variable), over a range from formal assent with private dissent to the more nuanced interaction between selected and interpreted beliefs and acted and justified experiences ... We are talking about characteristic elements of impulse, restraint, and tone: specifically affective elements of consciousness and relationships: not feeling against thought, but thought as felt and feeling as thought; practical consciousness of a present kind, in a living and interrelating continuity. (1977:132)

It is difficult to convey the passion and visceral quality of the Peronist conviction. One story I heard illustrates this passion. My friend's father had suffered a heart attack and later died, so moved was he to hear a recording of Eva Perón's last speech on the radio on the twenty-first anniversary of her death. He had not heard her voice in the eighteen years since Peronism had been banned.

Javier Auyero's *Poor People's Politics* (2000) is another study that pays careful attention to the actual practices of a particular sector of the Peronist masses. Auyero's ethnography of a Buenos Aires shanty town in the mid 1990s focuses on Peronist survival networks, in particular, clientelism. Auyero argues that Peronism is not what it once was, that it no longer occupies as central a place in the common sense of the destitute *villeros* he knew. He does however, like James (1988), use Williams's notion of structures of feeling to think about Peronist practice (2000).

Of course, Peronism and what Williams describes are different. Structures of feeling are emergent, inchoate, not yet realized. Peronism, on the other hand, has made such feelings its stock and trade, although no less real or potent for being sanctioned. The official ideology of Peronism may also have taken on greater potency because of its many years underground. As Auyero puts it, 'to be blunt, if in the 1940s Peronism offered a "heretical" (i.e., heterodoxical) reading of social relations of hierarchy and domination embedded in clientelist relation, today the official reading of Peronism reinforces and justifies personalized political mediation as a way of solving everyday problems. From being a heresy (a contestation of, among other things, clientelist arrangements), Peronism has become the orthodoxy (a justification of these institutionalized practices)' (2000:196). Perhaps we can think of Peronism as a sort of institutionalized structure of feeling.

The Menem years, yet again, elicited predictions of the demise of Peronism. For many observers, the politics and policies of Menem's presidency as a Peronist imperiled the future prospects of the party because of the gap between the policies he espoused as a candidate and those he has pursued in office. Yet Peronism survived almost eighteen years of prohibition and the death of its leader. It has proven remarkably flexible and resilient. The Peronist past will undoubtedly continue to shape Argentine political culture for some time.

Appendix B

Chronology

Juan Domingo Perón's first and second presidencies	1946–55
Perón overthrown	19 September 1955
General Eduardo Lonardi becomes president following coup	23 September 1955
Peronism outlawed	6 April 1955
Series of coups	1955–66
General Juan Carlos Onganía leads military coup	28 June 1966
Onganía takes office as president	29 June 1966
PEVE begins	1968
El Cordobazo	29–30 May 1969
General Alejandro Agustín Lanusse becomes president following coup	26 March 1971
Héctor J. Cámpora wins presidential elections	11 March 1973
Cámpora inaugurated	25 May 1973
Toma in José Ingenieros	May–June 1973
Perón returns (Ezeiza)	20 June 1973
Perón wins presidential elections	23 September 1973
Perón inaugurated	12 October 1973
Perón dies; María Estela de Perón (Isabel) becomes president by decree	1 July 1974
Inflation, social and economic upheaval	1974–6
General Jorge Rafael Videla becomes president through coup; he is also member of the ruling junta with Admiral Eduardo Emilio Massera and Brigadier General Orlando Ramón Agosti; *el proceso* begins	24 March 1976

NHD 17 kidnappings	24 March 1976
Allanamientos begin in José Ingenieros	1977
José Ingenieros passes from federal to provincial jurisdiction early	1978
José Ingenieros assigned a military administrator	mid-1978
Mass for Cirila Benítez	3 or 4 April 1978
Kidnappings of doctors and neighbourhood leaders in José Ingenieros	5 April 1978
Economic crisis escalates	1980
José Ingenieros returns to administration by residents' commissions	December 1980
General Roberto Viola succeeds Videla as president	29 March 1981
General Leopoldo succeeds Viola as president	22 December 1981
Malvinas (Falklands) War	2 April–14 June 1982
General (Ret.) Reynaldo B. Bignone becomes president	1 July 1982
Raúl Alfonsín wins presidential elections	30 October 1983
Alfonsín inaugurated; end of *el proceso*	10 December 1983
CONADEP report (later published as *Nunca Mas*) presented to Alfonsín	September 1984
Trials of the ex-commanders of the *proceso*	1985
Alfonsín attempts to introduce Obediencia Debida legislation	April 1986
Punto Final legislation passed	23 December 1986
Punto Final closing date	23 February 1987
Semana Santa uprising	14–19 April 1987
Obediencia Debida legislation passed	4 June 1987
Monte Caseros uprising	January 1988
Villa Martelli uprising	November–December 1988
MTP takeover of La Tablada	23 January 1989
Saqueos (food riots)	May 1989
Carlos Saúl Menem wins presidential elections	15 May 1989
Menem inaugurated	8 July 1989
First set of *indultos*	8 October 1989
Carapintada uprising	3 December 1990
Second set of *indultos*	29 December 1990

Glossary

AAA (Alianza Argentina Anticomunista)   Argentine Anticommunist Alliance
adjudicado/a   person assigned an apartment in José Ingenieros under PEVE
ajuste   adjustment (as in structural adjustment policies)
allanamiento ˌ search and seizure operation
aperturista   with respect to the economy, a strategy which opens it to foreign investment
asado   barbecue
asentamiento   organized squatter settlement
Asociación Vecinal Pro-policía   Neighbours' Pro-Police Association

Banco Hipotecario de la Nación   National Mortgage Bank
barrio   neighbourhood
blanqueado/a   passed to official status from clandestine detention; literally whitened

CAF (Centro de Acción Familiar)   Family Action Centre
calefón   water heater
Capital Federal   central Buenos Aires; federal capital
carapintada   group of rebellious junior officers; literally 'painted face'
carbonero   charcoal seller
carenciado   needy
Casa Rosada   presidential palace; literally 'pink house'
CdeO (Comando de Organización)   An armed Peronist Organization
CEC (Centro Educativo Complementario)   Complementary Educational Centre
CEDES (Centro de Estudio de Estado y Sociedad)   Centre for the Study of the State and Society

CELS (Centro de Estudios Legales y Sociales) Center for Legal and Social Studies

CGT (Confederación General de Trabajo) General Labor Confederation

changas odd jobs, such as performed by a handyman

CISP (Comitato Internazionale per lo Sviluppo dei Popoli) International Committee for Popular Development

CODESEDH (Comité para Defensa de la Salud, la Ética Profesional, y los Derecho Humanos) Committee for the Defence of Health, Professional Ethics, and Human Rights

comisaría police station

comisión vecinal neighbours' council

complejo housing complex

compra cooperativa buying coop

CONADEP (Comisión Nacional sobre la Desaparación de Personas) National Commission on Disappeared People

CONASE (Consejo Nacional de Seguridad) National Security Council

conurbano boroughs of metropolitan Buenos Aires, exclusive of federal capital

copamineto occupation

Cordobazo, El the uprising in Córdoba in 1969

desarollo, desarollista development, developmentalist

dos demonios two demons; describes the violence of the 1970s as a conflict between left and right

ERP (Ejército Revolucionario del Pueblo) Revolutionary People's Army

estafa rip-off

feria market

FONAVI (Fondo Nacional de Vivienda) National Housing Fund

gnocchi a person who receives pay for a job at which he or she does not work because of political connections; literally an Italian potato dumpling

Gran Buenos Aires Greater Buenos Aires; also *conurbano*

grupo de tarea work group; in the context of the repression, refers to groups which abducted people

guerra sucia dirty war; used to refer to dictatorship of 1976–82

indulto   pardon
Instituto de la Vivienda de Provincia   Provincial Housing Institute
intruso/a   squatter

Jardín de Infantes (jardín)   preschool
JP (Juventud Peronista)   Peronist Youth
juicio   trial
junta vecinal   neighbourhood council

lavadero   clothes-washing area
ley de obedencia debida   due obedience law

Madres de Plaza de Mayo   Mothers of the Plaza de Mayo; Mothers of
   the Disappeared; in the early 1990s Las Madres were divided into
   two groups: Linea Bonafini and Linea Fundadora
Malvinas   Falkland Islands
MAS (Movimiento al Socialismo)   Movement toward Socialism
maté, maté cocido   a tea-like drink consumed in the Southern Cone
mestizaje   cultural mixture, usually of indigenous and European
   cultural groups
militante   activist, party member
Ministerio de Bienestar Social   Social Welfare Ministry
MODIN (Movimiento por la Dignidad y la Independencia)
   Movement for Dignity and Independence
monobloc   apartment block
Montoneros, Montos   a Peronist guerrilla organization
MTP (Movimiento Todos por la Patria)   Everyone for the Fatherland
   Movement

negro/a   dark-skinned person, usually assumed to be poor and from
   the interior; literally black
NHD (Núcleo Habitacional Definitivo)   Definitive Residential
   Nucleus
NHT (Núcleo Habitacional Transitorio)   Transitional Residential
   Nucleus

obra social   organization operated by unions, providing social services such as health care to union members
olla popular   soup kitchen
operador/a **social**   social operator; social worker, but without the professional connotation

PAN (Plan de Alimentación Nacional)   National Food Plan
PC (Partido Comunista)   Communist Party
PCR (Partido Comunista Revolucionario)   Revolutionary Communist Party
PEN (Poder Ejecutivo Nacional)   National Executive Power; allowed the military to hold political prisoners for an indefinite time
Peronismo de Base   literally Base Peronism
PEVE (Plan de la Eradicacion de Villas de Emergencia en Capital Federal y Gran Buenos Aires)   Plan for the Eradication of Shanty Towns
pintada política   political grafitti painted very large
PJ (Partido Justicialista)   Peronist Party
PO (Partido Obrero)   Workers' Party
población de alto riesgo   high-risk population
porteño/a   resident of Buenos Aires
Proceso de Reorganización Nacional (*el proceso*)   Process of National Reorganization
promoción social   social promotion; social work, but without the professional connotation
proyecto de salud   health project
puntero/a político/a   political operator; political
Punto Final   final stop law; put an end to further prosecution of military, with some exceptions

quinela   illicit lottery
quinelero/a   person who runs the *quinela*; numbers runner

salita   clinic
saqueo   looting
Semana Santa   Easter week; holy week

taller   workshop
tallerista   workshop participant
toma   squatter occupation

UCR (Union Cívica Radical)   the Radical Party
unidad básica   local Peronist political office

villa, villa miseria, villa de emergencia   shanty town
villero/a   shanty town resident
viviendas transitorias   transitional housing; see NHT

Notes

Chapter 1

1 The neighbourhood is sometimes officially known as José Ingenieros II, to distinguish it from another with the same name. It probably acquired its name because of the eponymous train station nearby. The man himself (1877–1925), was 'the most eminent of Argentine positivists,' a sociologist who applied 'Spencerian social Darwinism' to Argentine history (Hale 1986:406–7). Ingenieros was also a committed and active socialist until about 1903.

2 The exact number of apartments is unknown. Although there were originally 2,493, the number increased because squatters continued to occupy available spaces. INDEC, the Argentine census bureau, kindly provided me with population and household census data. The census fractions match the boundaries of José Ingenieros. The 1991 INDEC data cover 2,782 households. The discrepancy between this figure and 2,493 may be explained by additional squatters, but it may also represent a small amount of slippage between the census fractions and the physical boundary of the neighbourhood. The precise population figure for 1991 is 11,698. All subsequent INDEC figures for José Ingenieros come from this same data set.

3 The term *porteño* refers to the residents of Capital Federal, the central part of Buenos Aires city, a port city.

4 An exception here is Alejandro Isla's article (1998) which undertakes a similar examination for Tucumán, Argentina.

5 This liberal view is powerfully and persuasively represented in the film *The Official Story* (Puenzo 1985), for example. For a discussion of the particular kinds of questions that anthropology raises about human rights see Wilson (1997).

6 Authors such as Asad (1993), following Foucault in part, emphasize that discourses are located in speech but also crucially in practices which represent and embody relations of power. Indeed, the Popular Memory Group, which popularized the term in English having borrowed it from Foucault, are thoroughly Marxian historians. They note that Foucault finally abandoned the term popular memory (Popular Memory Group 1982:218).

7 There is an enormous literature on the Holocaust, but four compelling and very different examples are Lantzmann's documentary *Shoah* (1986); Spiegelman's Pulitzer Prize–winning comic books *Maus* (1986, 1991); the volume edited by Passerini, *Memory and Totalitarianism* (1992); and Felman and Laub's *Testimony* (1992).

8 The widely used 'dirty war,' on the other hand, suggests violence run amok rather than the systematic exercise of violence as one of several strategies of social control on the part of the state.

9 Key texts in this 'rapprochement' (Ortner 1984) are Rosaldo 1980, Sahlins 1985, Price 1983, Fabian 1983, Taussig 1980. Wolf's *Europe and the People without History* (1982) figures prominently here, but is really embedded in the longer tradition of anthropological political economy. Among the most prominent of a much longer list are: Wolf 1959, 1969; Mintz 1974 [1960], 1985; Nash 1979. For treatments of the history of this connection, see especially Roseberry (1991) and Vincent (1990). This discussion seems to be back again more recently, see Sider and Smith (1997) and the debates in *Radical History* (Sider 1996b, 1996c, Buhle 1996, Cameron 1996, Stansell 1996), and *Focaal* (Kalb, Marks, and Tak 1996, Sider 1996a, Marks 1996).

Chapter 2

1 *Villa* properly means town or village, but the term is regularly used as the short form for the more cumbersome Argentine terms for shanty town: *villa de emergencia* (emergency settlement) or the more critical *villa de miseria* (town of misery).

2 A debate among field workers about how to identify the places and people they describe is ongoing. Some argue that changing names and identifying characteristics protects only the researcher from those who would question her or his findings since people in the communities where we work know to whom we speak. On the other hand, there are a few sobering stories of published ethnographic material being used by authorities to identify dissidents. People in José Ingenieros also had differing opinions on the matter. Few felt strongly about the question, but I was not always convinced that they understood exactly how I, or others, might use their stories. One polit-

ically active interviewee helped make up my mind. He suggested that although people in the know could often figure out who was being referred to, a pseudonym gave him the option of denying that the words quoted were his. On a 1994 visit I asked some of the key characters if they would like to pick names for themselves. When they chose names, I have used them here.

3 The youngsters include some born the year before the *toma* because of how the census data is grouped. However, descriptions of the *toma* indicate that squatters were already living in Buenos Aires by the time of the *toma* in 1973. Very young children would have been born in Buenos Aires, even if their parents were recent migrants.

4 The *hornero* is the name of a bird typical of the Argentine pampa and also of its distinctive nest made of sticks and clay. The bird is thought to be industrious, and its nest secure.

5 *Maté* is a beverage which is a strong marker of regional identity, shared particularly by those from Argentina and Uruguay, but also enjoyed in Paraguay, Brazil, and Chile with slight regional variations in the particulars of the ritual. In Argentina one fills the gourd three-quarters full with the *yerba* (literally herb, the highly caffeinated leaves employed), and then pours very hot water on top. One drinks *maté* through a metal straw, either sweet or bitter. In José Ingenieros people usually drank it sweet; I suspect this is a marker of social class, echoing Mintz's discussion of tea and sugar as food for the poor (1985:148ff.). Ideally, *maté* is drunk in a group; one person serves and the gourd is passed around. It thus connotes and even facilitates sociability.

6 Diego Maradona is the world-famous Argentine soccer player whose humble origins in a Buenos Aires *villa* and unparalleled ball-handling skills made him a national hero.

7 One woman told me she had masses of papers accumulated over the years, but would not allow me to look at them.

8 Some of the old debates in anthropology counterposed synchronic approaches to the study of culture which aimed for the fullest possible description at a particular moment in time, with a diachronic approach which focused on change over time.

9 This becomes a particular concern when people are ill and need to get to hospital.

10 These questions about identity and stigma resonate with those raised by Gregory for Lefrak City, Queens, New York, in an article evocatively titled 'Race, Rubbish and Resistance' (1994).

11 This low figure may be misleading. One imagines that people with univer-

sity degrees are more likely to have the economic means to leave the neighbourhood.

12 Literacy rates are very high in Argentina, especially in the cities, the legacy of the massive expansion of educational institutions in the Peronist era.

13 All the *complejos* identify apartments by a series of numbers and letters, although the units differ somewhat from one to the next. In 4-5-6, an address includes: apartment number, column number (1 or 2) and complex number. Residents use other clues to locate or place people. In response to a question about where someone lived, people said things like: 'in the yellow *monobloc*, in front of 7, where Antonio lives.'

14 There was no supermarket and only one store offered general grocery shopping.

15 While I was in the neighbourhood, the drugs which seemed to be circulating were cocaine (injected), marijuana, amphetamines, and barbituates. Glue sniffing was also a concern.

16 This was possible because the eduational system permitted independent schools to collect subsidies from the government and charge parents an additional fee; some of these schools had scholarships for needy children. On the other hand, the condition of the public schools worsened daily; they were painfully under-funded, and assailed by constant teachers' strikes.

17 The neighbourhood falls under the jurisdiction of the Municipalidad de La Matanza which is the name for the government of the Partido de La Matanza.

18 The low profile of the church may have been related to the current lack of a conveniently located church with sympathetic clergy.

19 The growth of evangelical and fundamentalist churches appears to be generalized in poorer sectors of Argentine society in recent years (Stoll 1990).

20 Each party has its own name for the places from which on-the-ground political work is carried out.

21 In José Ingenieros people were conscious of the attempts of politicians to manipulate them. Accustomed to getting what they could from the patronage system, people were capable of taking the goods without delivering the votes if they thought they could get away with it. For an ethnographic account of Peronist patronage in a Buenos Aires *villa*, see Auyero's *Poor People's Politics* (2000). Auyero demonstrates that clientelism is a much more complex and subtle process than most academic and journalistic accounts suggest.

22 For a more sustained discussion of politics and gender in José Ingenieros, see DuBois (1999).

23 Men represented 49.3 per cent of the population. Also surprising, women headed only 23 per cent of households in 1991.

24 As noted, there were local institutions that tried to pick up the slack for many families which were unable to schedule their days for the half-day system.

25 Las Madres have deservedly attracted considerable attention (cf. Diago 1988, Feijoó and Nari 1994, Fisher 1989, Navarro 1989, Oria 1987). They themselves publish and have a web page.

26 I met my husband, Daniel, through a friend who lived in José Ingenieros. Daniel was an outsider, however. When I started seeing him seriously, I consulted an older woman friend about the etiquette. Would it sully my reputation in the neighbourhood, I asked? 'Quite the contrary,' replied my friend, perhaps jokingly.

Chapter 3

1 By 1980 this figure was back down to 4 per cent (Yujnovsky 1984:334–64).

2 In practice, according to social workers involved, priority was given to flood-prone *villas* and *villas* which stood in the path of public works projects (shanty towns often spring up on public land). Some municipalities also exerted extra pressure to have their shanty towns removed.

3 The city of Buenos Aires has a special political status like that of Washington DC, thus the part of the project which addressed the central city fell under a distinct jurisdiction, and a separate administration.

4 The Federación de Villas y Barrios de Emergencia de la Capital (Federation of Shanty Towns of the Capital) was founded in 1958 and was associated with the Communist Party. The Frente Villero replaced the federation in 1972 and was later united with the Movimiento Villero Peronista (Peronist Shanty Town Dwellers' Movement) (Davolos et al. 1987: 21).

5 During the *proceso*, state agents also engaged in systematic attempts to eliminate *villas*. Violent, large-scale removals took place, this time without any alternate housing (Bellardi and De Paula 1986). In the early 1990s security forces and the police continued to see the *villas* as almost impenetrable.

6 People who had been on the administrative side of this process told me they had no good censuses of *villas* in La Matanza because the population was too transient to collect reliable data.

7 One study says some of the foreigners living in the *villas* were excluded (Davolos et al. 1987:23). Social workers involved in PEVE at the time disagree. They say that PEVE was different from FONAVI projects (Fondo Nacional de la Vivienda, the largest public housing agency) in that

FONAVI required the head of household to be naturalized, while PEVE did not. Some residents believe that there were also political biases penalizing those thought to be likely dissidents.

8 One wonders about the motivation for this change. Former residents of the *barrios transitorios* saw the time requirement as tied to a project of resocialization. Given delays in construction, it seems likely that it may also have been a bureaucratic way of slowing the process.

9 A radical Argentine architecture magazine, *Summa*, published at least three articles on designs for José Ingenieros (1971, 1973a, 1973b). Those calling for a new emphasis on the social content of architecture found merit in these designs.

10 According to the authors of a study on the *Villa 7* project (Davolos et al. 1987), preserving the existing community was a priority. Inclusion of all community members was considered essential as was the location of the new housing close to the original site. Planners, including both professionals and community members, considered the economic conditions of residents as well. Thus the construction was devised and executed to provide work for unemployed residents. In addition, payment plans were negotiated within the community so that those most able to pay were persuaded to take a ten-year instalment plan instead of the maximum thirty years (Davolos et al. 1987:37–43).

11 Throughout part one of this book I have relied on several authoritative accounts of the period. For general histories of the post-Peronist period, I especially depend on Rock (1987), Torre and Riz (1993), Graham-Yooll (1989), Cavorozzi (1992), and Andersen (1993). For economic history Torrado (1992) is especially important. On organized Peronist workers James (1988) is central.

12 Although Perón was not elected until 1946, Torrado uses 1945, when his rise to power was well under way, as the beginning of this period.

13 The gaps between the strategies, Torrado argues, point to moments when no clear economic scheme was in place. The third Peronist government, for example, did not change the socio-economic structure. Torrado also notes the considerable inertia inherent in shifts between strategies (1992:51).

14 Import substitution focused industrialization efforts on producing domestic products to replace foreign imports.

15 It was a hope only partly realized with Perón's short third presidency (12 October 1973 to 1 July 1974). The sense of unfulfilled promise may help to explain the extraordinary place that Evita continues to hold for Argentines today. She died of cancer on 26 July 1952. Perón remarried in exile. His new

wife, María Estela (known as Isabel), served as his vice president, becoming president on his death. I have heard Perón extolled, only to have the speaker stop and specify, 'That is Perón with Evita.'

16 From 17 November to 14 December 1972.

17 James suggests that guerilla organizations increased in importance, partly in response to the flagging of other pockets of resistance in the early 1960s, and the displacement of the most militant union activists and leaders by accommodationist union bureaucracies (1988:210).

18 In hospitals, for example, people attempted to invent a new form of collective management in which decisions (including treatment decisions) were made in committees made up of doctors, nurses, hospital staff (including cleaning staff), patients, and patients' relatives (Ernesto Jauretche, personal communication).

19 In 1973 reports appear in the large circulation newspapers *Crónica* (1973a, 1973b, 1973c, 1973d, 1973e, 1973f, 1973g, 1973h, 1973i, 1973j), *Clarín* (1973a, 1973b, 1973c, 1973d), and *La Nación* (1973a, 1973b, 1973c, 1973d).

20 These are all oral accounts. I sometimes found informants unreliable on dates, so whenever possible tried to confirm such information by asking how they related to memorable events of national importance like the massacre at Ezeiza or the period of Lanusse or Cámpora's presidency (26 March 1971 to 24 May 1973, and 25 May to 13 July 1973, respectively).

21 The neighbourhood has undergone a series of name changes with successive governments because of the political connotations of the various appellations. This is especially marked because the *monoblocs* are often referred to as part of Ciudad Evita.

22 According to a communique quoted in this article, a *'Zona de Emergencia'* had been declared. The army would carry out evictions in La Matanza, Belgrano, Ramos Mejía, Ciudadela, 'and others.' These are all *partidos* (roughly, boroughs) of Gran Buenos Aires.

23 Press reports cannot be assumed to be entirely accurate since errors suggest confusion about the particulars of these events.

24 When Susana says that they built a house, she probably means that they did it themselves, not that they had it built for them.

25 Here Susana uses the term *vivienda digna* which resonates with Peronist discourse on the essential rights of the worker.

26 This is not as improbable as it may seem to the North American reader, since government housing was a benefit quite often accorded to public employees of all types.

27 The generous lease agreements eventually accorded the *intrusos* stipulated that the apartment could not be resold until eight years had elapsed.

28 For example, a four-bedroom apartment in NHD 17 sold for about $9,000 US in 1992.

29 Most literature which tries to address these processes looks at particular organizations, and much of it is testimonial. Of the more analytic writing, the most authoritative is an account of the *Montoneros* (with useful information on the armed Peronist organizations active throughout this period), Gillespie's *Soldiers of Perón* (1982). See also Luvecce's study of *Peronismo de Base* (1993).

30 Rulli's story also demonstrates how occupations came to be seen as a strategy in political disputes. Having discovered that he would not be assigned a position he had been promised as the head of the Office of Culture [Dirección de la Cultura] in the new Peronist government, Rulli decided to take it by occupying the building (Anzorena 1989:191).

31 In 1973 it would have been particularly difficult to disentangle the Juventud Peronista from the Montoneros, since they were essentially parallel organizations at the time, Montoneros being the military organization whose members also constituted the hierarchy of the JP (Gillespie 1982, Anzorena 1989).

32 Given the nature of the moment, there were probably more organizations present, but these are mentioned repeatedly by residents.

33 Note José's conviction that every family had a right to own its own housing. Without rent control regulations, renters are vulnerable. Realtors generally charge a one-month fee annually, and rents can increase exponentially from lease to lease. Although landlords complain that eviction is a slow process, the fact that the laws are largely in their favour and the instability of the economy in general makes renting a very risky proposition for the tenant.

34 It has been asserted that groups in some sectors demanded payment from would-be squatters, evicting those who would not or could not pay and replacing them with better customers. It is impossible to assess the veracity of such claims: they are certainly conceivable, especially for households that may have fallen outside client groups. But this is also the kind of accusation that one political group might have flung at another. In any case, such practices do not seem to have been general in José Ingenieros.

35 Although snow is virtually unheard of in Buenos Aires, frost is not. The nearby subterranean Rio de La Matanza often adds an extra chill to the air in José Ingenieros.

36 The service station at the *rotonda* was an important source of water. Some people from the *chalets* also helped by allowing *intrusos* access to water from their homes.

37 The lack of a doorknob made it more difficult for people to enter apartments, so removing it acted as a primitive lock.

38 Images of civilians defending their country from British assault at the beginning of the nineteenth century, armed only with boiling oil, are part of national mythology.

39 Here she is probably confusing two groups, both of which were on the left: Peronismo de Base and Juventud Peronista.

40 *Mate cocido* is the other principal way of preparing the traditional *mate*. In this case *mate* is simply steeped like a tea.

41 The summer weather of New Year's Eve is ideal for outdoor parties; they tend to have a character similar to the festivities of Canada Day or the US Fourth of July.

42 This comes out in the bemused commentaries about the number of weapons that ended up in the trash during searches conducted at the beginning of the *proceso*.

43 I use real names here because they come from a published source (below).

44 Cañete is still remembered in the neighbourhood, and the consensus is that he was from CdeO.

45 These names were not so well remembered by those I spoke to.

46 That I know more about some groups than others is indicative of the way that these early political configurations continue to matter in the present. My alliances with certain people, as is always the case, affected my access to others with inside knowledge of particular groups. Also, I knew more people in *complejos* 4-5-6 and 17 than in 18 or 19, although I did know and interview people from all four sectors.

Chapter 4

1 On the evolution of repression in Argentina, see Rodríguez Molas (1985a, 1985b).

2 Here I condense a number of perspectives expressed by the military government but it is misleading to write about an ideological position in the singular. There have always been distinct, and sometimes incompatible, points of view within the Argentine armed forces. Some distinctions have been important ideological ones – pro versus anti-Peronist, nationalist versus pro-American – while others have been more arcane. These differences have often been defined in terms of membership in particular forces, or branches within forces. It was in light of this history of distinction and rivalry that the cooperation between the branches of the military at the

beginning of *el proceso* was so remarkable. Fissures reappeared with time (Munck 1998).

3 Disappearance refers to people kidnapped by military or police amidst systemic denials. Although some people later reappeared, the figures for disappeared people refer to those who were subsequently murdered. The official count of the Report of the Argentine National Commission on the Disappeared (CONADEP 1986) was 8,960 people disappeared between March 1976 and 1982. A 1992 edition included another 215 cases (*Página/12* 1992:10). The number is certainly higher, since the CONADEP counted only documented cases. Human Rights groups in Argentina often cite a figure of 30,000 disappeared, Amnesty International estimates 20,000 while other observers think 12,000 is a more accurate figure (Corradi 1985:120; Ranis 1986:30; Osiel 1986:145 n23). The imprecision must be blamed on the repressive apparatus itself. Many of the disappeared were buried in secret mass graves or thrown, some still alive, into the sea precisely to obfuscate (Verbitsky 1996).

4 The Permanent Assembly on Human Rights (APDH) estimates the number of dead over and above figures on the disappeared (Fernández Meijide 1988).

5 This repressive apparatus had an important ideological component, as I have argued elsewhere (DuBois 1990).

6 The founding Process of National Reorganization Act (point 8) suspends the collective (*gremial*) activities of all workers, business owners, and professionals.

7 The *obra social* is one of the most important vestiges of the unionization under Perón's first government. Argentine unions controlled vast benefits packages, including high-quality health care and recreational facilities. Removing the *obras sociales* from the control of the unions is to undermine one of the most important services unions offer their members.

8 I spoke to some members of this group, but never asked for any details about detention. The cases related to NHD 17 discussed here are relatively well documented because the members of the group survived their disappearances and many testified for national and international organizations and tribunals about their experiences. They did so at the Organization of American States in 1979, Amnesty International, the Hague, the Argentine CONADEP, and at various trials. They testified when it was politically important, and did not do so lightly. Robben (1996) addresses some of the complex methodological and ethical concerns in talking to victims and perpetrators of violence.

 9 Liwski's testimony appears in *Nunca Más* (CONADEP 1986:20–6) and in *El Diario del Juicio* (1985). Some sources spell his name Liwsky.

10 This interview was recorded, transcribed, and edited as part of a larger project on human rights and the transition to and consolidation of democracy in Argentina. The interdisciplinary project was undertaken by a team of researchers at CEDES in Buenos Aires.

11 In his testimony to CONADEP, he says the initial assault occurred on the 25th (in CONADEP 1986 [1984]:21) while in this later interview he says it was the 24th.

12 I use people's real names when they are part of the public record.

13 Although Liwski went on to discuss other activities in which he was involved (his work in an experimental school for disabled children, for example), in this interview, as well as in *Nunca Más* and testifying in the 1985 trial against the commanders of the military junta, he stressed that he was targeted for his work with poor communities. He testified to CONADEP that, just before torture began, 'I heard another voice. This one said he was a "Colonel." He told me they knew I was not involved with terrorism or the guerrillas, but that they were going to torture me because I opposed the regime, because: "I hadn't understood that in Argentina there was no room for any opposition to the Process of National Reorganization." He then added: "You're going to pay dearly for it ... the poor won't have any goody-goodies to look after them any more!"' (CONADEP 1986:22).

14 San Justo is the administrative centre of La Matanza.

15 The Southern Cone regimes had been cooperating for some time in the pursuit of those they believed to be their enemies.

16 The story of the mass was made particularly and tragically memorable by the events that followed. Working backward from published sources that describe subsequent disappearances as occurring on April 5, the mass seems to have been held on 3 or 4 April.

17 Some of these names are mentioned by Liwski in *Nunca Más* (CONADEP 1986:25). The abduction of the four doctors is reported in the *Buenos Aires Herald* (1978a, 1978b, 1978c) and once (1978a), remarkably, with a banner headline across the front page. The *Herald* was the only newspaper still reporting such occurrences at the time; presumably it was less tightly censored because it publishes in English. Its editor was eventually forced into exile, however (Graham-Yool 1982).

18 Of the twelve who remained, all but three were kept in San Justo. The other three were in the police station of Isidro Casanova. Then all twelve were sent on to the police station at Gregorio Laferrere where their situations

were semi-legitimized, in part because there was some national and international pressure, especially around the cases of the physicians from the World Medical Association. The next step for many was passage to PEN which signified their shift from disappeared to political prisoners within the official prison system (Liwski 1990:6–7).

19 Green (1999) describes how social suffering turned into illness for many of the Guatemalan widows with whom she worked.

20 For first-hand accounts of such experiences, see Partnoy's compelling tale (1986), Timerman (1981), and the fictionalized version by Bonasso (1988).

21 This was probably the Regiment of La Tablada, just across Camino de Cintura Avenue from José Ingenieros. Apparently it was quite common for people from the neighbourhood to go there when in search of missing people.

22 People who worked in the offices which administered the Nucleos Definitivos both before and after the transfer describe the process as disorganized. They say that most of the documentation from the early days of the neighbourhood was lost in the transfer. They recall a truck arriving one day, being loaded with files, and leaving. Those on the receiving end say the paperwork was tossed hodge-podge into a storage room and eventually disappeared.

23 The Ford Falcon was the model of car notoriously used by the death squads in Argentina.

24 Because these stairways are specific, addresses have been changed.

25 She refers here to an *allanamiento* (search and seizure operation) by using the word census.

26 The administrators she remembers are Lavela, Lieutenant-Colonel Angeloz, Alsina, and finally Luitenent-Colonel Coronel (*sic*).

27 Teresa describes this cooperation as including NHDs 17, 18 and 19, presumably leaving out 4-5-6 because it's administrative status was slightly different because of the greater number of *adjudicados*. Other accounts suggest that all four *complejos* were administered jointly by the interveners.

28 The *quinela* is a lottery. The *quinelero* sells the tickets. In this case, he would have been running a shadow *quinela* in which tickets were sold privately, but winners were determined by the official lottery's numbers.

29 In one scheme, the commission would buy each family a clothes-dryer to stop people hanging clothes on their balconies and window sills.

30 Argentines are notorious for their *che*, which acts as punctuation. In Katerina's account, the *che* connotes friendly informality as well.

31 Estela was uncomfortable speaking in front of a tape recorder, but agreed that I could take notes.

32 Raúl and Susana's account comes from a taped portion of an interview I conducted with them in December 1992. I discuss this interview more fully in chapter 7.
33 Jorge Rafael Videla became president of Argentina as the delegate of the military junta on 29 March 1976. Emilio Eduardo Massera was also part of this junta as admiral of the navy, and a particularly vocal ideologue of the repression. Menem was the president at the time of the interview. Don Fernando, a passionate Peronist, does not seem to approve of him.
34 This silence is significant. It is Don Fernando's solution to the problem of what to call the last dictatorship since each of the many labels people used implied a political position on it.
35 On humiliation, see Asad's 1993 *Genealogies of Religion*, especially chapter 4.
36 It is possible the invitation was meant to be ironic, but the story was repeatedly told to me as if it were not.

Chapter 5

1 Deborah Poole made this helpful point in comments on a panel at the American Anthropological Association meetings in 2002.
2 Although we cannot know precisely how people in José Ingenieros would have seen and interpreted the events described below, we can assume they were exposed to them. Most residents of José Ingenieros are literate enough to read newspapers. Almost everyone had a television, with one state-owned, and four privately-owned channels. Radio remained a powerful medium in Argentina. News and information stations were popular, and many were quite politically sophisticated. Much biting political commentary is expressed in comedy on very popular radio and television programs.
3 See Guber (2001) for a careful study of the Malvinas as national icon and (1999) for an analysis of the conflict as experienced and understood by ex-combatants.
4 Galtieri was mistaken on two key fronts: that Margaret Thatcher was willing to go to war, and that, notwithstanding the Monroe doctrine and School of the Americas, the United States would support Britain over Argentina in any dispute (Rock 1987: 374ff, Torre and Riz 1993:337ff). Many Argentines were shocked that the United States aided the British fleet by facilitating satellite images. When the Gulf War broke out in 1991, I heard many nationalist Argentines sympathize with Saddam Hussein's plight. They saw the Iraq situation as directly parallel to their own.
5 APDH is the Asemblea Permanente de Derechos Humanos. Human rights

organizations forced the issue into the collective consciousness and onto the political agenda. In addition to weekly marches at the Plaza de Mayo, and marches organized in response to specific events, the human rights movements' strategies included plastering life-sized silhouettes representing the disappeared all over downtown Buenos Aires.

6 General Videla and Admiral Massera received life sentences, General Viola seventeen years, Admiral Lamburscini eight years, and Brigadier Agosti three years and nine months. Once the trial against the juntas was completed, attention turned to the two thousand criminal complaints filed by private parties about human rights crimes committed during the *proceso*. Among these was a case brought against General Ramon Camps, chief of Buenos Aires Police, the country's largest security force which was responsible for action in Gran Buenos Aires, including La Matanza. In December 1986 Camps was sentenced to twenty-five years in prison.

7 These were known as Monte Caseros (January 1988), Villa Martelli (November and December 1988), and 3 December 1990.

8 The 3 December rebellion was not received the same way, perhaps because it was resolved much more quickly. It also occurred during Menem's Peronist presidency and after La Tablada.

9 Two members of MTP appear in photographs as being captured alive, but were counted among the dead. Several MTP prisoners say (and their testimony is supported by six draftees and a sergeant) they tried to surrender several times. Some of those who did surrender were tortured and even murdered (Schneider 1989:12).

10 Alfonsín thus violated his own National Defence Bill of April 1988 which explicitly forbade the armed forces from gathering domestic intelligence (Schneider 1989:12).

11 Legal actions continued in the restitution of children of the disappeared to their birth families. Also, by the end of the 1990s, there was a new wave of prosecutions, most often for kidnapping, in Argentine and foreign courts.

12 Opinion polls consistently showed 63 to 70 per cent of the population opposed it (cf. *Página/12* 1990a:10–11).

13 Journalists received death threats (*Clarín* 1991b:2, 1991c:19), and bombs were placed at the offices of the dailies *Clarín* (on 25 January 1991) and *Página/12* (on 22 February 1991). There were no injuries (*Clarín* 1991g:16, *Página/12* 1991b:4).

14 The foreign debt amassed during the *proceso* is particularly pernicious because of the regime that acquired it, but also because much of it was from private debt and 'statized.' When the government needed foreign currency, it encouraged private debtors to refinance through subsidies and guaran-

tees against future currency devaluations. The private debt was national-
ized when foreign credit was cut in August 1982 (Canitrot 1994:80).
15 Martínez de Hoz believed in the free market as an agent of social, political,
and economic transformation. He had remarkable longevity for an Argentine minister of finance, holding the position for five years (Schvarzer
1986:16). Collins and Lear (1995) describe a similar marriage of convenience
between the neoliberal economists, 'The Chicago Boys,' and Pinochet's
regime in Chile.
16 Hidden wage-earners are employees who work in such marginal conditions – in construction, for example – that they classify themselves as self-
employed. Marginal workers are those who, for lack of alternatives, do
changas, or pick up work: as street vendors, shining shoes or washing cars,
for example (Torrado 1992:238–9).
17 Cavallo stepped down in July 1996 in response to popular criticism of yet
another austerity package.
18 Consumer prices rose 171.7 per cent in 1991 and 24.9 per cent in 1992
(World Bank 1994:22).
19 A report in the economic supplement of the *porteño* newspaper *Clarín* made
special note of the rise in the importation of textiles and electronics. In 1989
and 1990 thread, yarn, and fabric represented the bulk of imports and manufactured goods a small minority; the trend was reversed by September
1991. Between 1990 and 1991, imported clothing and other manufactured
textile goods increased by 1,518 per cent (*Clarín* 1991a:6). Small wonder
goods made in Argentine were not in demand.
20 For an explanation of debates around different poverty measures, their use
in Argentina, and their implications, see Powers (1995b).
21 In Argentina at this time the poverty line was defined as double the price of
a basic shopping basket of food.
22 Unfortunately, this downward trend was temporary (see epilogue).
23 On a return visit in 1994 I found car services littering a landscape where
before they were nonexistent. With the lifting of very stiff import duties and
thus lower prices, many people had invested their severance packages in
cars they then drove for car services. These new endeavours transformed
the landscape of José Ingenieros as people changed bedroom windows into
store fronts and built garages onto spare bits of public space.
24 A sign of the desperation induced by the combination of growing poverty
and hyperinflation is the sudden outburst of food riots in some of the poorest sections of the country beginning in May 1989. People in José Ingenieros
date the closing of local supermarkets from these events. Georges Midré
describes the *saqueos* in an article on food aid in Argentina (1992:356–60).

25 As elsewhere in Latin America (Levenson-Estrada 1994) Coca-Cola paid
well for the privilege of non-unionized labour. According to this informant,
rigorous screening practices tried to keep it that way in Buenos Aires. He
worried about whether Coca-Cola would see his participation in El
Hornero as an asset or a liability.

Chapter 6

1 See *History Workshop Journal* in general and especially Selbourne 1980 and
Samuel 1980. See also Lindenberger and Wildt 1992; Johnson et al. 1982;
Brecher 1984. I have the impression that the history workshop is used quite
a lot throughout Latin America and Africa, but this remains an impression
(see the special issue of *Radical History Review* on South Africa, including
Witz 1990 and especially Bozzoli 1990). For Chile, see Paley 1993. In a different tradition, Myerhoff (1978) employed a similar technique in her work
with elderly people in a California Jewish community to great effect.
2 In Argentina the term *taller* is commonly used for activities that are supposed to be collective efforts as opposed to lecture-style. Sometimes the
term is used to convey a democratic air, even when meetings are not organized around working groups. Thus the *taller* idea is one with which people
are familiar. The prevalence of the workshop mode in Argentina may relate
to the importance of social psychology there. Conferences with a workshop
format with social psychologists as facilitators are common. One also
detects the influence of Brazilian Paolo Freire's 'pedagogy of the oppressed'
(1970).
3 After the first meeting, we did post signs, distribute flyers, and had the
meetings announced over local radio stations, but no one ever came to a
taller who had not been personally invited by one of the participants.
4 The group was young for history workshops, which often engage elder
members of a community. The group's youth is a result of one of the neighbourhood's peculiarities; there were few elders – only 5.7 per cent of the
population was over 60 (1991 INDEC data) – because most people involved
in the *toma* were quite young at the time. In the early 1990s leaders from the
1973 *toma* were still working; some also remained politically active. Their
current positions often curtailed their ability to participate in the *taller*.
5 On the problem of writing, The Popular Memory Group argue, 'For the
modern period there is a real problem of the implicitly non-popular effects
of focusing on formal history-writing, a practice largely colonized by academic and professional norms. (This is also the case with new methodologies, especially "oral history," which are sometimes seen as intrinsically

"popular" and democratizing.) If we retain this focus, we risk reproducing some very conservative forms: a closed circle of comment between left social historians and what Marx would have called "critical critics"' (1982:206).

6 Both *memoria* and *historia* have even more complex constellations of meaning in Spanish than do their English equivalents. *Memoria* means 'memory' in the English senses, and also 'memorial' and 'memoir.' *Historia* includes the various English meanings of 'history' but also 'story,' so does not necessarily have the same connotation of truth as does its English equivalent.

7 This was a stroke of luck caused by the fact that our meeting was held immediately after one on a crisis concerning the local sewage system. People from the earlier meeting were persuaded to participate in the *taller*. The Complementary Education Centre (CEC) had cancelled classes because sewage was actually backed up into the school building, so some CEC teachers also participated.

8 I taped the session, but since almost half the participants were speaking at any one time, the tape was indecipherable. Diagrams were copied onto smaller sheets by a pre-school teacher. Figures 6.1 and 6.2 are schematic versions.

9 Participants told me that there was a serious argument about the date of the *toma*. A woman who insisted that it was in 1972 threatened to leave when people contradicted her because she thought they were lying. Despite her passionate outburst, she stayed.

10 Because, as we have seen, the neighbourhood was built under a government plan, and shifted from federal to provincial authorities, residents have long had to deal with government bureaucrats. The neighbourhood has been officially classified as a high-risk population (*población de alto riesgo*). This brings certain advantages – the teachers get a bonus, for example – but also officially classifies residents as poor and needy, with all the negative implications these labels carry in the eyes of bureaucrats.

11 This experience was a reminder that memory is not just oral or visual, although the popular memory literature privileges these forms. For an exception, see Connerton (1989).

12 Chaffee suggests that the history of military rule is partially responsible for the lack of mural tradition in Argentina (1986:78 ff).

13 The mural was very inexpensive. We used acrylic paints because they dry quickly, are easy to work with, and are quite durable. Ladders were lent us by the *complejo*'s administration. Since the wall was quite small the cost of paint and other materials was about $45. The pre-school lent the *taller* the money, but this had to be paid back about half-way through when I put in

the cash. All the more-or-less steady participants were asked to donate $3. As this was decided only at the last minute, many did not have the money at that time, but I did eventually receive more than half. Although I said I was happy to cover the cost, some participants felt that sharing financial responsibility was a significant part of our collective effort. For some, the inability to collect this small amount of money was an impediment to starting a second mural.

14 There was a proposal to label each building but that idea was discarded.

15 There were practical and artistic reasons behind this division. The group that did the original design for the buildings worked in pencil and did not feel confident enough to brave the daunting task of drawing people. The group that did the silhouettes used a projector to cast shadows, tracing them onto paper.

Chapter 7

1 I know some readers will find this distinction troubling because all historical accounts are constructions. I have no quarrel with this view, but I do believe that there is an objective reality in relation to which, and out of which, such constructions are manufactured.

2 Various readers have taken exception to my use of the words 'mistake' and 'error' in this discussion, noting that it is dangerous to try to discern between true and false memories, and is generally positivist. Try as I might, I am unable to let go of the idea that certain events occurred in particular ways. This is not to argue that any of us has unmediated access to facts, or the truth, only that some approximations get closer than others. Further, it is precisely because we have persuasive evidence that the Madres de Plaza de Mayo formed and were active during the *proceso* years, not ten years earlier, for example, that we can know that Raúl and Susana are creatively reworking the past.

3 It was said that the centre was a front for some communist or socialist party, although this was not true and perhaps Susana and Raúl are too politically astute to have believed it.

4 The Peronist/Menemist candidate Eduardo Duhalde (originally Menem's vice-president) won as anticipated with 45 per cent of the vote, the Radical Pugliese received 24 per cent, and Rico received almost 10 per cent of the vote.

5 As the press noted, Rico's support came from the southern and western zones of the *conurbano*, 'precisely the hardest hit by the economic crisis and the industrial reconversion initiated in 1976' (*Clarín* 1991i:9). This result

poses questions that have yet to be adequately answered. Was this some kind of vote for authoritarianism? It seems likely that dissatisfied Peronists turned to Rico to register their protest against Menem's economic policy. The Radical Party's economic platform differed little from that of the party in power, and besides, for many of those who have been Peronist all their lives, voting Radical would be as inconceivable as switching soccer teams. It needs also to be said that Rico actually campaigned in these areas. In José Ingenieros at the time, Peronist *pintadas* (huge graffitis with electoral slogans) and rallies were ubiquitous; the 'Ricomobile,' a pick-up truck with speakers and the candidate on the back, made several passes through the neighbourhood; but workers from other parties were nowhere to be seen.

6 In the end, this was probably a bad bet politically, since the local office never got off the ground and MODIN's electoral support collapsed in subsequent elections.

7 One should recall that human rights violations have always accompanied military regimes in Argentina. For the present discussion, the important distinction is that as an officer during the *proceso* it would have been virtually impossible to avoid participation in, or at the very least knowledge of, such abuses.

8 An article on the 'antagonistic memories' of Jews and non-Jews in Berlin (Stern 1992) makes an argument which is suggestive. Stern shows that given the radically different shape of the social world for the two groups during the war – and thus the significance of allied bombing raids, for example – their memories were almost irreconcilable afterwards.

9 Here, also, Raymond Williams's caution against the dangers of romanticization is worth bearing in mind. Speaking of Welsh identity, he reminds us: 'It is easy to speak of proud independent people. The rhetoric warms the heart. But you can be proud without being independent; you often have to be. In the older epochs of colonialism, and in the modern epoch of industrial capitalism, there hasn't been that much choice. The self-respect, the aspirations, were always real and always difficult. But you don't live for centuries under the power of others and remain the same people' (1989:101).

10 'These testimonies,' Passerini notes, 'are first and foremost statements of cultural identity in which memory continuously adapts received traditions to present circumstances' (1987:17).

11 For Gramsci, 'common sense' is the collection of beliefs, prejudices, and principles which each of us encounters and absorbs as we become social beings (1971:323). It is the 'product of history and a part of the historical process' (1971:326). Common senses are thus specific to particular times,

places, and social contexts. Further, common sense is inherently 'disjointed and episodic' (1971:324). It thus contrasts both with the relatively coherent dominant ideologies and religions, and with critical thought which takes 'common' and 'good' sense as its starting point for the building of coherent philosophies and interpretations of the world (1971:323–25, 423, 199).

Chapter 8

1 This increase is probably tied to the period of hyperinflation and general economic crisis.
2 He had just associated 'delinquents' with drugs and drug addicts.
3 One study of press coverage of crime in Argentina between 1983 and 1989 found that the frequency of reports increased and decreased in relation to the needs of the police forces; increasing amid demands for higher salaries for police officers, for example (Oliveira and Tiscornia 1990).
4 The Asociación was restricted to NHD 4-5-6 for political and historical reasons. Inés's sphere of influence was mainly limited to 4-5-6 where she lives. She saw herself as a natural leader and over the years undertook various administrative tasks. Her most conspicuous role in 1991 and 1992 was in collecting payments for and dealing with the power company and trying to take care of the ailing water pumps in the wells which supply the *complejo*. Both of these jobs are more complex than they appear. These expenses were billed to the *complejo* as a whole, and many people did not feel compelled to pay their share. The job thus entailed considerable and varied forms of persuasion applied both to neighbours and to officials at the companies and in the municipal and provincial governments.
    These roles should have been taken on by an administration but 4-5-6 had been rudderless in this sense for some time. Previous administrators left amid accusations of corruption. Existing lawsuits from administration employees (for non-payment of indemnification) have precluded the formation of a new administration which would assume these old debts. Also, it was unclear who had sufficient credibility to take on such a role without immediately falling victim to new accusations of corruption.
5 The mall in *complejo* 18 has a *velatorio* which local families can use for funerals free of charge. The two families received mourners there together.
6 The Argentine version of the *empanada* is a favourite and cheap fast food. The victim's father, then, was a small merchant known by most people in the community.
7 Such overkill was not uncommon. A famous case that occurred in July was back in the papers at the time. After an autopsy twenty police were being

brought up on charges for killing four young people after the robbery of a corner store: Jorge Villafañe (fourteen), Esteban Duarte (fifteen), Gabriel Montovia (seventeen), and Roberto Méndez (eighteen). The twenty police fired 128 times, and forty-six bullets found their marks in the four boys, several in the palms of their hands (*Clarín* 1991d, 1991e, 1991g).

8 The question was rhetorical. When I asked how many, he did not know: 'a lot,' he said.

9 This phrasing might suggest that the 'guilty' victim's death was less tragic. This sense was implicit in Tito's account.

10 Tito was also lucky that the provincial police did not notice that he had an outstanding warrant in the capital.

11 People often go to police headquarters on bureaucratic errands: for example, for permissions to sell beer in a public place.

12 In fact, some neighbours criticized Inés's privileged access to the police. They noted that she had a police radio in her apartment, and that police officers often visited her there. It was even said that she supplied a list of local youth she considered delinquents.

13 Like other recipients of public funding, health care institutions have suffered from the rollback of the state. A formerly excellent public health system has been nearly run into the ground. This is popularly believed to have been caused by a combination of underfunding and corruption.

14 The Spanish title of the health project is: '*Asistencia, promoción y desarrollo para la población materno-infantil en situación de emergencia económica-social.*' It is worth noting how this portrays poor mothers and children as the (innocent? blameless?) needy. The title had some constraining effects, but those involved in developing the project in José Ingenieros actively read it in the broadest sense, making it about community health.

15 CISP stands for Comitato Internazionale per lo Sviluppo dei Popoli (International Committee for Popular Health). The complex acronym of the Argentine NGO stands for Comité para Defensa de la Salud, la Etica Profesional, y los Derechos Humanos (Committee for the Defense of Health, Professional Ethics and Human Rights). CODESEDH organizes around health and human rights precisely because health issues are a way of expanding the issues of human rights. CODESEDH has published materials on a similar course (CODESEDH 1989).

16 The other was a mothers' organization in an *asentamiento* (organized squatter settlement).

17 El Hornero, like all officially recognized nonprofit organizations, was required to have a specific hierarchical administrative structure. In practice, governance was more informal and based on consensus, although there

were internal conflicts. In general the most active participants in the centre, those staffing the office, organizing events, and teaching classes, were the officers of the association. For example, since I offered my computer for the production of typed documents, taught English, and sometimes staffed the office, I became part of this inner circle, although I never held a post. The time I had to contribute was key.

18 An initial proposal had suggested setting up a clinic in NHD 4-5-6, in the building housing El Hornero, but this plan was eventually scrapped because of the Italian requirement that no projects be established that would require ongoing funding, in this case staff for the *salita*.

19 In Argentina the cholera scare took on an important symbolic role. It was clear from the way cholera was thought to come from Bolivia, and the 'Indians' in the north, that it was seen as an indicator of the Latin Americanization (i.e. impoverishment) of Argentina. Powers notes that it evoked discussion of poverty in Argentina (1995:85). The cholera scare thus added another level of anxiety about what the problem of the sewage represented for local identity.

20 *Complejo 4-5-6* had been without such an administrator since the late 1980s.

21 Abortion was still illegal in Argentina.

22 I did not tape this meeting, so the quotes are reconstructed from notes and my memory. They should thus be taken as reflecting the tenor, and general content, but not the specific words of those speaking.

23 People were shocked to discover that I did not charge for the English classes I taught, for example.

24 Although she had been personally invited, Doña Inés did not attend the meeting described above.

25 It is also possible that, because he himself was from outside José Ingenieros, he really believed himself to be talking to social workers, or some other variety of outsider, rather than neighbours.

26 CODESEDH had experience with this sort of project (see CODESEDH 1989).

27 It was thought that nurses, especially those who worked in José Ingenieros, would benefit from the course – that is, that some would benefit from a more community-oriented, less technical view of health. A couple of nurses attended some sessions. I was also permitted to take the course.

28 Topics covered included participatory planning and community self-diagnosis, water treatment, mental health, children's growth and development, pregnancy, adolescence, drug addiction, dental health, and birth control.

29 The most evident conflict was in the class on drug addiction. The instructor made statements such as: 'In general, one combats drugs from the ethical-

juridical perspective and when the drug addict returns to his community he returns to drug consumption.' And with respect to drug use, 'The family is an important institution and there is a risk of drug use in families where everyone works, and the adolescent is often alone' (class handout). His position on these questions was clearly much closer to that of Doña Inés than of people like Marisa, who had been central in constructing the curriculum. One wonders whether he gave much thought to his audience; poor families often have no choice but for both parents to work. Another conflict arose when the class scheduled to address birth control discussed fetal development instead.

30 Until the course began, Liwski had not even walked through José Ingenieros in the intervening years. He did not have much daily involvement in the project, but did participate in the course itself as an instructor. It must also have been a complex experience for him.

31 A perverse effect of this repression is a kind of survivor's guilt. There are those on the left who assume that all the 'best' people, the people with integrity, have died.

32 This is not meant as an apology for the evident brutality and violence, however.

33 Friends in the neighbourhood told me about these events.

34 This is similar to the findings of both Sacks (1988) and Gregory (1994) for the United States.

35 The reader may recall that Raúl had recently lost his Peronist political appointment in the municipality.

36 Harvey (1995) addresses precisely this question in an article on Raymond Williams. He quotes Williams: what begins, 'as local and affirmative ... was always insufficiently aware of the quite systematic obstacles which stood in the way' (1989:115). The problem here is that the notions of community and solidarity of which Williams writes so passionately and persuasively are about what Harvey calls 'militant particularisms' rooted in experience that does not (perhaps cannot) see the processes occurring at another level of abstraction.

Epilogue

1 Former President Menem was under house arrest in 2001, accused of illicit enrichment through illegal arms deals.

2 The poverty line in 2001 was set at 470 pesos a month for a family of four. Extreme poverty is characterized as a family of four earning less than 200 pesos a month (INDEC in Bermudez 2001:23).

Appendix A

1 'The third position' was the idea that Argentina should locate itself apart from the super powers, at equal distance from the United States and the Soviet Union: as a popular Peronist slogan put it, '¡Ni yankis, ni marxistas, peronistas!' It thus is reminiscent of the non-aligned movement. This third way also implied an economic system somewhere between capitalism and communism. The 'Organized Community' was to avoid the excesses of both models, guaranteeing private property as long it fulfilled a 'social function' (Gillespie 1982:17–18).

2 This was the CGT (Conferederación General de Trabajo) from 1946 to 1955 and the '62 Organizations' from 1957 to 1973. Richard Gillespie describes a 'defacto Youth Branch' between 1971 and 1974 led mostly by left-wing Peronist militants (1982:19).

3 There are also a growing number of case studies of particular unions or factories which of necessity give more nuanced and careful attention to the particular Peronism of the rank and file in these contexts. See, for example, Pozzi (1988) and Cangiano (1996).

4 These developments were not all due to factors internal to Argentina. Global economic processes dramatically affected both exports and imports and consequently the Argentine economy.

5 He won by 52.4 per cent to 42.5 per cent, defeating José Tamborini, the candidate representing the Unión Democrática, an anti-Peronist coalition (Rock 1993:238–40).

6 Wages increased as a share of national income from 40.1 per cent in 1946 to 49 per cent in 1949, and this trend held despite the economic crisis at the end of Perón's second presidency (James 1988:10–12).

7 In assessing the Peronist development strategy in the context of subsequent regimes, Torrado notes: 'The Peronist model did not induce large overall economic development nor notable modernization in the division of labour, but it had the merit of neither segmenting labour markets, nor excluding important sectors of the population from the fruits of the development which it did achieve' (1992:414).

8 Also telling was the peculiar, but not entirely implausible, story that the aerial view of Ciudad Evita revealed a portrait of the leader herself. Some local people insisted that the curving streets of the subdivision had clearly outlined her profile until the image was marred by the interventions of later developments wrought in anti-Peronist eras. Looking at a local map, it seemed to me possible that this were true. Some also asserted that José Ing-

enieros had been placed to obstruct the view of Ciudad Evita from the heavily trafficked thoroughfare.

9 This point was brought home to me as I watched friends struggle to maintain a household on the money they brought in doing piece-work. When they needed to buy a new machine they found their employer was their only available source of credit. They were then obligated to sew for him at a relatively low rate until they had managed to pay him back and obtain the note on the machine.

10 Most who engage in this form of piece-work are women. This is probably even more true of the first Peronist period, although it is hard to tell, since everyone assumes that those sewing are women. When I lived in Argentina I knew men who sewed. This was not a desirable choice, though, and it may have been a recent result of the deterioration of job prospects in traditionally male domains.

11 James writes that 'much of the Peronist state's effort between 1946 and its demise in 1955 can be viewed as an attempt to institutionalize and control the heretical challenge it had unleashed in the earlier period and to absorb this challenge within a new state-sponsored orthodoxy. Viewed in this light Peronism was, in a certain sense, a passive, demobilising social experience for workers' (1988:34).

Bibliography

Abiad, Pablo, and Leonardo Torresi. 2001. 'Jueces federales denunican torturas en las investigaciones policiales. *Clarín* (Buenos Aires), 9 August 2001. http://www.clarin.com.ar/diario/2001-08-09/s-03215.htm

Abrams, Philip. 1988 [1970]. 'Notes on the Difficulty of Studying the State.' *Journal of Historical Sociology* 1(1): 58-89.

Accorinti, Vicente et al. 1990. *Los Ferroviarios que perdimos el tren.* Buenos Aires: Secretaría de la Nación, Dirección Nacional del Libro, Ministerio de Educación.

Acuña, Carlos H., et al. 1994. 'Politics and Economics in the Argentina of the Nineties (Or; Why the Future No Longer Is What It Used to Be).' Pp. 20–73 in William C. Smith, Carlos H. Acuña, and Eduardo A. Gamarra, eds., *Democracy, Markets, and Structural Reform in Latin America.* New Brunswick, NJ: Transaction (North-South Center).

Acuña, Carlos H., et al, eds. 1995. *Juicio, castigos y memorias: Derechos humanos y justicia en la política argentina.* Buenos Aires: Nueva Visión.

Acuña, Carlos H., and Catalina Smulovitz. 1995. 'Militares en la transición Argentina: del gobierno a la subordinación constitucional.' Pp. 21–99 in Carlos H. Acuña et al., eds., *Juicio, castigos y memorias: Derechos humanos y justicia en la política argentina.* Buenos Aires: Nueva Visión.

Alvarez, Lilian, et al. 1989. *Los talleres de historia por dentro.* Buenos Aires: Secretaría de la Nación, Dirección Nacional del Libro, Ministerio de Educación.

Andersen, Martin Edwin. 1993. *Dossier Secreto: Argentina's Desaparecidos and the Myth of the 'Dirty War.'* Boulder, CO: Westview.

Anderson, Benedict. 1991 [1983]. *Imagined Communities: Reflections on the Origin and Spread of Nationalism.* New York: Verso.

Antze, Paul, and Michael Lambek, eds. 1996. *Tense Past: Cultural Essays in Trauma and Memory.* New York: Routledge.

Anzorena, Oscar R. 1989. *JP: Historia de la Juventud Peronista (1955/1988)*. Buenos Aires: Ediciones del Cordón.

Asad, Talal. 1993. *Genealogies of Religion: Discipline and Reasons of Power in Christianity and Islam*. Baltimore: Johns Hopkins University Press.

Auyero, Javier. 2000. *Poor People's Politics: Peronist Survival Networks and the Legacy of Evita*. Durham, NC: Duke University Press.

Bellardi, Marta, and Aldo De Paula. 1986. *Villas miserias: Origen, erradicación y respuestas populares*. Buenos Aires: Centro Editor de América Latina, Biblioteca Política, No. 159.

Bermudez, Ismael. 2001. 'En un año, subió en 413.000 personas el número de pobres en Capital y GBA.' *Clarín* (Buenos Aires), 17 August, 23.

Bonasso, Miguel. 1988. *Recuerdo de la muerte*. Buenos Aires: Puntosur.

–. 1990. *La Memoria en Donde Ardía*. Buenos Aires: El Juglar Editores : Editorial Dialéctica : Editorial Contrapunto.

Boyarin, Jonathan, ed. 1994. *Remapping Memory: The Politics of TimeSpace*. Minneapolis: University of Minnesota Press.

Bozzoli, Belinda. 1990. 'Intellectuals, Audiences and Histories: South African Experiences, 1978–88.' *Radical History Review* 46(7): 237–63.

Brecher, Jeremy. 1984. 'How I Learned to Quit Worrying and Love Community History: A "Pet Outsider's" Report on the Brass Workers History Project.' *Radical History Review* 28(30): 187–201.

Buenos Aires Herald. 1978a. 'Another Doctor Reported Kidnapped.' *Buenos Aires Herald*, 13 April, 1.

–. 1978b. '"Missing" Doctors in Police Custody.' *Buenos Aires Herald*, 14 June, 11.

–. 1978c. 'Physician on Call Abducted.' *Buenos Aires Herald*, 11 April, 11.

Buhle, Paul. 1996. 'Bread and Roses: A Response.' *Radical History Review* 65: 84–90.

Caldeira, Teresa P.R. 1996. 'Building up Walls: The New Pattern of Spatial Segregation in Sao Paulo.' *International Social Science Journal* 147: 55-66.

Cameron, Ardis. 1996. 'Comments on "Cleansing History."' *Radical History Review* 65: 91–7.

Cangiano, Maria Cecilia. 1996. 'What Did It Mean to Be Revolutionary? Peronism, Classism and the Steel Workers of Villa Constitución, Argentina, 1945–95.' PhD diss., State University of New York at Stoneybrook.

Canitrot, Adolfo. 1994. 'Crisis and Transformation of the Argentine State (1978–1992).' Pp. 75–102 in William C. Smith, Carlos H. Acuña, and Eduardo A. Gamarra, eds., *Democracy, Markets, and Structural Reform in Latin America*. New Brunswick, NJ: Transaction (North-South Center).

Carlson, Eric Stener. 1996. *I Remember Julia: Voices of the Disappeared*. Philadelphia: Temple University Press.

Cavarozzi, Marcelo. 1992. *Autoritarismo y democracia (1955–1983)*. Buenos Aires: Centro Editor America Latina.

CEDES (Centro de Estudios de Estado y Sociedad). 1990. Primera Entrevista a Norberto Liwski. 25/9/90. Buenos Aires, Argentina.

CEPA (Comite Ejecutivo para el Estudio de la Pobreza en la Argentina). 1994. 'Mapas de la pobreza en la Argentina.' Documento de Trabajo No. 4. Buenos Aires: Ministerio de Economía y Obras y Servicios Públicos, Secretaría de Programación Económica.

Chaffee, Lyman. 1986. 'Poster Art and Political Propaganda in Argentina.' *Studies in Latin American Popular Culture* 5: 78–89.

–. 1989. 'Political Graffiti and Wall Painting in Greater Buenos Aires: An Alternative Communicative System.' *Studies in Latin American Popular Culture* 8: 37–60.

CISEA/Centro Editor de América Latina. 1984. *Argentina 1983*. Buenos Aires: Centro Editor América Latina.

Clarín. 1973a. 'Actuó el ejército en el barrio General Belgrano.' *Clarín* (Buenos Aires), 18 May, 1, 14.

–. 1973b. 'Incidentes por la ocupación de un complejo de viviendas.' *Clarín* (Buenos Aires), 28 May, n.p.

–. 1973c. 'Más de 900 personas viven a la intemperie.' *Clarín* (Buenos Aires), 19 May, 10.

–. 1973d. 'Villeros ocupan la Comisión Municipal de la Vivienda.' *Clarín* (Buenos Aires), 25 May, 14.

–. 1991a. 'Cada vez menos gente conforma a la clase media.' *Clarín* (Buenos Aires), 29 September, 6.

–. 1991b. 'Denuncia de un periodista.' *Clarín* (Buenos Aires) 6 July, 2.

–. 1991c. 'Denuncian violencia contra la prensa.' *Clarín* (Buenos Aires), 22 March, 19.

–. 1991d. 'Fueron 20 los policías que balearon a los cuatro chicos en Pacheco.' *Clarín* (Buenos Aires), 4 August, 31.

–. 1991e. 'La Policía insiste en que la muerte de los chicos fue en un enfrentamiento.' *Clarín* (Buenos Aires), 3 August, 26–7.

–. 1991f. 'Muchos quioscos, un síntoma.' *Clarín* (Buenos Aires), 15 November, 16.

–. 1991g. 'Preventiva para 5 policías acusados de homicidio.' *Clarín* (Buenos Aires), 11 August, 31.

–. 1991h. 'Repudios por la bomba contra Clarín.' *Clarín* (Buenos Aires), 26 January, 16.

–. 1991i. 'Rico tuvo apoyo en los distritos más pobres.' *Clarín* (Buenos Aires), 10 September, 6.

–. 1992. 'Acto y festival para repudiar las advertencias de Menem.' *Clarín* (Buenos Aires), 17 July, 9.

–. 2001. 'Casos de picana eléctrica, bastonazos y amenazas.' *Clarín* (Buenos Aires). 9 August (cited 11 August 2001). (www.clarin.com.ar/diario/2001-08-09/s-03302.htm)

Clark, A. Kim. 1998. *The Redemptive Work: Railway and Nation in Ecuador, 1895-1930.* Wilmington, DE: Scholarly Resources Press.

Cockroft, Eva Sperling, and Holly Barnet-Sánchez, eds. 1990. *Signs from the Heart: California Chicano Murals.* Venice, CA: Social and Public Art Resource Center.

Cockroft, Eva, John Weber, and Jim Cockcroft, eds. 1977. *Toward a People's Art: The Contemporary Mural Movement.* New York: E.P. Dutton & Co.

CODESEDH (Comité para la Defensa de la Salud, la Etica Profesional y los Derechos Humanos). 1989. *La salud: Diálogo del pueblo. Curso de atención primaria de salud y participación popular.* Buenos Aires: CODESEDH.

Cole, Jennifer. 1998. 'The Work of Memory in Madagascar.' *American Ethnologist* 25(4): 610-33.

Collins, Joseph, and John Lear. 1995. *Chile's Free Market Miracle: A Second Look.* Oakland, CA: Food First.

Comaroff, John, and Jean Comaroff. 1992. *Ethnography and the Historical Imagination.* Boulder, CO: Westview.

CONADEP (Argentine National Commission on the Disappeared). 1986 [1984]. *Nunca Más: The Report of the Argentine National Commission on the Disappeared.* Trans. Writers and Scholars International. New York: Ferrar Straus Giroux in association with Index on Censorship.

Confino, Alon. 1997. 'Collective Memory and Cultural History: Problems of Method.' *American Historical Review* 102(5): 1386–1403.

Connerton, Paul. 1989. *How Societies Remember.* Cambridge: Cambridge University Press.

Corradi, Juan E. 1985. *The Fitful Republic: Economy, Society, and Politics in Argentina.* Latin American Perspectives Series, No. 2. Boulder, CO: Westview Press.

Corradi, Juan E., Patricia Weiss Fagen, and Manuel Antonio Garretón, eds. 1992. *Fear at the Edge: State Terror and Resistance in Latin America.* Berkeley: University of California Press.

Crane, Susan A. 1997. 'Writing the Individual Back into Collective Memory.' *American Historical Review* 102(5): 1372-85.

Crónica. 1973a. 'Casas: Hambre y sangre por la ocupación: Ocupación de comisión de viviendas.' *Crónica* (Buenos Aires), 12 June, 1, 10–11.

–. 1973b. '"Caza" de viviendas: Villeros desesperados coparon otro barrio.' *Crónica* (Buenos Aires), 27 May, 20.

–. 1973c. 'Copan oficina municipal: Recurren al expeditivo medio, angustiados villeros.' *Crónica* (Buenos Aires), 24 May, 7.

–. 1973d. 'Ejército cerca a humilde barriada.' *Crónica* (Buenos Aires), 27 May 10–11.

–. 1973e. 'Ejército y policías desalojan a un barrio.' *Crónica* (Buenos Aires), 17 May, 1.

–. 1973f. 'Esperanzas a la intemperie: Llega ayuda a barrio Gral. Belgrano.' *Crónica* (Buenos Aires), 19 May, 1, 20.

–. 1973g. 'No ceden "invasores" de viviendas: grave planteo en los mono-bloques.' *Crónica* (Buenos Aires), 30 May, 5.

–. 1973h. 'Ocupan departamentos que estaban asignados.' *Crónica* (Buenos Aires), 27 June, 3.

–. 1973i. 'Viven en un basural: Drama de desalojos del "General Belgrano."' *Crónica* (Buenos Aires), 18 May, 24.

–. 1973j. 'Viviendas a desalojados. Dejan el barrio Gral. Belgrano.' *Crónica* (Buenos Aires), 21 May, 24.

Daniel, Valentine. 1996. *Charred Lullabies: Chapters in an Anthropology of Violence.* Princeton, NJ: Princeton University Press.

Davolos, Patricia, Marcela Jabbaz, and Estela Molina. 1987. *Movimiento villero y estado (1966–1976).* Buenos Aires: Centro Editor América Latina, Biblioteca Politica, No. 178.

Diago, Alejandro. 1988. *Hebe Bonafini: Memoria y esperanza.* Buenos Aires: Ediciones Dialéctica.

Dirección Nacional de Investigación y Desarollo Socio-económico Habitacional y Urbano, Secretaría de Estado de Desarollo Urbano y Vivienda, Argentina. 1978. *Diseño y modos de uso de conjuntos habitacionales: Informe por la dirección nacional de investigación y desarollo socio-económico habitacional y urbano.*

Douglas, Mary. 1984 [1966]. *Purity and Danger.* New York: Routledge.

DuBois, Lindsay. 1990. 'Torture and the Construction of an Enemy: The Example of Argentina 1976–1983.' *Dialectical Anthropology* 15: 317–28.

–. 1997. 'Past, Place and Paint: A Neighbourhood Mural Project in Suburban Buenos Aires.' *Anthropologica* 34(1–2): 7–15.

–. 1999. 'Valiant Ladies: Gendered Dispositions in Argentine Working Class Memories.' *Social Analysis* 43(3): 6-25.

–. 2000. 'Memories Out of Place: Dissonance and Silence in Historical Accounts of Working Class Argentines.' *Oral History* 28(1): 75–87.

El diario del juicio (Buenos Aires). 1985a. 'Carezco de futuro: Mi futuro es una celda.' *El diario del juicio* (Buenos Aires), 8 October, 25.

–. 1985b. 'Contribuí a que las Fuerzas Armadas lograron el triunfo.' *El diario del juicio* (Buenos Aires), 22 October, 434–5.

–. 1985c. 'La acusación.' *El diario del juicio* (Buenos Aires), 8 October, 1–24.

–. 1985d. 'La orden secreta de Videla.' *El diario del juicio* (Buenos Aires), 3 December, 529–32.

Fabian, Johannes. 1983. *Time and the Other: How Anthropology Makes Its Object.* New York: Columbia University Press.

Fagen, Patricia Weiss. 1992. 'Repression and State Security.' Pp. 39–71 in Juan E.Corradi, Patricia Weiss Fagen, and Manuel Antonio Garretón, eds. 1992. *Fear at the Edge: State Terror and Resistance in Latin America.* Berkeley: University of California Press.

Feijoó, María del Carmen, and Marcela María Alejandra Nari. 1994. 'Women and Democracy in Argentina.' Pp.109–30 in Jane Jacquette, ed., *The Women's Movement in Latin America.* 2nd ed. Boulder, CO: Westview Press.

Felman, Shoshana, and Dori Laub. 1992. *Testimony: Crises of Witnessing in Literature, Psychoanalysis, and History.* New York: Routledge.

Fernández Meijide, Graciela. 1988. *Las cifras de la guerra sucia.* Buenos Aires: Asamblea Permanente de Derechos Humanos.

Fisher, Jo. 1989. *The Mothers of the Disappeared.* London: Zed Books.

Foucault, Michel. 1980 [1977]. 'Truth and Power.' Pp. 109–33 in *Power/Knowledge: Selected Interviews and Other Writings, 1972–1977.* Trans. and ed. Colin Gordon. New York: Pantheon.

Fraser, Ronald. 1984. *In Search of a Past: The Rearing of an English Gentleman, 1933–1945.* New York: Atheneum.

Freire, Paulo. 1970. *Pedagogy of the Oppressed.* Trans. Myra Bergman Ramos. New York, Herder and Herder.

Friedman, Jonathan. 1992a. 'Myth, History and Political Identity.' *Cultural Anthropology* 7(2):194–210.

–. 1992b. 'The Past in the Future: History and the Politics of Identity.' *American Anthropologist* 94: 837–59.

Frisch, Michael. 1990. *A Shared Authority: Essays on the Craft and Meaning of Oral and Public History.* Albany: State University of New York Press.

Geertz, Clifford. 1983. '"From the Native's Point of View": On the Nature of Anthropological Understanding.' Pp. 55–70 in Clifford Geertz, *Local Knowledge.* New York: Basic Books.

Gill, Lesley. 2000. *Teetering on the Rim: Global Restructuring, Daily Life, and the Armed Retreat of the Bolivian State.* New York: Columbia University Press.

Gillespie, Richard. 1982. *Soldiers of Perón: Argentina's Montoneros.* Oxford: Clarendon Press.

Gillis, John R., ed. 1994. *Commemoration: The Politics of National Identity*. Princeton, NJ: Princeton University Press.

Gledhill, John. 1995. *Neoliberalism, Transnationalism and Rural Poverty: A Case Study of Michoacán, Mexico*. Boulder, CO: Westview Press.

–. 1997. 'Liberalism, Socio-economic Rights and the Politics of Identity.' Pp. 70–110 in Richard A. Wilson, ed., *Human Rights, Culture and Context: Anthropological Perspectives*. London: Pluto Press.

Graham-Yooll, Andrew. 1982. *A Matter of Fear: Portrait of an Argentine Exile*. Westport, CT: Lawrence Hill and Company.

–. 1989. *De Perón a Videla*. Buenos Aires: Legasa.

Gramsci, Antonio. 1971. *Selections from the Prison Notebooks*. Trans. and ed. Quintin Hoare and Geoffrey Nowell Smith. New York: International.

Grant, Bruce. 1995. *In the Soviet House of Culture: A Century of Peristroikas*. Princeton, NJ: Princeton University Press.

Green, Linda. 1999. *Fear as a Way of Life: Mayan Widows in Rural Guatemala*. New York: Columbia University Press.

Gregory, Steven. 1994. 'Race, Rubbish and Resistance: Empowering Difference in Community Politics.' Pp. 366–91 in Steven Gregory and Roger Sanjek, eds., *Race*. New Brunswick, NJ: Rutgers University Press.

Guber, Rosana. 1991. *El salvaje metropolitano*. Buenos Aires: Legasa.

–. 1999. 'From Chicos to Veterans: Memory and the Nation in the Making of Malvinas Post-war Identities.' PhD diss., Johns Hopkins University.

–. 2001. *¿Por qué Malvinas?* Buenos Aires: Fondo de Cultura Económica.

Hale, Charles A. 1986. 'Political and Social Ideas in Latin America, 1870–1930.' Pp. 367–441 in Leslie Bethell, ed., *The Cambridge History of Latin America*. Vol. 4. Cambridge: Cambridge University Press.

Hall, Stuart, C. Critcher, T. Jefferson, J. Clarke, and B. Roberts. 1978. *Policing the Crisis: Mugging, the State, and Law and Order*. New York: Holmes and Meier.

Harvey, David. 1989. *The Condition of Postmodernity*. Cambridge: Basil Blackwell.

–. 1995. 'Militant Particularism and Global Ambition: The Conceptual Politics of Place, Space, and Environment in the Work of Raymond Williams.' *Social Text* 42: 69–98.

Herbel, Gustavo A. 1993. 'Operatividad del sistema penal en el conurbano bonaerense.' *Delito y societal* 2(3): 97–110.

Hobsbawm, Eric, and Terence Ranger, eds. 1983. *The Invention of Tradition*. Cambridge: Cambridge University Press.

INDEC (Instituto Nacional de Estadísticas y Censos). 1990. *La pobreza urbana en la Argentina*. Buenos Aires: INDEC.

Isla, Alejandro. 1998. 'Terror, Memory and Responsibility in Argentina.' *Critique of Anthropology* 18(2): 134–56.

James, Daniel. 1987. '17 y 18 de Octubre de 1945: El Peronismo, la protesta de masas y la clase obrera argentina.' *Desarollo económico* 27(107): 445–60.

–. 1988. *Resistance and Integration: Peronism and the Argentine Working Class, 1946–76.* Cambridge: Cambridge University Press.

–. 1997a. 'Meatpackers, Peronists, and Collective Memory: A View from the South.' *American Historical Review* 102(5): 1404–12.

–. 1997b. '"Tales Told Out on the Borderlands": Doña Maria's Story, Oral History and Issues of Gender.' Pp. 31-52 in Daniel James and J.D. French, eds., *The Gendered Worlds of Latin American Women Workers.* Durham, NC: Duke University Press.

–. 2000. *Doña María's Story: Life History, Memory, and Political Identity.* Durham, NC: Duke University Press.

Johnson, Richard, G. McLennan, Bill Schwartz, and David Sutton, eds. 1982. *Making Histories: Studies in History Writing and Politics.* Minneapolis: University of Minnesota Press.

Joseph, Galen. 2000. 'Taking Race Seriously: Whiteness in Argentina's National and Transnational Imaginary.' Identities: Global Studies in Culture and Power, 2000, 7, 3,Sept, 333–371.

Joesph, Gilbert M., and Daniel Nugent, eds. 1994. *Everyday Forms of State Formation: Revolution and the Negotiation of Rule in Modern Mexico.* Durham, NC: Duke University Press.

Kalb, Don, Hans Marks, and Herman Tak. 1996. 'Historical Anthropology and Anthropological History: Two Distinct Programs.' *Focaal* 26/27: 5–16.

Kaufman, Ester. 1991. 'El ritual jurídico en el juicio a los ex-comandantes: La desnaturalización de lo cotidiano.' In Rosana Guber, ed., *El salvaje metropolitano.* Buenos Aires: Legasa.

Kaufman, Michael. 1997. 'Differential Participation: Men, Women and Popular Power.' Pp. 151–68 in Michael Kaufman and Haroldo Dilla Alfonso, eds., *Community Power and Grassroots Democracy.* London and Ottawa: Zed Books and International Development Research Centre.

La Nación. 1973a. 'Cesan desde hoy las zonas de emergencia.' *La Nación* (Buenos Aires), 19 May, 1.

–. 1973b. 'Desalojáse a los intrusos de varios monobloques.' *La Nación* (Buenos Aires), 18 May, 4.

–. 1973c. 'La ocupación de un grupo de viviendas.' *La Nación* (Buenos Aires), 20 May.

–. 1973d. 'La ocupación ilegal de viviendas urbanas.' *La Nación* (Buenos Aires), 17 May, 11.

Lantzmann, Claude, dir. 1986. *Shoah.* Writ. Claude Lantzmann. Hollywood, CA, Paramount Home Video.

LeGoff, Jacques. 1992. *History and Memory.* Trans. Steven Randall and Elizabeth Claman. New York: Columbia University Press.

Levenson-Estrada, Deborah. 1994. *Trade Unionists against Terror: Guatemala City, 1954–1985.* Chapel Hill: University of North Carolina Press.

Lindenberger, Thomas, and Michael Wildt. 1992. 'Radical Plurality: History Workshop as a Practical Critique of Knowledge.' *History Workshop Journal* 33: 73–99.

Loveman, Brian, and Thomas M. Davies, Jr, eds. 1989. *The Politics of Antipolitics: The Military in Latin America.* Lincoln: University of Nebraska Press.

Luvecce, Cecilia. 1993. *Peronismo de Base.* Buenos Aires: Centro Editor de América Latina.

Malkki, Liisa H. 1995. *Purity and Exile: Violence, Memory and National Cosmology among Hutu Refugees in Tanzania.* Chicago: University of Chicago Press.

Mallon, Florencia. 1995. *Peasant and Nation: The Making of Postcolonial Mexico and Peru.* Berkeley: University of California Press.

Marcus, George E. 1994. 'The Official Story: Response to Julie Taylor.' Pp. 204–8 in Michael Ryan and Avery Gordon, eds., *Body Politics: Disease, Desire and the Family.* Boulder, CO: Westview Press.

–. ed. 1993. *Perilous States: Conversations on Culture, Politics, and Nation.* Chicago: University of Chicago Press.

Marks, Hans. 1996. 'Tempi, Loci and People: Conclusions.' *Focaal* 26/27:183–90.

Marx, Karl. 1963. *The 18th Brumaire of Louis Bonaparte.* New York: International Publishers.

Massey, Doreen. 1994. *Space, Place and Gender.* Minneapolis: University of Minnesota Press.

McClenaghan, Sharon. 1997. 'Women, Work and Empowerment: Romanticizing Reality.' Pp. 19–35 in Elizabeth Dore, ed., *Gender Debates in Latin America: Debates in Theory and Practice.* New York: Monthly Review Press.

Midré, Georges. 1992. 'Bread or Solidarity? Argentine Social Policies, 1983–90.' *Journal of Latin American Studies* 24(2): 343–73.

Ministerio de Bienestar Social de Argentina. 1968. *Plan de Erradicación de las Villas de Emergencia de la Capital Federal y del Gran Buenos Aires: Primer programa, erradicación y alojamiento transitorio.* Buenos Aires: Ministerio de Bienestar Social, Poder Ejecutivo Nacional, Republica de Argentina.

Mintz, Sidney W. 1974 [1960]. *Worker in the Cane: A Puerto Rican Life History.* New York: W.W. Norton.

–. 1985. *Sweetness and Power: The Place of Sugar in Modern History.* New York: Penguin Books.

Minujin, Alberto. 1992. 'En La Rodada.' Pp. 15–44 in Alberto Minujin, ed., *Cuesta Abajo. Los nuevos pobres: Efectos de la crisis en la sociedad argentina*. Buenos Aires: Unicef/Losada.

Munck, Gerardo L. 1998. *Authoritarianism and Democratization: Soldiers and Workers in Argentina, 1976-1983*. University Park, PA: Pennsylvania State University Press.

Murmis, Miguel, and Silvio Feldman. 1992. 'La heterogeneidad social de las pobrezas.' Pp. 45–92 in Alberto Munijin, ed., *Cuesta abajo. Los nuevos pobres: Efectos de la crisis en la sociedad argentina*. Buenos Aires: Unicef/Losada.

Myerhoff, Barbara. 1978. *Number Our Days*. New York: Touchstone.

Nash, June. 1979. *We Eat the Mines and the Mines Eat Us: Dependency and Exploitation in Bolivian Tin Mines*. New York: Columbia University Press.

Navarro, Marysa. 1989. 'The Personal Is Political: Madres de Plaza de Mayo.' Pp. 241–58 in Susan Eckstein, ed., *Power and Popular Protest*. Berkeley: University of California Press.

Noticias del país (Buenos Aires). 1973. 'San Justo: Violencia por las viviendas.' *Noticias del país* (Buenos Aires), 14 December, 6.

Nugent, David. 1997. *Modernity at the Edge of Empire: State, Individual, and Nation in the Northern Peruvian Andes, 1885-1935*. Stanford, CA: Stanford University Press.

O'Brien, Jay, and William Roseberry, eds. 1991. *Golden Ages, Dark Ages: Imagining the Past in Anthropology and History*. Berkeley: University of California Press.

Oliveira, Alicia, and Sofía Tiscornia. 1990. *La construcción social de imágenes de guerra*. Buenos Aires: Cuadernos de CELS (Centro de Estudios Legales y Sociales).

Oria, Piera Paola. 1987. *De la casa a la plaza*. Buenos Aires: Editorial Nueva América.

Ortner, Sherry. 1984. 'Theory in Anthropology Since the Sixties.' *Comparative Studies in Society and History* 26(1): 126–66.

Osiel, Mark. 1986. 'The Making of Human Rights Policy in Argentina: The Impact of Ideas and Interests on a Legal Conflict.' *Journal of Latin American Studies* 18: 135–78.

–. 1997. *Mass Atrocity, Collective Memory, and the Law*. New Brunswick, NJ: Transaction Press.

Página/12. 1990. 'A contrapelo de la gente.' *Página/12* (Buenos Aires), 30 December, 10–11.

–. 1991a. 'El nuevo orden peronista.' *Página/12* (Buenos Aires), 15 March 2–6.

– 1991b. 'Una bomba en la madrugada.' *Página/12* (Buenos Aires), 23 February, 4.

–. 1992. 'Se suman 215 desaparecidos a la lista de CONADEP.' *Página/12* (Buenos Aires), 5 May, 10.

Paley, Julia. 1993. 'Popular History Workshops in Chile: Reflections on the Politics of Knowledge.' Paper presented at the Conference of the Committee for Historical Studies, New School for Social Research, New York, 30 April.

Parelli, Carina. 1994. 'Memoria de Sangre: Fear, Hope, and Disenchantment in Argentina.' Pp. 39–66 in Jonathan Boyarin, ed., *Remapping Memory: The Politics of TimeSpace*. Minneapolis: University of Minnesota Press.

Partnoy, Alicia. 1986. *The Little School: Tales of Disappearance and Survival in Argentina*. Trans. Alicia Partnoy with Lois Athey and Sandra Braunstein. Pittsburgh, PA: Cleis Press.

Passerini, Luisa. 1987. *Fascism in Popular Memory: The Cultural Experience of the Turin Working Class*. Trans. Robert Lumley and Jude Bloomfield. Cambridge: Cambridge University Press.

– ed. 1992. *Memory and Totalitarianism. International Yearbook of Oral History and Life Stories*. Oxford: Oxford University Press.

Perlman, Janice. 1976. *The Myth of Marginality*. Berkeley: University of California Press.

Popular Memory Group. 1982. 'Popular Memory: Theory, Politics and Practice.' Pp. 205–52 in Richard Johnson, G. McLennan, Bill Schwartz, and David Sutton, eds., *Making Histories: Studies in History Writing and Politics*. Minneapolis: University of Minnesota Press.

Portelli, Alessandro. 1991. *The Death of Luigi Trastulli and Other Stories: Form and Meaning in Oral History*. Albany, State University of New York Press.

Powers, Nancy R. 1995a. 'The Politics of Poverty in the 1990s.' *Journal of Interamerican Studies and World Affairs* 37(4): 89–137.

–. 1995b. 'Poverty Looks at Democracy: Material Interests and Political Thinking in Contemporary Argentina.' Ph.D diss., Notre Dame University.

–. 2001. *Grassroots Expectations of Democracy and Economy: Argentina in Comparative Perspective*. Pittsburgh, PA: University of Pittsburgh Press.

Pozzi, Pablo. 1988. *Oposición obrera a la dictadura*. Buenos Aires: Contrapunto.

Pratt, Mary Louise. 1990. 'Women, Literature and National Brotherhood.' Pp. 48–73 in Emile Bergmann et al., eds., *Women, Culture, and Politics in Latin America*. Berkeley: University of California Press.

Price, Richard. 1983. *First-Time: The Historical Vision of an Afro-American People*. Baltimore: Johns Hopkins University Press.

Puenzo, Luis. 1985. *The Official Story (La Historia Oficial)*. Writ. Luis Puenzo and Aida Bortnik. Argentina, Fox/Lorber; Almi Pictures.

Ranis, Peter. 1986. 'The Dilemmas of Democratization in Argentina.' *Current History* 30: 29–33.

Rappaport, Joanne. 1994. *Cumbe Reborn: An Andean Ethnography*. Chicago: University of Chicago Press.

Restivo, Nestor. 2001. 'El Gobierno tuvo que pagar entre 14 y 16% para conseguir US$ 850 milliones.' *Clarín* (Buenos Aires), 11 July, 8.

Robben, Antonius C.G.M. 1996. 'Ethnographic Seduction, Transference, and Resistance in Dialogues about Terror and Violence in Argentina.' *Ethos* 24(1): 71-106.

Robert, Karen Joyce. 1997. 'The Argentine Babel: Space, Politics and Culture in the Growth of Buenos Aires. 1856–1890.' PhD diss., University of Michigan.

Rock, David. 1985. *Argentina, 1516–1982: From Spanish Colonization to the Falklands War*. Berkeley: University of California Press.

–. 1987. *Argentina, 1516–1987: From Spanish Colonization to Alfonsín*. Berkeley: University of California Press.

–. 1993. *Authoritarian Argentina: The Nationalist Movement, Its History and Its Impact*. Berkeley: University of California Press.

Rodríguez Molas, Ricardo. 1985a. *Historia de la tortura y el orden represivo en la Argentina*. Buenos Aires: EUDEBA.

– ed. 1985b. *Historia de la tortura y el orden represivo en la Argentina: Textos documentales*. Buenos Aires: EUDEBA.

Rosaldo, Renato. 1980. *Ilongot Headhunting, 1883–1974: A Study in Society and History*. Stanford, CA: Stanford University.

Roseberry, William. 1991. *Anthropologies and Histories: Essays in Culture, History, and Political Economy*. New Brunswick, NJ: Rutgers University Press.

–. 1994. 'Hegemony and the Language of Contention' Pp. 355–66 in Gilbert M. Joseph and Daniel Nugent, eds., *Everyday Forms of State Formation: Revolution and the Negotiation of Rule in Mexico*. Durham, NC: Duke University Press.

Sacks, Karen. 1988. 'Gender and Grassroots Leadership.' Pp. 77–94 in Sandra Morgan and Ann Bookman, eds., *Women and the Politics of Empowerment*. Philadelphia: Temple University Press.

Sahlins, Marshall. 1985. *Islands of History*. Chicago: University of Chicago Press.

Samuel, Raphael. 1980. 'On the Methods of the History Workshop: A Reply.' *History Workshop Journal* 9: 162–76.

Sarlo, Beatriz. 1994. 'Argentina under Menem: The Aesthetics of Domination.' *NACLA Report on the Americas* 28(2): 33–7.

Schild, Veronica. 1997. 'The Hidden Politics of Neighborhood Organizations: Women and Local Participation in the Poblaciones of Chile.' Pp. 126–48 in Michael Kaufman and Haroldo Dilla Alfonso, eds., *Community Power and Grassroots Democracy*. London and Ottawa: Zed Books and International Development Research Centre.

–. 1998. 'New Subjects of Rights? Women's Movements and the Construction of Citizenship in the "New Democracies."' Pp. 93–117 in Sonia E. Alvarez et al., eds., *Cultures of Politics / Politics of Cultures: Re-visioning Latin American Social Movements*. Boulder, CO: Westview Press.

Schneider, Joe. 1989. 'The Enigma of La Tablada.' *NACLA Report on the Americas* 23: 9–13.

Schocklender, Sergio M. 1992. 'La cárcel, factores de criminalización y reincidencias.' *Delito y sociedad*. 1(1): 57–66.

Schvarzer, Jorge. 1986. *La política económica de Martínez de Hoz*. Buenos Aires: Ediciones de CISEA, Hyspamérica.

Scott, Joan Wallach. 1988. *Gender and the Politics of History*. New York: Columbia University Press.

Selbourne, David. 1980. 'On the Methods of the History Workshop.' *History Workshop Journal* 9: 150–61.

Shumway, Nicolas. 1991. *The Invention of Argentina*. Berkeley: University of California Press.

Sider, Gerald M. 1996a. 'Anthropology and History: Opening Points for a New Synthesis.' *Focaal* 26/27: 127–34.

–. 1996b. 'Cleansing History: Lawrence Massachusetts, the Strike for Four Loaves of Bread and No Roses, and the Anthropology of Working-class Consciousness.' *Radical History Review* 65: 48–83.

–. 1996c. 'In Reply... ' *Radical History Review* 65: 108–17.

Sider, Gerald M., and Gavin Smith, eds. 1997. *Between History and Histories: The Making of Silences and Commemorations*. Toronto: University of Toronto Press.

Smith, Gavin. 1991. 'The Production of Culture in Local Rebellion.' Pp. 180–207 in William Roseberry and Jay O'Brien, eds., *Golden Ages, Dark Ages: Imagining the Past in Anthropology and History*. Berkeley: University of California Press.

–. 1997. 'Pandora's History: Central Peruvian Peasants and Re-covering the Past.' Pp. 80–97 in Gerald Sider and Gavin Smith, eds., *Between History and Histories: The Making of Silences and Commemorations*. Toronto: University of Toronto Press.

Smith, William C. 1989. *Authoritarianism and the Crisis of Argentine Political Economy*. Stanford, CA: Stanford University Press.

Spence, Donald P. 1982. *Narrative Truth and Historical Truth, Meaning and Interpretation in Psychoanalysis*. New York: W.W. Norton.

Spiegelman, Art. 1986. *Maus I, A Survivor's Tale: My Father Bleeds History*. New York: Pantheon Books.

–. 1991. *Maus II, A Survivor's Tale: And Here My Troubles Began*. New York: Pantheon Books.

Stansell, Christine. 1996. 'Response to "Cleansing History."' *Radical History Review* 65: 103–7.

Steedman, Carolyn Kay. 1987. *Landscape for a Good Woman: A Story of Two Lives.* New Brunswick, NJ: Rutgers University.

–. 1995. 'Difficult Stories: Feminist Auto/biography.' *Gender and History* 7(2): 321–6.

Stern, Frank. 1992. 'Antagonistic Memories: The Post-War Survival and Alienation of Jews and Germans.' Pp. 21–43 in Luisa Passerini, ed., *Memory and Totalitarianism, International Yearbook of Oral History and Life Stories.* Oxford: Oxford University Press.

Stoll, David. 1990. *Is Latin America Turning Protestant? The Politics of Evangelical Growth.* Berkeley: University of California Press.

Striffler, Steve. 2002. 'Communists Communists Everywhere! Forgetting the Past and Living with History in Ecuador.' Pp. 107–20 in Belinda Leach and Winnie Lem, eds., *Culture, Economy, Power: Anthropology as Critique, Anthropology as Praxis.* Albany: State University of New York Press.

Summa. 1971. Proyecto PEVE NHD 4-5-6.

–. 1973a. Proyecto PEVE NHD 17.

–. 1973b. Proyecto PEVE NHD 19.

Swedenburg, Ted. 1991. 'Popular Memory and the Palestinian National Past.' Pp. 152–79 in William Roseberry and Jay O'Brien, eds., *Golden Ages, Dark Ages: Imagining the Past in Anthropology and History.* Berkeley: University of California Press.

–. 1995. *Memories of Revolt: The 1936–1939 Rebellion and Palestinian National Past.* Minneapolis: University of Minnesota Press.

Taussig, Michael T. 1980. *The Devil and Commodity Fetishism in South America.* Chapel Hill: University of North Carolina Press.

Taylor, Diana. 1997. *Disappearing Acts: Spectacles of Gender and Nationalism in Argentina's 'Dirty War.'* Durham, NC: Duke University Press.

Taylor, Julie M. 1979. *Eva Perón: The Myths of a Woman.* Chicago: University of Chicago Press.

–. 1993. 'The Outlaw State and the Lone Ranger.' Pp. 283–303 in George E. Marcus, ed., *Perilous States: Conversations on Culture, Politics and Nation.* Chicago: University of Chicago Press, Late Editions.

–. 1994. 'Body Memories: Aide-Memoires and Collective Amnesia in the Wake of the Argentine Terror.' Pp. 193–203 in Michael Ryan and Avery Gordon, eds., *Body Politics: Disease, Desire and the Family.* Boulder: Westview Press.

Timerman, Jacobo. 1981 [1980]. *Prisoner without a Name, Cell Without a Number.* Trans. Tony Talbot. New York: Vintage Books.

Torrado, Susana. 1992. *Estructura social de la Argentina: 1945–1983*. Buenos Aires: Ediciones de la Flor.

Torre, Juan Carlos, ed. 1995. *El 17 de octubre de 1995*. Buenos Aires: Ariel.

– and Liliana Riz. 1993. 'Argentina since 1946.' Pp. 243–363 in Leslie Bethell, ed., *Argentina since Independence*. Cambridge: Cambridge University Press.

Trouillot, Michel-Rolph. 1996. *Silencing the Past: Power and the Production of History*. Boston: Beacon.

United Nations Development Program. *Human Development Report 2003; Millenium Development Goals: A Compact among Nations to End Human Poverty*. http://hdr.undp.org/reports/global/2003.

Vázquez, Enrique. 1985. *La Ultima: Origen, apogeo y caída de la dictadura militar*. Buenos Aires: Eudeba.

Verbitsky, Horacio. 1985. *La posguerra sucia: un análisis de la transición*. Buenos Aires: Legasa.

–. 1996 [1995]. *The Flight: Confessions of an Argentine Dirty Warrior*. New York: New Press.

Villareal, Juan. 1984. 'Los hilos sociales del poder.' Pp. 201–83 in Eduardo Jozani et al. eds., *Crisis de la dictadura Argentina*. Buenos Aires: Siglo XXI.

Vincent, Joan. 1990. *Anthropology and Politics: Visions, Traditions, and Trends*. Tuscon: University of Arizona Press.

Wallace, Michael. 1996. *Mickey Mouse History and Other Essays on American Memory*. Philadelphia: Temple University Press.

Walter, E. V. 1969. *Terror and Resistance: A Study of Political Violence*. New York: Oxford University Press.

Williams, Raymond. 1977. *Marxism and Literature*. Oxford: Oxford University Press.

–. 1989. 'The Importance of Community.' Pp. 111–19 in Raymond Williams, *Resources of Hope: Culture, Democracy, Socialism*. London: Verso.

Wilmsen, Edwin, and Patrick McAllister, eds. 1996. *The Politics of Difference*. Chicago: University of Chicago Press.

Wilson, Richard A., ed. 1997. *Human Rights, Culture and Context: Anthropological Perspectives*. London: Pluto Press.

Witz, Leslie. 1990. 'The Write Your Own History Project.' *Radical History Review* 46(7): 377–87.

Wolf, Eric R. 1959. *Sons of the Shaking Earth*. Chicago: University of Chicago Press.

–. 1969. *Peasant Wars in the Twentieth Century*. New York: Harper & Row.

–. 1982. *Europe and the People without History*. Berkeley: University of California Press.

World Bank. 1994. 'Argentina.' Pp. 17–23 in World Bank, *Trends in Developing Economies*. Washington: World Bank.

Yujnovsky, Oscar. 1984. *Claves políticas del problema habitacional argentino: 1955–1981*. Buenos Aires: Grupo Editor Latinoamericano.

Index

Abrams, Philip, 17–18
Alfonsín, Raúl: and democracy, 115; economic policy of, 123–24; and human rights, 115–17, 119
anthropology: ethics, 238–39n2; and history, 16–17
Argentine culture, 5–9; affect of immigration, 6–7; Argentine sense of difference, 6, 8; European influence, 5–6; importance of beef, 6; indigenous people, 6; literacy, 240n12; and *maté*, 239n5; pauperization, 6; and Peronism, 221–22
Auyero, Javier, 222, 228–29

Balbín, Oscar Eduardo, 58
Banco Hipotecario de la Nación (the National Mortgage Bank), 83
Bignone, Reynaldo, 114
Bufano, Bishop, 91

Cámpora, Hector, 57–58, 59
carapintadas, 116–17. *See also* Rico, Aldo
Cavallo, Domingo, 124, 125, 214
CEDES (Centro de Estudios de Estado y Sociedad), 90

CdeO (Comando de Organización), 68, 75, 81; and the *toma*, 69
class. *See* working class
Clemente, Hebe, 134
CODESEDH (Comité para Defensa de la Salud, la Ética Profesional, y los Derecho Humanos), 190–91, 198, 257n15
Collins, Joseph, 206
CONADEP (Comisión Nacional sobre la Desaparación de Personas), 115, 246n3, 247n13
CONASE (Consejo Nacional de Seguridad), 19
Comisión Municipal de la Vivienda, 50
community. *See* José Ingenieros
community organizations: and apathy, 100; La Asociación Vecinal Pro-Policía, 179, 182–84, 256n4; corruption of, 96; and the coup, 89–91; difficulties with, 138–39, 195–97, 201–2; and gender, 203; El Hornero, 23, 257–58n17; in José Ingenieros, 37, 76–77, 81–82; limited resources of, 187–88; memory and, 198–200; *el proyecto de salud,*

189–91; resistance to, 183–84, 186–89, 194–95. *See also* José Ingenieros

El Cordobazo, 57

Corradi, Juan, 88, 123

corruption: and the police, 185–86; and repression, 99; of local officials, 4

coup (24 March 1976), 86, 206

crime, 216–17; and the economic crisis, 181, 215; and fear, 184–86. *See also* police

culture: and power, 205, 209

culture of fear, 211; and silence, 93, 171–72, 177

de Hoz, Martínez, 121, 251n15

de la Rúa, Fernando, 214

dictatorship. *See* proceso

dirty war, the, 238n8. *See also proceso*

disappeared, the, 246n3; from José Ingenieros, 89–95

Douglas, Mary, 110

Duhalde, Eduardo, 163, 219

economic policies. *See* Alfonsín, Raúl; Menem, Carlos; neoliberalism; Perón, Juan Domingo; *proceso*

ERP (Ejercito Revolucionario del Pueblo), 68, 117

Ezeiza, 57, 58

Falklands War. *See* Malvinas War

FONAVI (Fondo Nacional de la Vivienda), 241–42n7

Frente Justicialista de la Liberación, 58

Frente Villero de la Liberación Nacional, 50

Galtieri, Leopoldo, 114, 216, 249n4

gender: and community participation, 41–42, 203; and division of labour, 40–41; and identity, 41–42, 212; and memory, 148, 174; and the state, 40, and the *toma*, 75–76

Gill, Lesley, 10, 18

Gillespie, Richard, 221–22

Gledhill, John, 8, 10

Gobierno de la Revolución Argentina, 49

Gramsci, Antonio: and common sense, 173, 205, 255–56n11; and hegemony, 176

Green, Linda, 10

Guber, Rosana, 3

Hall, Stuart, 180–81

Harvey, David, 259n36

health: clinics, 82; project, 189–200; sewage crisis, 192–93; training, 197–98, 258–59n29

historical ethnography: and historical accounts, 14; importance of, 17. *See also* popular memory

history: and anthropology, 16–17; ethnographic approach to, 9–11; and hegemony, 138; as space and place, 154

history workshops (the *taller*): activities of, 141–54; critiqued by residents, 155–56; demographics of, 136, 140, 252n4; limitations of, 175; as methodology, 139, 141, 252–53n5; mural project, 149–54, 218–19; participation in, 136–38; and silence, 144–46; and the state, 134–35; *taller de memoria*, 139–41, time lines, 141–46

human rights, 11–13; under Alfonsín, 115–17; exile, 91; extradition of violators, 216; violent repression of, 12; unintended consequences of, 12

human rights organizations, 11, 247–48n18, 249–50n5; APDH (Asemblia Permanente de Derechos Humanos), 115; CISP (Comitato Internazionale per lo Sviluppo dei Popoli), 190–91, 257n15. *See also* Liwski, Norberto; *Nunca Más*; Madres de Plaza de Mayo

Illia, Arturo, 55
inflation, 123, 251nn18–19, 251n24; fear of, 128–29, 181
Ingeniero Santos vigilante case, 11–12
Instituto de la Vivienda, 72, 100–101

James, Daniel, 56, 161–62, 222–23, 225, 229
José Ingenieros: administration of, 36–37, 95, (during *proceso*), 100–102; architecture of, 27–28, 53–54, 242n9; armed patrols at, 73; as barrio, 26–27; and the church, 37–38; as community, 29; crime in, 179–80; demographics of, 3–5, 22, 237n2; education levels in, 30–31; and gender, 39–43; and globalization, 217–18; and inflation, 126; legality of, 65, 82–83; organization of, 71–77; and Peronism, 38–39, 221; and public health, 189–91; as refuge, 102–3; relative location, 28; self-sufficiency of, 34–36; sewage crisis, 192–93; as space and place, 154; and the state, 206, 253n10; underground economy, 36. *See also* community organizations

José Ingenieros II, 237n1
Joseph, Galen, 8
JP (Juventud Peronista), 67, 68
juicio a los excomandantes, 115–16, 138; resistance to, 116–17

Lear, John, 206
LeGoff, Jacques, 209
Liwski, Norberto, 89–92, 116, 148–49, 173, 190, 198, 199–200, 247n13. *See also* human rights; human rights organizations
Luder, Italo, 115

Madres de Plaza de Mayo, Las, 12, 42, 114–15, 241n25; as cautionary tale, 120. *See also* human rights organizations
Malvinas War, 114, 143, 249n4
Maradona, Diego, 239n6
Mason, Carlos, 216
Massera, Emilio, 165, 216
Massey, Doreen, 154
McClenaghan, Sharon, 40
memory: contradictory memories, 165–67; and chronology, 174; and community organizations, 198–200; as gendered, 148, 174; and history, 140; mistakes and meanings, 161–65, 254n2; and narrative, 209; as political project, 209; and the state, 148. *See also* popular memory
Menem, Carlos, 4, 119–20, 123–24, 214, 219; economic policy of, 124 (*see also* neoliberalism); and Peronist identity, 124, 229; presidential pardons (*indulto*), 119; repression under, 120; support for, 128–29; and the war on drugs, 181
military, 87–89, 180–81, 206, 245–

46n2;. *See also* La Tablada; state
Ministerio de Acción Social y
Familia, 23
Ministerio de Bienestar Social, 50, 53,
65, 73
MODIN (Movimiento por la
Dignidad y la Independancia),
160, 163. *See also* Rico, Aldo
Montoneros, 58, 67, 244n29
moral panics, 180, 204
MTP (Movimiento Todos por la
Patria), 28, 117–19

narrative: and audience, 167–70; and
historical truth, 158, and silence,
170–72. *See also* memory
neighbourhoods: as political spaces,
68. *See also* José Ingenieros
neoliberalism, 121–23; and globalization, 216; under Menem, 124–29,
206–7; social costs of, 125–27; and
the state, 206–8, 214
Neustadt, Bernardo, 12
La Noche de los Lapices, 120–21
Nugent, David, 18
Nunca Más, 87, 115, 138, 247n13. *See
also* human rights; human rights
organizations

Onganía, Juan Carlos, 55–56
order: as ideology 107–11, 203

Partido Justicialista, 38, 221. *See also*
Peronism; Menem, Carlos
Passerini, Luisa, 157, 171
PC (Partido Comunista), 68, 70
PCR (Partido Comunista Revolucio-
nario), 68, 70
PEVE (Plan de la Eradication de
Villas de Emergencia en Capital

Federal y Gran Buenos Aires), 49–
54, 203, 241–42n7; resistance to, 50
Perlman, Janice, 26
Perón, Eva Duarte de, 38, 221, 223,
228, 242–43n15, 260–61n8; Eva
Perón Foundation, 227–28; and
race, 7, 226
Perón, Isabel, 86, 242–43n15
Perón, Juan Domingo, 38, 56, 221,
242–43n15; death of, 86; economic
policy, 260n7; and organized
labour, 224–25; return of, 58–59 (*see
also* Ezeiza)
Peronism: and identity, 163–65, 212;
and politics, 38–39, 221; and
neoliberal ideology, 121–22; and
patronage, 38–39, 240n21; prohibition of, 56; and working class, 38
Peronist Party. *See* Partido Justicialista
police, 180–81; and crime statistics,
180; and corruption, 185–86;
increase in, 215, 256n3; and violence, 256–57n7
popular memory, 13–17; as collective identity, 155; as contradictory,
210; as methodology, 15; and official history, 173–75; the past-
present relation, 15–16, 189
Popular Memory Group, the, 15,
140–41, 155, 176–77
Portelli, Alessandro, 157, 161–62
poverty: pauperization, 125–26; poverty rates, 214–15; structural poverty, 125–26. *See also* neoliberalism
proceso (Process of National Reorganization): academic accounts of,
14; *allanamientos* (search and seizure operations), 29, 104–7; and
the cold war, 86; community resis-

tance to, 91; and economic crisis, 250–51n14; end of, 114–15; memory of, 111; and organized labour, 88–89

Radical Party, 55, 58, 115, 123, 129. *See also* Alfonsín, Raul
repression: of intellectual middle class, 12; in José Ingenieros, 29; of middle class, 12; under Onganía, 56; policies of, 5; and the state, 87; targets of, 87, 92. *See also* violence
Rico, Aldo, 160, 163; and Peronism, 160–61, 164; support for, 254–55n5. *See also* MODIN
Riz, Liliana, 56
Rock, David, 7, 89
Roseberry, William, 18

Sarlo, Beatriz, 124, 128–29
Schild, Veronica, 41, 207
Schneider, Joe, 119
Smith, Gavin, 29, 176, 178
Smith, William, 113, 207
Spence, Donald, 158
squatter invasion (the *toma*), 4, 59–62; and gender, 75–76; and local identity, 47; media coverage of, 60–62; political-economic context, 54–55, 65–70, 243n18, 244n30; political organization of, 62–63
state, 17–18; control of media, 110; and gendered division of labour, 40; and the military, 206; and memory, 148; and social workers,

100, 206, 241–42n7. *See also* human rights; violence
Steedman, Carolyn, 211–12, 227
Striffler, Steve, 10
Swedenburg, Ted, 209

Tablada, La, 117–19, 144
Taylor, Julie, 222–23
Thatcher, Margaret, 249n4
toma. *See* squatter invasion
Torrado, Susana, 54–55, 121, 122
Torre, Juan Carlos, 56
trial of the generals. *See juicio a los excomandantes*

UCR (Unión Civica Radical). *See* Radical Party

Videla, Jorge Rafael, 86–87, 122, 216
violence: and class, 92; death squads, 5; and politics, 78–81; and the *proceso*, 85; and the state, 87–89, 180–81, torture, 87. *See also* human rights; military; police

Williams, Raymond, 138, 140, 205, 211–12, 259n36; structures of feeling, 210–13, 228–29
Wolf, Eric, 26
women: and community work, 212–13; and resistance, 94, 96
working class: and gender, 40; and history, 172–73; and memory, 176; and neoliberal policy, 122; and Peronism, 222–29

Anthropological Horizons

Editor: Michael Lambek, University of Toronto

Published to date:

1 *The Varieties of Sensory Experience: A Sourcebook in the Anthropology of the Senses*
   Edited by David Howes
2 *Arctic Homeland: Kinship, Community, and Development in Northwest Greenland*
   Mark Nuttall
3 *Knowledge and Practice in Mayotte: Local Discourses of Islam, Sorcery, and Spirit Possession*
   Michael Lambek
4 *Deathly Waters and Hungry Mountains: Agrarian Ritual and Class Formation in an Andean Town*
   Peter Gose
5 *Paradise: Class, Commuters, and Ethnicity in Rural Ontario*
   Stanley R. Barrett
6 *The Cultural World in Beowulf*
   John M. Hill
7 *Making It Their Own: Severn Ojibwe Communicative Practices*
   Lisa Philips Valentine
8 *Merchants and Shopkeepers: A Historical Anthropology of an Irish Market Town, 1200–1991*
   Philip Gulliver and Marilyn Silverman
9 *Tournaments of Value: Sociability and Hierarchy in a Yemeni Town*
   Ann Meneley
10 *Mal'uocchiu: Ambiguity, Evil Eye, and the Language of Distress*
   Sam Migliore
11 *Between History and Histories: The Production of Silences and Commemorations*
   Edited by Gerald Sider and Gavin Smith
12 *Eh, Paesan! Being Italian in Toronto*
   Nicholas DeMaria Harney
13 *Theorizing the Americanist Tradition*
   Edited by Lisa Philips Valentine and Regna Darnell
14 *Colonial 'Reformation' in the Highlands of Central Sualwesi, Indonesia, 1892–1995*
   Albert Schrauwers

15 *The Rock Where We Stand: An Ethnography of Women's Activism in Newfoundland*
Glynis George

16 *Being Alive Well: Health and the Politics of Cree Well-Being*
Naomi Adelson

17 *Irish Travellers: Racism and the Politics of Culture*
Jane Helleiner

18 *Writing and Colonization in Northern Ghana: The Encounter between the LoDagaa and the 'World on Paper,' 1892–1991*
Sean Hawkins

19 *An Irish Working Class: Explorations in Political Economy and Hegemony, 1800–1950*
Marilyn Silverman

20 *The Double Twist: From Ethnography to Morphodynamics*
Edited by Pierre Maranda

21 *Of Property and Propriety: The Role of Gender and Class in Imperialism and Nationalism*
Edited by Himani Bannerji, Shahrzad Mojab, and Judith Whitehead

22 *Guardians of the Transcendent: An Ethnography of a Jain Ascetic Community*
Anne Vallely

23 *The House of Difference: Cultural Politics and National Identity in Canada*
Eva Mackey

24 *The Hot and the Cold: Ills of Humans and Maize in Native Mexico*
Jacques M. Chevalier and Andrés Sánchez Bain

25 *Figured Worlds: Ontological Obstacles in Intercultural Relations*
Edited by John Clammer, Sylvie Poirier, and Eric Schwimmer

26 *Revenge of the Windigo: The Construction of the Mind and Mental Health of North American Aboriginal Peoples*
James B. Waldram

27 *The Cultural Politics of Markets: Economic Liberalization and Social Change in Nepal*
Katherine Neilson Rankin

28 *A World of Relationships: Itineraries, Dreams, and Events in the Australian Western Desert*
Sylvie Poirier

29 *The Politics of the Past in an Argentine Working-Class Neighbourhood*
Lindsay DuBois